Chinese Migration and Economic Relations with Europe

This book explores how far existing networks of overseas Chinese and new flows of migrants act as drivers of economic relations between China and the host countries. It considers migration, trade, the flow of capital and foreign direct investment, includes both skilled and unskilled migrants and outlines the complex different waves of migration flows. It includes detailed case studies, based on extensive original research, on the position in a range of European countries and concludes with policy-oriented analysis and with an overall assessment of how far the Chinese diaspora matters in stimulating increased bilateral economic activity and stronger bilateral economic relationships.

Marco Sanfilippo is Assistant Professor at the Institute of Development Policy and Management, University of Antwerp, Belgium.

Agnieszka Weinar is a Research Fellow at the European University Institute, Florence, Italy.

Routledge Contemporary China Series

Chinese Migration and Economic Relations with Europe

Edited by
Marco Sanfilippo and Agnieszka Weinar

Routledge
Taylor & Francis Group

LONDON AND NEW YORK

First published 2016 by Routledge

2 Park Square, Milton Park, Abingdon, Oxfordshire OX14 4RN
711 Third Avenue, New York, NY 10017

Routledge is an imprint of the Taylor & Francis Group, an informa business

First issued in paperback 2017

British Library Cataloguing in Publication Data
A catalogue record for this book is available from the British Library

Library of Congress Cataloging-in-Publication Data
Chinese migration and economic relations with Europe / edited by
    Marco Sanfilippo and Agnieszka Weinar.
       pages cm. — (Routledge contemporary China series ; 129)
    Includes bibliographical references and index.
  1. China—Emigration and immigration—Economic
aspects.   2. Europe—Emigration and immigration—Economic
aspects.   3. China—Foreign economic relations—Europe.   4. Europe—
Foreign economic relations—China.   5. Investments, Foreign—
China.   6. Investments, Foreign—Europe.   I. Sanfilippo,
Marco.   II. Weinar, Agnieszka.
   JV8701.C55 2016
   337.5104—dc23
   2015006620

ISBN: 978-1-138-81940-5 (hbk)
ISBN: 978-0-8153-5597-7 (pbk)

Typeset in Times New Roman
by Apex CoVantage, LLC

Contents

xiv *Contents*

Figures

xvi *Figures*

Tables

Contributors

Annette Bongardt is currently a Visiting Senior Fellow at the London School of Economics (European Institute). She has been a Senior Member at St Antony's College, Oxford University, and a Visiting Fellow at the Robert Schuman Centre for Advanced Studies of the European University Institute (EUI) in Florence since 2012. She has been Associate Professor at *Universidade Fernando Pessoa* and Professor and Head of European Studies at the Portuguese National Institute for Public Administration. After receiving her PhD in Economics at the EUI in 1990, she was a Schuman Fellow of the European Commission at CEPS, Assistant Professor at the Rotterdam School of Management, Senior Research Fellow at ICER (Turin) and Academic Visitor and consultant of the European Commission. She was also Visiting Professor at the Universities of Aveiro, Pisa, Roma (II) and Victoria, BC, Canada, and Católica, Lisbon. Her publications include several co-authored and edited books on issues such as the single market, competition policy and migration policies and articles on the Lisbon and Europe 2020 strategies, environmental policy and economic sustainability.

Gabi Dei Ottati is Professor of Applied Economics in the Department of Economics and Management at the University of Florence (Italy) and Professor of Local Development in the Doctorate in Economics at the University of Florence. Her main research interests focus on industrial organization and especially on the industrial district model of organization and the role of industrial districts in the Italian economy. On these topics, Gabi Dei Ottati has published several books and more than 50 articles, many of them in international journals such as *Cambridge Journal of Economics* and *European Planning Studies*. In more recent years, her research activity has extended to immigrant businesses in Italian industrial districts and in particular to Chinese entrepreneurs in Prato.

Paweł Kaczmarczyk is Deputy Director of the Centre of Migration Research at the University of Warsaw and Assistant Professor at the Faculty of Economic Sciences, University of Warsaw. He is a fellow at IZA, the Institute for the Study of Labor in Bonn, Germany, and with TFMI, the Transcontinental Forum on Migration and Integration. He also serves as a SOPEMI correspondent for

Poland at the OECD. His research focuses on the drivers and consequences of labor migration, highly skilled mobility, the methodology of migration research, labor economics, population economics, demography, international economics and migration policy.

Frank N. Pieke studied cultural anthropology and Chinese studies at the University of Amsterdam and the University of California, Berkeley, where he received his PhD in 1992. After lectureships in Leiden and Oxford, he was appointed chair professor in modern China studies at Leiden University in 2010. Pieke is coordinator of the Leiden University research profile area *Asian Modernities and Traditions* and director of the University's Modern East Asia Research Centre. Pieke's work on contemporary Chinese society and politics focuses on the changing role of the Chinese Communist Party. His most recent book is *The Good Communist: Elite Training and State Building in Today's China* (Cambridge University Press, 2009). Pieke's other specialization is Chinese international migration. In 2004, he published *Transnational Chinese: Fujianese Migrants in Europe* with Stanford University Press. Pieke's current research revolves around foreign immigrant groups in China.

Marco Sanfilippo holds a PhD in Development Economics at the University of Florence, Italy. Currently, he is an Assistant Professor at the University of Antwerp, Belgium, and an Associate Fellow at the Italian Institute of International Affairs. Before joining Antwerp, he worked for some years as a research fellow at the European University Institute in Florence and worked/consulted for the Bank of Finland, University of Eastern Piedmont, UNICEF, UNIDO and UNU-Wider, among the others. His main research interests are in the field of development and international economics, focusing in particular on the globalization of Chinese firms and the implications for recipient countries, with a geographic focus on Europe and Africa.

Miguel Santos Neves holds a PhD from the London School of Economics and Political Science (LSE). Between 1995 and 2013, he was Director of the Asia Programme and the Migrations Programme at the Institute of International and Strategic Studies in Portugal (IEEI). Previous jobs include positions as Economic Counselor at the Ministry of Foreign Affairs in Portugal, Adviser to the Governor of Macau and expert to the Sino-Portuguese Joint Liaison Group on Macao. He has coordinated several research projects on EU–China relations looking at both formal track I and informal channels, in particular focusing on the dynamics and role of the Chinese business community in Portugal, its ties both with other communities in the EU and with China and on the paradiplomacy of Chinese provinces and EU regions. He has published books and articles on these topics in various international journals.

Yun Schüler-Zhou is Associate Research Fellow at the German Institute of Global and Area Studies (GIGA), Institute of Asian Studies. She received her PhD in Business Administration from the University of Hamburg. Her research interests focus on the internationalization of Chinese enterprises and the economic relations between China and the EU. She also works as an independent researcher and consultant with a focus on Chinese investment in the EU.

Margot Schüller is Senior Research Fellow at the German Institute of Global and Area Studies (GIGA) and Deputy Director of the GIGA, Institute of Asian Studies. She is regular lecturer on Chinese and East Asian economics at universities in Germany and abroad, and frequently consults governmental and private institutions. Her current research focusses on China's economic development, especially the transition of the banking and state sector, and its economic relations with neighbouring countries in Asia, China's innovation system, and the globalization of Chinese companies.

Ekaterina Selezneva graduated from St. Petersburg State University (Russia) in 2001. In 2003, she was awarded a Master of Arts in Economics from the CORIPE Piemonte (Turin, Italy) and in 2005 from the European University in St. Petersburg (Russia). In January, 2009 Ms Selezneva completed her PhD studies at the University of Turin (Italy). Ms Selezneva's scientific interests include applied research related to labour market, gender economics topics and subjective well-being studies. Ekaterina works at the Department of Economics of the Institute for East and Southeast European Studies in Regensburg (Germany) since 2009.

Tabitha Speelman graduated with an MA in Chinese Studies from Leiden University in 2013. In 2014, she completed a fellowship at the International Institute of Asian Studies, researching the social impact of high-speed rail development in China. Her publications on contemporary Chinese society have appeared in the *Atlantic*, the *Wall Street Journal, Caixin* and various Dutch publications. Speelman is currently based in China, working as a correspondent for Dutch daily newspaper *Trouw*.

Monika Szulecka is an Associate of the Centre of Migration Research, the University of Warsaw. She graduated from the Faculty of Applied Social Sciences and Resocialisation, University of Warsaw. Her research interests include economic integration of migrants, irregular migration and the role of migration policy in creating, preventing or combating it, and migration-related criminal phenomena, such as trafficking in persons, forced labour and human smuggling. She participated in a number of research projects conducted by international bodies (incl. FRA, ICMPD) or Polish institutions and organisations (e.g. Batory Foundation, Association for Legal Intervention).

Joanna Tyrowicz is an Assistant Professor at the University of Warsaw and an advisor in the Economic Institute at National Bank of Poland. She holds an MA from Katholieke Universiteit Leuven and a PhD from the University of Warsaw. She was a Fulbright Scholar at Columbia University and a Mellon Fellow at the Netherlands Institute for Advanced Studies.

Agnieszka Weinar received her PhD from the Department of Political Science of the University of Warsaw, where she also served as Assistant Professor at the American Studies Center and as a researcher at the Center for Migration Research. She worked in the European Commission (DG HOME) from 2007 to 2010. Since 2011, she has been a research fellow at the European University Institute, Florence, Italy. In 2014, she received a Marie Curie Outgoing International Fellowship and is currently seconded to Carleton University in Ottawa, Canada. Her research interests include emigration and diaspora policies, mobility and migration policy development, migration and liberal states, Europeanisation of migration policy, migration in international relations, as well as issues of citizenship and integration.

Haiyan Zhang is Associate Professor at NEOMA Business School and University of Antwerp and research fellow at the College of Europe. He holds a MA and a PhD in public administration and management from the University of Antwerp. His research interests include international business activities of Chinese- and overseas Chinese–owned enterprises, management issues of international joint ventures in transition economies, high-tech industrial agglomeration in China, Chinese outward FDI in Europe, EU–China FDI relations and the like. He has published in journals such as the *Management International Review* and has contributed to books on foreign direct investment in China and the internationalisation of Chinese multinational enterprises. He has consulted for trade associations, government institutions and multinational companies on various topics, such as U.S. direct investment in Belgium, strategic management of bilateral cooperation with Chinese local authorities, merger and acquisition in China and so forth.

Acknowledgements

The book is a result of a pilot research project conducted at and funded by the Migration Policy Centre (MPC), European University Institute in 2012–2013. The editors would like to thank Professor Philippe Fargues and Professor Alessandra Venturini for their intellectual guidance. We also thank co-organizing institutions and participants to the 6th Chinese in Prato and 4th Wenzhouese Diaspora Symposia on "Chinese migration, entrepreneurship and development in the new global economy" held at Monash University Prato, October 2013, during which preliminary versions of some of the chapters were presented and discussed.

Introduction

Chinese migrations and economic relations with Europe

Marco Sanfilippo and Agnieszka Weinar

Over the last three and a half decades, China undertook rapid transformations, moving from an underdeveloped economy to the most dynamic economic superpower in the world. This extraordinary pattern of growth presents characteristics that are almost unique among the major economies in the world. Since 1978, China has adopted pragmatic reforms that proved successful. In a relatively short period, China has experienced efficiency gains in agriculture and a tremendous expansion of international trade and has been able to absorb external technology and know-how together with consistent inflows of capital through high levels of inward foreign direct investment (FDI) (Naughton 2007). This unusual performance has certainly been helped by the country's favourable demographic conditions as well as by the simultaneous opening up of the global economy.

Since the start of the reforms, and with greater intensity after the country's accession to the World Trade Organization (WTO) in 2001, the international integration of China has become a widely debated issue in both the academic literature and policy circles. At the same time, in conjunction with the launch of the tenth 5-year plan, the Chinese government has announced its "*zou chu qu*" ("Going Out") strategy, whose purpose is to encourage domestic actors to invest abroad and, at the same time, relax the central authorities' control of the financial sector. Following the "Going Out" strategy, the country is emerging as a major source of FDI, rapidly moving from the status of net recipient to that of exporter of capital to third countries, both developed and developing.

Despite the considerable attention that has been given to traditional channels of integration such as trade and FDI, still relatively little is known about the role of international migration and the existing networks of Chinese communities in the world and how they interact with the aforementioned channels, contributing to the development pattern of the country – including, for instance, to the recent upgrading of competencies and assets. The economic reforms and political changes that have occurred in China's history have through time stimulated different waves of migration, both within and outside the country. According to more recent estimates, there are currently approximately 40 million overseas Chinese (*haiwai huaren*) all over the world, the largest share of which is based in the rest of Asia. Recently, however, they are increasingly concentrated in more advanced economies in North America, Oceania and Europe.

Chinese networks began to appear during the first wave of migration at the end of the nineteenth century and in turn contributed to the attraction of new flows of migrants, which became massive after 1978. After the reforms started, in fact, Chinese migration flows were officially permitted, a measure that paved the way for their direct involvement in the country's development strategy, including as sources of capital, skills and new technology from different areas of the world. Most of the time, these flows of people consisted of low-skilled workers looking for new opportunities abroad or of students allowed to obtain advanced instruction in developed countries. After 2001, with the deepening of China's integration into the world economy, new forms of migration flows following the flows of Chinese capital abroad also rose, generating a new wave of Chinese skilled migrants, such as managers, employees and workers living abroad, often on a temporary basis.

In the context in which China's globalization is rapidly progressing, this book is intended to provide a fresh look at the complex relationships among migration, factor mobility, trade and investment. Based on original research and country case studies, the main objective of this edited volume is to offer a multi-level comparison between different contexts and to account for developments over time.

The focus of this volume is on China's relations with continental Europe. European countries are among China's most relevant partners in terms of economic relations and host a large number of Chinese nationals, who come at different stages and with different motivations (see section 3). Current populist debates on China in the European Union (and in Russia, for that matter) oscillate around three issues: the Chinese diaspora and its role in the European economy (Chinese workers are often accused of "taking the jobs from Europeans"); the "exporting of jobs" to China by European companies; and the risks posed by Chinese investment in the key European industries.

The main question the book strives to answer has to do with the role of the existing networks of overseas Chinese and new flows of migrants, both unskilled and skilled, as drivers of economic relations between China and the host countries. This is still a partially unexplored area of study, despite its high relevance to strategic interactions between China and Europe and the policy implications that are likely to arise as a result. Both traditional smaller-scale activities established during the first waves of Chinese migration into Europe and more consistent capital flows in the form of bilateral trade and FDI are considered in order to evaluate the potential of different waves and types of Chinese migration in Europe. Whether increasing economic flows from China, especially in the wake of the financial crisis, give rise to new migration flows and affect the dynamics of European labour markets is also an object of the analysis.

1. Research framework

1.1. Background

This volume is based on a multi-disciplinary approach that studies the relationship between human mobility and economic relations between political entities in the context of China's interactions with Europe. Our research framework, developed to construct a case study–based analysis, is theoretically grounded in two main strands of the literature: transnationalism from the migration studies perspective and a more economic approach based on transaction-costs theory and the international movement of the main factors of production.

The study of the relationship between migrants and their country of origin has developed in various disciplines over the last 60 years or so. Diaspora studies have looked at migrants and their connection to the homeland mainly from the point of view of the country of origin: primarily exploring issues of diaspora-building and brain drain (Adams & Rieben 1968; Zahlan 1981). Migration studies have brought new dynamics to the field by trying to provide a theoretical frame for the relationship between the migrant (individual), the country of destination and the country of origin. In this volume, we focus on the specific theoretical contribution of migration studies, that is, transnationalism.

Transnationalism is one of the approaches traditionally practiced in the realm of international relations. The term refers to the trans-border relations of various actors: individuals, organizations, companies and governments. Sociological research focusing on migrant behaviour has used this term while analysing their interactions in a global space (Basch, Schiller, & Blanc 1994; Schiller, Basch, & Blanc-Szanton 1992; Vertovec & Cohen 1999). According to this logic, migrants live their lives in transnational spaces (VanWey & Faist 2000) – i.e. durable, dense, and stable processes (activities and practices) that link them to both their country of origin and destination – but without actually fully integrating into any of them. This triangular structure (Bauböck & Faist 2010) creates a specific environment in which unique social phenomena take place and thus where transnational economic relations are forged. The structure is composed of many actors: individuals, groups (families), organizations (e.g. employer organizations, trade unions, migrant associations) and various levels of government at the place of origin and destination. They all influence the way relations develop.

The role of the country of origin in developing and nurturing these links has been deeply examined only recently, within a worldwide revival of interest in migration and development agenda (Agunias & Newland 2007; de Haas 2005; de Haas & Novib 2006). The research on the economic relations of individual migrants in transnational contexts thus takes into account impacts at both the destination (traditional migration studies approach) and the origin (development studies approach). The key elements of economic transnationalism are remittances, investment that uses transnational financing and the trade of specialized goods and services. So far, these relations have been analysed at micro level, from the migrant perspective, but the role of the transnational companies and trans-border states is still not fully integrated into the equation. The way these actors can on the one hand influence migrants' economic activities at a destination, and on the other, make use of migrants to further their own economic expansion abroad remains to be studied.

However, in the domain of economics and entrepreneurship studies, the literature has looked into transnational ties much earlier. Migrants are able to reduce transaction costs associated with selling and producing overseas through the creation of business networks that are a main source of information (Kugler &

Rapoport 2007). Migrants facilitate the development of social and business networks, which, in turn, can improve exchanges between their countries of origin and destination by providing information and matching services that the market fails to supply. Communities of migrants have increasingly been recognized as important factors in overcoming informal barriers to international trade, including shortages of information about international trade opportunities, a lack of local knowledge of export markets, a weak international legal environment for contract enforcement and so on. In fact, it should be stressed that migrants and their communities can bridge the institutional divides that exist between countries that have markedly different institutional and business environments. Migrants are well placed to act as middlemen on account of their superior language skills and their knowledge of consumer preferences, business practices, market structures and laws. In addition, migrant business networks can help with contract enforcement by enforcing community sanctions, which can in turn reduce opportunistic behaviour such as contract violation.

In the present volume, we thus attempt to link two scholarly traditions. We discern the links between two levels of transnational interactions: those of transnational companies and trans-border states and those of social actors (i.e. individual migrants). Our hypothesis is that the former actors interact with the social actors, establishing and using migrant networks while forging transnational economic relations and *vice versa*. Our case studies further explore whether this strategic interaction differs between two specific categories of environments: the ethnic enclave economy and the global economy.

The first category consists of specific socio-economic spaces that have emerged as a consequence of immigration. Ethnic enclaves have been broadly discussed in the literature (Ndofor & Priem 2011; Neckerman, Carter, & Lee 1999; Portes 1995; Portes & Zhou 1993; Sanders & Nee 1987; Waldinger 1993). Their main characteristics are: a high concentration of one ethnic group; a local economy based on low-skilled workers (usually undocumented) doing low-skilled jobs that add low value in the value chain; and local entrepreneurs who act as middlemen between the enclave and the outside world and use transnational migrant networks to maximise profits. The global economy category sits on the other end of the spectrum. It comprises the transnational relations of big multinational companies that follow transnational strategies of investment. These companies usually rely on workers who bring high value added to the production chain. These two categories of economic activity thus reflect two different types of Chinese migrants and two different impacts that Chinese migration could have on the EU economy and labour market.

It is clear that the ethnic enclave pushes transnational entrepreneurs to rely more heavily on migrants and diaspora networks than in the case of transnational companies. Two factors shape this outcome: China's rise in the global economy and migration policies of the countries to which Chinese migrants migrate.

China has developed significant economic clout over the last three and a half decades. Chinese companies invest abroad on a large scale. This financial capital is often supported by the inflow of human capital (highly skilled workers). As the results of the studies included in this book demonstrate, these types of actors act as post-national global investors and do not necessarily rely on the diaspora or on Chinese migrants.

The rise of China has had little influence on ethnic enclave economies. Increases in import-export opportunities and in the flexibility of gathering needed capital are the main changes.

In both cases, the interlinkages between investment and migrants are to a great extent determined by migration policies at destination. Ethnic enclaves rely on migration policies, which shape legal and undocumented entries. At the moment, in all the countries studied in this volume, entry for low-skilled migrants is not easy: the current policy allows seasonal and temporary workers to enter for short periods and according to defined conditions. Chinese migrants residing in the enclave are rarely these types of workers. As a result, they tend to use other gateways – most notably family reunification streams. Entrepreneurs from China, on the other hand, can use special investor visas, which are available in many EU countries.[1]

All EU countries have some kind of special treatment reserved for highly skilled workers: namely researchers, students or specialists. In addition, EU–level directives regulate the rights of these categories of migrants, as well as those of intra-corporate transferees (ICTs).[2] These categories of migrants are encouraged to stay, provided that they find an employer. In fact, the number of students and highly skilled workers admitted to the EU from China over the last five years has increased significantly (EMN 2013). But their presence has not necessarily been related to an increase of big-scale investment from China in the same period. Big transnational Chinese companies rely primarily on intra-corporate transfers and only to a small extent on already established high-skilled workers of Chinese origin. Contract workers brought to work on specific projects under a bilateral agreement (e.g. construction workers brought to Poland or factory workers brought to Russia) are a special category.

1.2.   *Framework*

The rest of this volume is structured around two main parts which examine the research questions at two different layers. At a more general level, this volume aims at dissecting existing linkages between China's foreign and economic policies, which foster investment and development at home and Chinese communities in different contexts within geographical Europe. In this respect, the first part of the book establishes the context of the research and a general description of how diaspora networks of overseas Chinese have contributed to the enforcement of political and economic relations between China and host countries.

At a more specific level, our aim is to assess the role of migration and overseas Chinese in shaping economic relations between selected European countries and China. The second part of the book is based on new evidence collected for the research project, which covers a number of European countries, including three from Western Europe (Germany, Italy and Portugal) and two from Eastern Europe

(Poland and Russia). Country case studies are intended to provide fresh evidence by describing the most recent dynamics affecting economic relations between China and the host country and the ways in which these dynamics interrelate with Chinese migration and existing diaspora networks. Evidence from the case studies covers a number of different dimensions related to migration and capital flows from China, providing a quantitative assessment of these flows and further qualitative analysis, in some cases based on the results of ad-hoc surveys with representatives of Chinese companies based in the countries.

Country case studies are structured in a common way: they first assess whether the host country is well representative of the pattern followed by China in other countries within the region and if economic and/or migration flows from China are a relatively new phenomenon or a more established one. Second, the analysis moves to larger details that add original contributions to the existing knowledge of the interconnections between economic and migration flows in the host country. In this respect, each country case study provides information on (1) whether, to what extent and through which mechanisms the Chinese migrants or the existing diaspora have contributed to the attraction of Chinese capital flows, including by facilitating trade and large-scale investments by reducing transaction costs or by attracting new entrepreneurs, fostering the diffusion of small business activities at the local level; and (2) whether, to what extent and through which mechanisms rising capital flows from China – especially in the form of investment (either at a large or at a smaller scale) – have generated new flows of Chinese migrants into the country.

2.   Chinese migration and economic relations with Europe

The picture that emerges from the aggregate analysis is that even since the start of the economic and political reforms in China, Chinese migration trends have been extremely diverse in terms of the people involved, their origins and motivations and their relevance to the government's overall development strategies. At the very beginning of the reforms, Chinese migrants became high on the policy agenda. Migrants' access to foreign capital, know-how and markets made them valuable assets that had to be carefully cultivated. And initially, this approach yielded rich dividends: since the start of the reforms, overseas Chinese have in fact generated the largest shares of inward overseas investment in China.

Following a period of low emphasis, other important stepping stones in Chinese support for international migration can be identified in the early 1990s: permission to study abroad for self-funding individuals; and the early 2000s: the "Going Out" policies, which strengthened the economic dimension of foreign migration, especially for workers sent abroad to work in contracted projects. Overall, however, an assessment of policies made in Pieke and Speelman's contribution (Chapter 1) shows that the Chinese authorities have reacted pragmatically to the events without making any real attempt to construct a coherent and transparent framework of policies and institutions to deal with emigration, Chinese populations living abroad or return migration. The authors highlight the main characteristic of Chinese migration policy making: its fragmentation. Policy responses to the changing character of Chinese migration (its globalisation, its intensity and its commercialisation) have been elaborated at various levels of government and by various actors. In fact, the authors claim that since it no longer makes sense to talk about Chinese migration per se, it is equally difficult to talk about any kind of a Chinese policy towards these mobile individuals. The blurred division between the administration and politicians and between the public and private makes it difficult to come up with a uniform response to the needs of emigrants, the Chinese diaspora abroad and returnees. The authors meticulously reconstruct the development of various policies and frameworks over the decades, as well as the roles of institutions and private actors, and conclude that China cannot be expected to run a coherent policy approach in this domain, as it does in many other domains. The simple reason is its internal multilevel governance structure.

Chinese migration into Europe does not represent an exception to the trends discussed. Over the last decades, European countries have hosted different types of Chinese migrants, who in turn had diverse links with their country of origin.

2.1. Chinese communities in Europe and the role of the crisis

Europe has long been the destination of Chinese migrants seeking employment or trading opportunities, often in a specific Chinese sector of the economy. Starting with unskilled employment, their aim has been to later become the owners of a business, for instance a restaurant, store or workshop. This is a quite common pattern in most European countries, even if the patterns of specialization of Chinese entrepreneurs have been found to vary across geographic areas, with trade-related activities concentrated in Eastern Europe, food activities in the north and low-value-added textile productions in the south. Interestingly, for the purposes of our research, and as deeply documented in Zhang's contribution (Chapter 2), this original type of migration has opened the way to the establishment of an agglomeration of Chinese small-scale business activities in the continent. The availability of ethnic businesses, entrepreneurial networks and strong cultural ties and historic links with the home country are likely to present locational advantages, especially for small firms when they enter and operate in a foreign business environment. These firms tended to co-locate with firms from the same home country in European cities where there is a high concentration of overseas Chinese. Cases of clusters of Chinese firms in labour-intensive industries in South and Eastern Europe such as Prato in Italy, Elche in Spain or Budapest in Hungary well illustrate such trends, and have generated high concern about unfair competition, as well as rising tensions between ethnic Chinese entrepreneurs and local businesspeople. The case of the small city of Prato, in Italy, is probably the most clear example of this early trend of Chinese migration into Europe and, as such, it has been the object of a large strand of academic and policy research. Dei Ottati's contribution (Chapter 3) to this volume critically reviews some of the most challenging positions presented in the existing literature with the aim of providing new perspectives that can contribute to building up a more comprehensive interpretation of the businesses set up by Chinese immigrants in Prato. While the existing debate on the role of Chinese migrants and businesses in Prato has been polarized into positions in favour of or against integration, the chapter clearly shows that even though the development of the Chinese "fast fashion" production system introduced in Prato arose separately from the rest of the local economy, it has nevertheless revitalized the declining economic system linked to the activities of the local production system. The development of Chinese fast fashion, together with the multiplication of Chinese businesses, has meant that investments in such businesses have also increased. So far, it seems that these financial and commercial flows have mainly favoured China, which is above all due to the fact that the Prato Chinese system is characterized by greater integration with the Chinese homeland rather than with the local economy. Since the outbreak of the global financial crisis, the outcomes of these complex relations are nonetheless revealing some significant changes, including a process of diversification of Chinese businesses towards services and quality upgrading in textiles production. The latter change is encouraging Chinese firms to establish a wider range of relations with locals as employees, consultants, agents and suppliers. The ways in which the financial crisis has affected the dynamics of long-standing low-skill communities of Chinese migrants and businesses is at the heart of Bongardt and Neves's contribution (Chapter 4) based on an ad-hoc survey with Chinese businessmen in Portugal. Chapter 4 shows that the crisis had a significant impact on the existing Chinese small business community, not only by stimulating the adoption of a variety of coping strategies, which generated disparities in performance, but also by triggering some changes and new trends that touch on the very insertion of the community into the domestic and global economy. These changes are related to increasing signs of exit from the ethnic economy to a more diversified pattern of internationalisation to countries other than China. As a function of the crisis's impact, the small business community became more heterogeneous and less cohesive. Interestingly, exits from the ethnic economy, which result from a re-direction of segments to new products, imply a greater integration in the Portuguese economy.

2.2.   *New patterns of Chinese migration in Europe*

The other group of Chinese migrants in Europe is a much more recent development. Chinese are increasingly coming to Europe to study at a university, vocational school or training programme or coming as expatriate employees of Chinese firms or organizations. With the arrival of these new migrants, especially international entrepreneurs, students and highly skilled professionals and expatriate managers of Chinese multinational companies, the characteristics of the Chinese ethnic community in Europe are evolving. Students are a major source of this new wave of Chinese migrants, who are mostly concentrated in Western Europe and especially in the UK, France and Germany. Together, these countries account for more than 80 per cent of the total number of Chinese students in Europe (Latham & Wu 2013). The role of Chinese students can be key to allowing

European host countries to attract high-quality human capital and larger-scale investments from China. This potential correlation is well highlighted in Schüller and Schüler-Zhou's contribution (Chapter 5), which is based on an original survey designed to look at the interconnections between different types of Chinese migration to Germany with different types of capital flows from China. They show that the number of Chinese students in Germany has increased rapidly since 2001, with a strong focus on engineering, machinery, business and natural sciences. Although most of these students return to China after graduation, they possess specific knowledge about German business culture and institutions that enables them to fulfil a bridging role between companies from both countries. Those Chinese students who decide to stay in Germany tend to set up their own companies, relying on their acquired expert knowledge and cultural understanding.

Further interesting developments can also be associated with the role of Chinese high-skilled workers brought by Chinese multinational enterprises investing in Europe. The increase of Chinese direct investment has created new migration flows of managers, employees, workers and their family members. Although the expatriate communities within Chinese-owned enterprises, especially the state-owned enterprises, are quite different from the ethnic communities of traditional migrants – and often co-exist only in parallel – these Chinese expatriates have re-enforced the presence of Chinese migrants in Europe and created additional links between the overseas Chinese community and their home country. According to Kaczmarczyk, Szulecka and Tyrowicz's contribution (Chapter 6), these new flows of high-skilled migrants stemming from Chinese FDI are becoming significant for example in Poland, which although not a major destination of Chinese early migrants has become a key location for Chinese outward FDI in search of a large and potentially expanding market, proximity to the EU and a still relatively cheap labour force compared to the rest of Europe.

Russia–China relations comprise a category of their own, which gives an additional dimension to our discussions and provides a wider context for other case studies. The underlying question tackled in Selezneva's contribution (Chapter 7) is whether being China's neighbour changes the dynamics of migration and economic relations. What is striking is that the answer seems to be no. Despite the declared special status of the two countries in each other's economy and geopolitical spheres, the relationship between investment and migration is to a large extent the same as in the EU countries. Russia and China are neighbours, both with the status of emerging state-run economies. On a political level, the governments have claimed that the two economies are compatible due to Russia's abundant natural resources and China's mobile labour force, but implementation of this alleged compatibility has lagged behind. Chinese workers in Russia are predominantly low-skilled workers working either in Chinese companies or in ethnic enclave businesses. They also dominate in the small border trade between the two countries. With regard to higher segments of employment, a plethora of bilateral agreements on cooperation has primarily benefited the Chinese labour market, with more Russian skilled workers working in China than Chinese working in Russia.

2.3.   The way ahead: the role of Chinese capital flows in shaping new migration patterns

Though the evidence on such new trends is still scarce and inconclusive, it may have a significant impact on the economic relationship between China and Europe on the one hand and on the migrant policy of European host countries on the other.

Overall, the picture emerging from these case studies seems to suggest that Chinese migration in Europe is clearly linked to economic activities, though with some relevant distinctions that are related to the different geographical areas and, especially, to the different modalities of capital investment or entrepreneurship involved. It seems possible to say that there is certainly a kind of spontaneous form of co-agglomeration between small-scale activities run by Chinese nationals and the size of the local Chinese communities, as illustrated by the existence of large clusters of Chinese firms in certain locations within Europe. On the other hand, perhaps due to the novelty of the phenomenon, the location choices of large-scale investments in the form of FDI do not seem to take advantage of the existence of Chinese communities. This is quite evident in the case of Portugal (described in Chapter 4), where the Chinese business community's structure has changed with the addition of a new large-scale segment, made up by investors (mainly state-owned enterprises, or SOEs) who are interested in acquiring the strategic resources of the country in the aftermath of the crisis. The (so far) clearly weak linkages between the two segments of the Chinese community in Portugal has given rise to a dualistic structure of the business community with stark contrasts between the two segments in terms of their size and fields of activities. There are, however, some notable exceptions. The case of Germany (discussed in Chapter 5) clearly shows that there is a key role for local communities, especially through the organization of business associations or by higher-skilled migrants, such as students; both can function as bridges, facilitating the entry of large-scale investors in the country as predicted by the transaction-cost related theory discussed in section 2. In addition, large-scale investments from China are likely to themselves become an instrument that attracts a new, highly skilled class of Chinese migrants, as discussed in the case of Poland (Chapter 6).

In Chinese policy making, investment and migration are considered separate policy issues. Chinese residents abroad may find employment with Chinese-invested companies or may even join smaller investments as partners. While this might be useful to these particular companies, it is not a central consideration for the Chinese government or Chinese businesses. Chinese skilled and unskilled contract workers employed by Chinese-invested firms or projects are an important exception: in these cases, people quite intentionally follow capital. However, such labour migration is explicitly intended to be temporary and remain separate from the local communities of Chinese residents.

Notes

1 The difference lies in the requirements: e.g. in Portugal, the investor has to invest a minimum of 500,000 EUR in a property or business, while in Germany, he or she must invest 1,000,000 EUR in a business and create a minimum of 10 German jobs.
2 The UK, Denmark and Ireland are not part of these EU directives.

References

Adams, W., & Rieben, H. (1968) *L'Exode des cerveaux*. Lausanne: Centre de recherches européenes.

Agunias, D. R., & Newland, K. (2007) *Circular Migration and Development: Trends, Policy Routes, and Ways Forward*. Washington, DC: MPIS.

Basch, L., Schiller, N. G., & Szanton Blanc, C. (1994) *Nations Unbound: Transnational Projects, Postcolonial Predicaments, and Deterritorialized Nation-States*. New York: Gordon and Breach.

Bauböck, R., & Faist, T. (2010) *Diaspora and Transnationalism: Concepts, Theories and Methods*. Amsterdam: Amsterdam University Press.

De Haas, H. (2005) International Migration, Remittances and Development: Myths and Facts, *Third World Quarterly*, 26 (8), 1269–84.

De Haas, H., & Novib, O. (2006) *Engaging Diasporas: How Governments and Development Agencies Can Support Diaspora Involvement in the Development of Origin Countries*. Oxford: International Migration Institute, University of Oxford.

EMN Synthesis Report. (2013) *Immigration of International Students to the EU*, available at: http://ec.europa.eu/dgs/home-affairs/what-we-do/networks/european_migration_network/reports/docs/emn-studies/immigration-students/0_immigration_of_international_students_to_the_eu_sr_24april2013_final_en.pdf

Kugler, M., & Rapoport, H. (2007) International Labour and Capital Flows: Complements or Substitutes? *Economics Letters*, 94, 155–62.

Latham, K., & Wu, B. (2013) *Chinese Immigration into the EU: New Trends, Dynamics and Implications*. London: Europe China Research and Advice Network.

Naughton, B. (2007) *The Chinese Economy: Transitions and Growth*. Cambridge, MA: MIT University Press.

Ndofor, H. A., & Priem, R. L. (2011) Immigrant Entrepreneurs, the Ethnic Enclave Strategy, and Venture Performance, *Journal of Management*, 37 (3), 790–818.

Neckerman, K. M., Carter, P., & Lee, J. (1999) Segmented Assimilation and Minority Cultures of Mobility, *Ethnic and Racial Studies*, 22 (6), 945–65.

Portes, A., & Zhou, M. (1993) The New Second Generation: Segmented Assimilation and Its Variants, *The Annals of the American Academy of Political and Social Science*, 530 (1), 74–96.

Portes, A. (1995) Economic Sociology and the Sociology of Immigration: A conceptual Overview. In Portes, A. (Ed.) *The Economic Sociology of Immigration*. New York: Russell Sage Foundation, pp. 1–41.

Sanders, J. M., & Nee, V. (1987) Limits of Ethnic Solidarity in the Enclave Economy, *American Sociological Review*, 52 (6), 745–73.

Schiller, N. G., Basch, L., & Blanc-Szanton, C. (1992) Towards a Definition of Transnationalism. *Annals of the New York Academy of Sciences*, 645 (1), ix–xiv.

VanWey, L., & Faist, T. (2000) The Volume and Dynamics of International Migration and Transnational Social Spaces, *Social Forces*, 79 (2), 793.

Vertovec, S., & Cohen, R. (1999) *Migration, Diasporas and Transnationalism*. Cheltenham: Edward Elgar.

Waldinger, R. (1993) The Ethnic Enclave Debate Revisited, *International Journal of Urban and Regional Research*, 17 (3), 444–52.

Zahlan, A. B. (Ed.) (1981) *The Arab Brain Drain*. London: Ithaca Press.

1 Chinese investment strategies and migration – does diaspora matter?

Frank N. Pieke and Tabitha Speelman

Abstract

The first section of this chapter outlines the main changes in the Chinese migration order since roughly 1980. In the second section, the chapter turns to a discussion of Chinese emigration and settlement in Europe (by which we mainly refer to the EU countries), whose similarities and contrasts help us highlight the range of permutations in recent emigration from China. The third section turns to China's administration, management and institutional and legal framework for dealing with the many different Chinese migratory flows and their ramifications for China, both domestically and for its rising global presence. Section 1.4 is a brief conclusion including some reflections on future trends.

Introduction

After the victory of the Chinese Communist Party (CCP) in 1949, China rapidly shut itself off from the rest of the world. Emigration from China, already much reduced due to the Great Depression and the Second World War, diminished even further and came to an almost complete standstill in the 1960s, with the important exception of illegal emigration across the border into Hong Kong.

This situation contrasts sharply with Chinese migration today. China now is one of the most important sending countries and has recently also become increasingly significant as a destination for international migrants from the whole world. The most important fact about Chinese international migration is perhaps the incredible diversity of migration. The interaction among the many different Chinese migratory flows and migrant communities is clearly crucial in shaping the way that new migrants insert themselves in receiving societies. Unlike 30 years ago, migrants are now from all kinds of social and cultural backgrounds, hail from all over China and include business and government expatriates, investors and entrepreneurs, students, professionals, contract workers, unskilled job seekers and family migrants. Chinese migrants fan out all over the world in search of employment, business opportunities, educational qualifications, marriage or family reunification. Added to this must be the vastly larger number of Chinese who travel abroad for shorter periods as tourists or visitors on business, on exchange programmes, as members of delegations or for family reasons. The world is indeed becoming a Chinese space, with long-term emigration being a vital but by no means the only component.

In the first section of this chapter, we outline the main changes in the Chinese migration order since roughly 1980. In the second section, we turn to a discussion of Chinese emigration and settlement in Europe (by which we mainly refer to the EU countries), putting it in a wider context of Chinese migrations from China. The third section turns to China's administration, management and institutional and legal framework for dealing with the many different Chinese migratory flows and their ramifications for China, both domestically and for its rising global presence. Section 1.4 is a conclusion including some reflections on future trends.

1.1.   Chinese international migration trends

The most important change in the Chinese emigration order in the last 40 years obviously has been the resumption of emigration from the People's Republic of China (PRC). The main driver, at least initially, of the new migration from the PRC was a gradual but fundamental relaxation of the country's emigration policy from the early 1970s onward. From an almost total ban on officially endorsed emigration, the PRC moved to a policy framework that now allows foreign travel and emigration to virtually all Chinese citizens who can produce a visa or other evidence of the right of legitimate entry to a foreign country. The frequent chastening of China for not letting its citizens out is now but a vague memory of a distant Cold War past.

Between the early 1970s and late 1980s, the new Chinese migration from the PRC consisted of two very different types. The first one was the resumption of emigration from areas where, before 1949, the majority of overseas Chinese came from. These new overseas Chinese first went to communities of overseas Chinese established before 1949 but gradually branched out to other destinations in search of opportunities. The chief examples of this are migrants from the Taishan area in Guangdong province to the United States and from the Wenzhou/Qingtian area in Southern Zhejiang province to Europe. Only somewhat later did emigration from the central part of Fujian province start. Despite being an old overseas area with communities in Southeast Asia, Central Fujian had no pre-existing ties with North America and Europe. Nevertheless, those became the chief destination areas of new migrants from Fujian.

The second initial flow of new Chinese migrants consisted of students and visiting scholars. Chinese students chiefly went to the United States, with smaller numbers accepted by other developed countries (Japan, Canada, Western Europe, Australia, New Zealand) as well. At this time, almost all Chinese students were postgraduates, accepted and supported on exchange programmes or Western scholarships; few Chinese could as yet afford the costs of study abroad themselves.

This relatively ordered pattern of Chinese international migration, with reasonably well-defined flows and areas of origin and destination, changed fundamentally in the 1990s and 2000s. Some of these changes were at least partially path dependent in that they followed from the impact that ongoing migration had on policy making and social and economic development in sending and receiving areas. However, change has equally much been driven by fundamental changes in Chinese society. Economic reform in the cities really began to bite in the early 1990s, weaning increasing numbers of urban Chinese from the dependence and restrictions of the Chinese "work unit" system. Reform and foreign trade also generated unprecedented economic growth, in turn creating a new entrepreneurial elite and middle class with a lifestyle and expectations to match. In terms of social and spatial mobility, Chinese now have almost as much freedom as residents of non-socialist countries. However, as China's market reform creates an increasingly level playing field, it produces not only winners but also losers: rural dwellers in the interior or otherwise isolated places, farmers in peri-urban areas losing their land to development projects and urban residents shed by state enterprise reform without much hope of finding comparable employment elsewhere.

The overall result of these developments has been that the types, origins and destinations of Chinese migration have changed and proliferated, both within China itself and abroad. Emigration is no longer limited to a few pockets of Chinese society but has become an option that can be entertained by Chinese across the country and from a wide range of backgrounds. In other words, these migratory flows have to be understood as transnational aspects of domestic patterns of geographical and social mobility resulting from the fundamental changes that have taken place in Chinese society rather than a "culture of migration" that produces emigration in traditional overseas Chinese areas.

The universalization of migration across China, therefore, emphatically does not entail that the number of Chinese migrants is now only limited by the obstacles that sending and receiving countries manage to put in their way – many factors impinge on migratory decisions, opportunity being one and only one of them. Universalization does, however, mean that Chinese migration has become highly diverse, making it increasingly difficult to speak about Chinese migration in the singular in any analytically meaningful sense. In what follows, we will briefly review the most important of these changes in the Chinese migration order. We will start with (1) commercialization of emigration and then discuss (2) the involvement of local government before moving on first to (3) the globalization of Chinese migration and then (4) the rise of education and professional migration.

1.1.1. Commercialization of emigration

The emigration business has become a world-wide phenomenon that includes everything from schools for language or professional training in preparation for work or study abroad to emigration agencies that advertise in newspapers or on the Internet to the gradual commercialization of assistance originally given free of charge to friends or family. The commercialization and professionalization of emigration was pioneered by Fujianese migrants to the United States in the 1980s. The first things that may very well come to mind here are illegal migration, asylum abuse or human smuggling and trafficking organized by "snakeheads", but commercialization is actually a much broader issue. In recent years and in response to increasingly successful attempts at cracking down on people smuggling from China, smugglers in Fujian branched out from transport by sea and over land to organized flights using counterfeit documents. When that became increasingly difficult as well, smugglers started arranging for genuine visas for fake marriage, business or study abroad (Chu 2010; Pieke et al. 2004).

Emigration from Fujian foreshadowed developments in China's Northeast (also known as Manchuria) and other provinces, which in the late 1990s suddenly put themselves on the Chinese emigration map. The Northeast in the 1990s was a rust belt of ill-performing state-owned enterprises. Emigration provided urban workers a much needed escape from unemployment; in their wake, rural dwellers also quickly availed themselves of the opportunities to go abroad. Commercial agencies that facilitate travel and emigration abroad drive much of the emigration from the Northeast and elsewhere. These agencies are fully legal and operate in full view of the authorities. The bulk of their work consists of Chinese contract workers destined for temporary employment in, for instance Japan, South Korea or Africa, but especially in the European context, this often shades into facilitating the legal entry of emigrants who, after the expiration of their visas, remain illegally (Pieke & Xiang 2010).

1.1.2. Local government

Local government is involved in Chinese emigration in ways that are often not condoned by policy or law of the central government. Central Fujian province provides the best-documented example. Informally, individual officials of local government in coastal central Fujian had been involved in the illegal emigration business already from the early 1980s (one of the key reasons emigration could flourish in this area), but the government could not openly be seen to be involved.[1]

In many other places beyond the overseas Chinese areas, local government (rather than individual officials) is in fact one of the key agents in the spread of mass emigration. The first example from Pieke's research dates from 1990 in the interior of Fujian province (principally Mingxi County), an industrial centre dating from Mao Zedong's "Third Front" strategy of the 1960s and early 1970s but also an area without any overseas Chinese tradition. Acutely aware of the success of international migration very nearby in coastal Central Fujian, the authorities were keen to raise the local standard of living through migration just as had happened along the coast. At the time, the local government's encouragement of emigration still had to be carefully weighed against the provincial government's displeasure and the general sensitivities arising from Fujian's illegal emigration business, and the local government could not openly facilitate emigration. Later, however, the county government felt confident enough to establish a migration guarantee fund. This fund gave loans to potential migrants to help them pay for their migration overseas. Money for the fund was provided by the county's International Economic and Trade Office, the Agricultural Bank and the Department of Finance. Subsequently, a new policy allowed banks to fund migration directly rather than through this government fund, thus even further widening the scope of such practices and fully integrating migration into the local economy. With the backing of the local authorities, the area quickly became an important sending area of Chinese migrants to Europe (Pieke et al. 2004, ch. 2).

1.1.3.   Globalization

The third key feature of the new Chinese migration order is the globalization of migration. Until the late 1980s, individual Chinese migratory flows tended to target specific destination areas with well-established Chinese ethnic sectors and communities from the same area of origin, only gradually expanding into adjacent areas, thus minimizing competition between Chinese groups. Starting in the mid-1980s, the Fujianese were the first to break through this mould. By focussing on the United States and later Western Europe, Fujianese migrants entered the territories of entrenched communities of Chinese from Hong Kong, Guangdong or Zhejiang, where they were mostly treated with hostility and as cheap, expendable labour. In the late 1980s and early 1990s, this example was quickly followed by the Zhejiangese, who aggressively expanded from their traditional stronghold in Western (and more recently Southern) Europe. In the 1990s, Zhejiangese appeared in new frontier areas, such as Eastern Europe or Africa. They also established a foothold in the UK and North America.

1.1.4.   Educational and professional migration

Globalization of Chinese migration is also a consequence of the rise of educational and professional migration, which is the fourth aspect of the new Chinese migration order that we would like to highlight here. In the 1990s and 2000s, Chinese educational migration proliferated, both in terms of sheer numbers and in the range of student backgrounds, destinations and degrees pursued. As China got richer, foreign study came within reach of the offspring of China's burgeoning entrepreneurial elite and even the salaried middle classes (Fong 2011).

Chinese professional migration is to a large extent the by-product of educational migration, when graduates seek employment in the country of study (or perhaps elsewhere abroad) rather than returning home. This pattern is particularly pronounced in the United States, but is significant in, for instance, Western Europe and particularly Japan as well.[2] Direct immigration of professionals from the PRC is also significant and on the rise not only to regions and countries where one might expect it (North America, Western Europe, Australia and New Zealand, Singapore and Hong Kong) but also to African countries that perhaps seem non-obvious to a Western observer.

1.1.5.   The changing face of Chinese migration

Since the late 1970s and accelerating in the early 1990s, Chinese migration has changed almost beyond recognition. Some old overseas Chinese areas (for instance, in Southern Fujian or much of the Pearl River Delta) that were able to tap into the opportunities for employment and entrepreneurship in New Economic Zones close by have conspicuously failed to generate new flows of mass migration. However, other, less well-located overseas Chinese areas (Central Fujian, Southern Zhejiang and, to a lesser extent, the Sze Yep area in Guangdong) have instead capitalized on their overseas links and have generated commercialized migration flows with a truly global reach. In these areas, emigration has become virtually universal: migrating abroad is the number-one choice for success for all but the very rich and the very poor.

Simultaneously, emigration has also become a much more generally available avenue for social mobility for people across China and from all kinds of backgrounds. For them, a decision to emigrate follows from diverse educational, employment or entrepreneurial strategies in which emigration is carefully weighted up against domestic employment, entrepreneurship or higher education, all of which may also include possible migration elsewhere in China. In other words, these migratory flows have to be understood as aspects of general domestic patterns of geographical and social mobility created by the fundamental changes that have taken place in Chinese society. Migrants of this type aspire to find white-collar employment or self-employment, although a considerable number may actually end up having to settle for low-skilled work abroad, either in the ethnic Chinese sector or else as day labourers in agriculture, manufacturing or food processing (Pieke & Xiang 2010). The numbers involved in these migratory flows can be large and are most likely to grow in absolute terms, but we would expect that only a very small percentage of the potential migration base will ever actually emigrate. For the vast majority, opportunities in China itself will continue to be less risky and expensive and more attractive, realistically available, or in tune with one's preferred lifestyle.

1.2. Migration from China to the European Union member states in a global context

Migration is a factor that is often discussed in the context of China's involvement in Central and Southeast Asia, on the African continent and in Latin America, regions where China is suspected of expansionist, hegemonic or even neo-colonial ambitions. In the discussion that follows, we will make some reference to these concerns without however wishing to imply that there is a plan for Chinese world domination in which Chinese emigration is one strategic component. Chinese migration (and investment and trade) is simply too diverse and too much subject to individual, local or sectorial agency to be subordinated to Beijing's agenda. Conversely, in China, different policy priorities compete with each other that make it very difficult to arrive at a sustained and coordinated approach to migration and its strategic implications.

Chinese living in the European Union can be divided into two main categories. Europe has long been the destiny of Chinese migrants seeking employment or trading opportunities, often in a specific Chinese sector of the economy.

The aim usually is to start in menial, unskilled employment and then work one's way up to become the owner of a business, for instance a restaurant, store or workshop. The other group of Chinese residents is, on the whole, a much more recent development. Chinese are increasingly coming to Europe to study at a university, vocational school, training programme or high school. In addition, an unknown number of wealthy Chinese own a second home in Europe, are here as expatriate employees of Chinese firms or organizations, have immigrated or stayed behind after graduation as professionals or have married a European resident.

Meaningful and reliable figures on the total number of Chinese in Europe are notoriously hard to get. This is not a new problem, yet little seems to be done about it. Eurostat collects and compiles data from its member states; a recent report details that China, with 97,000 new immigrants in 2008, was the second largest source of immigrants into the EU (after Morocco with 157,000). The same report states that Chinese were the tenth most numerous group of foreign citizens resident in the EU, with 2.1 per cent of EU total foreign population in 2008. With a reported total number of foreign nationals in EU member states (including nationals from other EU states) of 31,860,300, this percentage yields a total of 669,066 Chinese nationals in the EU in 2008 (Eurostat 2011).

National statistical bureaus of individual European countries often (but not always) provide numbers on their Chinese population. However, individual countries employ different definitions and methodologies to divide their population up into ethnic or national categories. The UK, for instance, employs ethnic self-identification in its censuses. In 2011, this yielded a total number of resident ethnic Chinese in England and Wales of 393,141.[3] The Netherlands, in its population records, uses country of birth of self and/or parents: a 2011 study yielded a total number of Chinese of 71,500 in 2010, almost two thirds Dutch nationals (Gijsberts et al. 2011).

One Chinese estimate of the total number of Chinese in Europe (however that might have been defined or measured) ranges between 2.6 and 3.2 million in 2010. Of this group, 800,000 are said to be "new migrants" who plan to stay in Europe (excluding illegal migrants and students).[4] This estimate, while probably generous, seems not too far off the mark when compared to the Eurostat, UK and Dutch figures, especially if not taken too literally and used merely as a point of comparison with similarly derived figures for Africa and other places.[5]

1.2.1. *Labour migration*

In all, five major groups of Chinese labour migrants have fanned out across Europe. In the nineteenth century, the first to come to Europe were small traders from two adjacent areas in southern Zhejiang: the hinterland of the port city of Wenzhou and the rural area around the town of Qingtian (Thunø 1999). Emigration from Zhejiang subsided after the Great Depression, the Second World War and the founding of the People's Republic of China in 1949 but quickly gained pace again after roughly 1974.

The second group are the Cantonese from the Pearl River Delta who came to the major ports in Northwestern Europe (London, Liverpool, Rotterdam, Amsterdam, Antwerp and Hamburg) as seamen. By the end of the Second World War, most had left Europe, but a few stayed on. They were joined in the 1950s by fellow Cantonese from the New Territories of Hong Kong who came to Britain in large numbers to find work in the Chinese catering trade (Watson 1977). From Britain they spread first to the Netherlands and later to Belgium, France, Germany, Scandinavia, Italy, Spain and Portugal.

The third group of Chinese in Europe are from former European colonies in Southeast Asia and other regions. After the fall of the United States–backed regimes in Vietnam, Laos and Cambodia in 1975, 75,000 Chinese from Indochina fled to France; smaller numbers of refugees were accepted by other Western European countries. Approximately 10,000 Chinese from Indonesia arrived in the Netherlands after Indonesian independence in 1947 and the Chinese pogroms in the 1950s and 1960s. Finally, relatively small numbers of Chinese from other former colonies, such as Singapore, Malaysia, Mozambique, Macao and Suriname, also found their way to Europe.

A fourth group of Chinese are immigrants from Central Fujian province who appeared in Europe in the second half of the 1980s. Their arrival was a direct consequence of the activities of human smugglers in Fujian. Originally, most of those who ended up in other European countries either could not afford passage to America, were abandoned halfway or were simply given no other choice. Only in the 1990s did Europe become the target of migratory flows from Fujian specifically destined for one or more countries in Europe, most commonly Britain or (in the case of Fujianese from Mingxi county) Central Europe or Italy (Pieke et al. 2004).

The fifth and final wave of Chinese immigrants are city dwellers, initially mainly from Northeast China but not much later from all over the country. Their presence became first apparent in Central and Eastern Europe immediately after the fall of communism there. Particularly in the initial phases, their migration often was an individual rather than a family decision. Many built on contacts with state enterprises and trading networks in China to provide goods and services to the undersupplied economies in the former Soviet bloc (Nyíri 1999). Soon, however, urban Chinese appeared all over Europe.

Specialization in specific sectors of the economy has given the Chinese populations in each region of Europe its own characteristics. In Western Europe, the catering trade and the ethnic sector continue to dominate. In Eastern Europe, the importation, wholesale and retail of cheap Chinese manufactured goods is the main activity of the Chinese population. In Southern Europe, Chinese specialize in small workshops that produce leather goods, garments or other products specifically aimed at local tastes and fashions.

For labour migrants from old and new overseas Chinese areas, employment in Chinatown or more generally the Chinese ethnic sector, such as the catering trade or leather goods or garment sweatshops in Europe, is not merely a second-choice option but in fact the main pull factor. Immigration of large numbers of Chinese willing to accept often gruelling working and living conditions revitalized the ethnic enclave economies and spurred their growth and spread.

What is unusual about the case of recent Chinese labour immigration is the sheer force and volume of the migration push generated by the high degree of commercialization of emigration in China. This has led to a surplus of Chinese labour and an even further deteriorating bargaining position of recent immigrants versus potential employers in the countries of destination. The obvious consequence has been an even further worsening of wages and working conditions. Migrants, especially if they stay and work illegally, are also vulnerable to extortion and protection rackets. Migration pressure in Britain recently has also had the effect of pushing Chinese migrants into employment outside the ethnic enclaves, which, in the case of women, also includes prostitution (Gao 2010).

1.2.2.   Students and highly skilled migrants

Young Chinese travel to Europe not only for a post-graduate degree at a top-level research university but also for undergraduate degrees, high school diplomas, pre-university courses or short-term certificate courses in English or other vocational skills. Europe is attractive not only for the quality of the education received but also for the relatively modest fees that universities charge, especially compared to the usual number-one choice, the United States. Chinese students currently are by far the largest group of foreign students in most European countries, whose governments and educational institutions energetically compete in this profitable growth market (Bohm et al. 2004).

According to a recent report of the European Commission and the Chinese Ministry of Education, the total number of Chinese students in the EU in 2010 was between 118,700 and 120,000, or about six times more than in 2000. This number is comparable to that in the United States, which had 127,600 Chinese students in 2010. Of the total number of Chinese students in the EU, 40 per cent were in the UK, 23 per cent in France and 20 per cent in Germany.[6] In the UK, China is the number one foreign country of origin for higher education students.[7] There is some doubt whether this high number will continue in the future. Chinese universities have been expanding fast, and Chinese parents and students often rank good universities in China higher than European universities. In the UK in the mid-2000s, considerable disquiet existed among Chinese students at third-tier institutions, while English-language training centres were often found to be mere fronts for labour immigration.[8] Recently, the rescinding of post-study work visas has threatened to make the UK less attractive to Chinese students.[9]

The aspect of the Chinese presence in Europe that is least known about is investments and enterprises and the associated immigration of Chinese professionals and their families (and quite unlike Africa, where it is the aspect that receives the most attention). Chinese-invested enterprises fall roughly into two categories. Larger Chinese corporate subsidiaries are more concentrated in Western Europe. Smaller individual entrepreneurial firms predominate in Eastern Europe, although they are by no means absent in Western Europe. The smaller firms tend to be concentrated in wholesale or retail trade; the larger firms focus on knowledge-intensive sectors. Smaller firms, usually privately owned, are more likely to have been set up in close co-operation or even partnership with local Chinese, who thus play a crucial role in bringing these investments to Europe. Larger investments are strategic, aimed at accessing European technology, brands, markets and skills. They may employ local ethnic Chinese or Chinese from Hong Kong or Taiwan for their familiarity with Western culture and business practices, but their business partners tend to be non-Chinese (Zhang et al. 2011).[10]

1.3. China's governance of international migration

For a correct understanding of China's governance of international migration, the basic observation should first be made that China knows no uniform, comprehensive and consistent approach. Instead, there are many, each associated with certain parts of the administration (usually a ministry, sometimes a CCP department). To add to the confusion, local governments often pursue their own agenda, which may (or may not) be at odds with priorities entertained by the Centre. The only consolation is the fact that this true for all policy areas in China. Fragmentation is intrinsic to China's system of government, in which there is no distinction between politics and administration. As a result, all administration is politicized; conversely, all politics is administratively informed.[11]

Emigration, migrants and return migration are aspects of many policy fields. Most important among these are overseas Chinese affairs, strengthening China's role in the world, development assistance to foreign countries, economic development in China itself, attracting high-end foreign and returnee talent, avoiding the "middle-income trap", national security and maintenance of the leading role of the CCP and no doubt several more. We will not be able to do justice to all of these but will focus on just a few that seem most germane to the purposes of this book.

1.3.1. Overseas Chinese affairs

Since the end of the nineteenth century, policies of China's governments toward emigrated Chinese and their descendants have wavered between two opposing notions, one inclusive, the other restrictive. The inclusive notion recognizes all Chinese worldwide, regardless of nationality or residence (and sometimes even ethnicity), as belonging to the Chinese nation. The opposite is a restricted notion of "Chinese" that only includes those who live in China, often further restricted in terms of either having Chinese descent or else citizenship.

After 1955, when at the Bandung Conference China committed itself to a leadership role in the movement of non-aligned countries, the People's Republic of China adopted a severely restricted notion of Chineseness in its dealings with emigrants, returned migrants and their descendants. This was a concession to Indonesia and other Southeast Asia countries in particular that were very weary of China's potential involvement in their very large and influential Chinese communities.

A cornerstone of the policies that followed from this choice was the refusal to allow dual citizenship. This was a sharp break with the past. Both the Qing dynasty in the last decades of its rule and the Republic of China after the fall of the Qing in 1912 were committed to a policy of automatic Chinese citizenship for all ethnic Chinese. Now suddenly, overseas Chinese were encouraged to adopt the nationality of their country of residence and to give up their Chinese nationality. Overseas Chinese affairs (*qiaowu*) thus was limited to Chinese abroad who had retained Chinese citizenship (termed "overseas Chinese", *Huaqiao*), dependents left behind in China (called *qiaojuan*) and overseas Chinese who had returned to China (*guiqiao*). All other "ethnic Chinese" (*Huaren*) were considered foreign nationals beyond China's responsibility. The main objective of this policy was to limit the diplomatic fallout on the PRC's relations with countries where ethnic Chinese resided, particularly in Southeast Asia. A secondary objective was to ensure the flow of remittances that supported overseas Chinese dependants in China while insulating socialist China from unchecked bourgeois influences emanating from the overseas Chinese (Pieke 1987; Wang 1993; Wang et al. 2006).

In 1977, after the turmoil of the Cultural Revolution period, China formally reinstated these notionally restrictive policies, but immediately their scope was widened in practice to include significant elements of the other, inclusive notion of Chineseness. Compared to the pre–Cultural Revolution period, the privileges and profile of overseas Chinese and returned overseas Chinese were expanded in an effort to strengthen their attachment and dedication to the land of their ancestors. Overseas Chinese and ethnic Chinese were encouraged to make charitable donations to their native place. They also were encouraged to return to China for visits to their place of origin and for tourism, study or business.

With reform and opening up, overseas Chinese had become much more than a liability that had to be managed. Their access to foreign capital, know-how and markets made them a valuable asset that had to be carefully cultivated. It no longer was particularly relevant whether a particular overseas Chinese investor, businessman or academic held Chinese or a foreign nationality: all were now kith and kin to be welcomed back in the embrace of the land of the ancestors (*zuguo*). This approach yielded rich dividends: since the start of reform, overseas Chinese have generated the vast bulk of inward overseas investment in China. Furthermore, by formally hanging on to a restrictive approach to overseas Chinese, China can choose to involve itself in the internal affairs of overseas Chinese communities and their countries of residence only to the extent that this conforms to China's own interests. There is no obligation, unless China wants to do so, to represent overseas Chinese interests outside China's own borders, with the exception of the interests of Chinese passport holders. Because of the ban on dual citizenship that China continues to hang on to, the latter are almost all recent migrants. They are therefore relatively powerless both in China itself and in their country of residence (Barabantseva 2005; Thunø 2001).

As we have seen in the preceding sections, with the onset of reform, an end also came to the PRC's highly restrictive emigration policies. Already in the early 1970s, the almost complete ban on emigration was lifted, followed by progressively further relaxation after 1978. A milestone was the 1985 "Law of the People's Republic of China on the control of exit and entry of citizens", in 2012 incorporated into the "Exit and entry administration law of the People's Republic of China".[12] The regulations turned exit by Chinese citizens into a normal event in principle within reach of all Chinese citizens, although they explicitly stopped short from granting the automatic right to exit. Chapter 2 of the law requires Chinese citizens to apply for a passport and gain permission to travel abroad, giving almost unlimited scope to the authorities to refuse such permission if they wish to do so. Nevertheless, by the early 2000s, the government increasingly treated exit and entry, as Xiang Biao put it, "as an area of service rather than of control" (Xiang 2003: 22).

However, a key issue regarding Chinese citizens who have left China for purposes of long-term or permanent residence abroad remains the fact that they lose their household registration in their place of residence in China (Lynn-Ee Ho 2011). With that, they and their children also forfeit a very extensive range of rights to settlement, housing, education and welfare; their rights and legal status are therefore not much different from those of returning ethnic Chinese with foreign citizenship. If they were to choose to return to China, they will therefore have to do so as overseas Chinese rather than as ordinary Chinese citizens returning home, and the local overseas Chinese affairs office is responsible for making arrangements, such as housing and schooling.[13]

Initially, the largest number of what in the 1990s became known as China's "new migrants" came from China's old overseas Chinese areas. These new migrants could therefore relatively easily be accommodated with the existing policy and institutional framework established for overseas Chinese affairs. Overseas Chinese affairs are fully integrated in the dense and complex mesh of Chinese administration. Usually at all levels of administration, from the Centre down to the county or even the township level, these include the government Office of Overseas Chinese Affairs (*Qiaoban*), the Overseas Chinese Federation (*Qiaolian*), the People's Congress Overseas Chinese Commission (*Huaqiao Weiyuanhui*) and the People's Political Consultative Conference's Taiwan, Hong Kong, Macao and Overseas Chinese Affairs Commission (*Zhengxie Tai-Ao-Gang Qiaowei*). Furthermore, one of China's eight so-called democratic parties that participate in the rule of China under the guidance of the CCP, the *Zhigongdang* (a name usually not translated but roughly meaning "party dedicated to the public cause"), represents returned overseas Chinese and the relatives of overseas Chinese (Barabantseva 2005). Finally, the Chinese Communist Party's United Front Department (*Tongzhanbu*) has overall responsibility for guidance, supervision and coordination of overseas Chinese affairs work across the administration.

1.3.2. Going out

After the 1980s, the old overseas Chinese and their native places ceased to be a government priority. From the perspective of the central government, new overseas Chinese migration, both from the traditional overseas Chinese areas and from other parts of China, often was more of an issue to be managed than an asset to be developed. The connection with illegality, asylum seeking and human smuggling made unskilled and unregulated overseas Chinese emigration a diplomatic head-ache for the central government in its dealings with receiving countries, especially those in the developed world. These insisted, reasonably or unreasonably, on a Chinese crackdown on "snakeheads" and a cooperative attitude in the admission of repatriated illegal immigrants and refugees who had been refused asylum.

An altogether different matter is the migration of students, skilled profession-als, businesspeople and, increasingly, organized contract workers. In Chinese discussions, as far as Chinese enterprises, investments and contract labour are concerned, these new foreign connections and migratory flows are usually con-nected to the government's so-called "going out" (*zou chuqu*) drive to strengthen China's economic presence abroad.

"Going out" was initiated in the latter half of the 1990s in the run-up to China's WTO accession in 2002. At the time, the Asian financial crisis of 1997 had left China largely unaffected, putting the country in a relatively favourable position to take advantage of business opportunities abroad. The surge in student and professional migration, however, predates the "going out" drive by at least five years, when in the early 1990s the Chinese government allowed self-funded study abroad (as distinct from students on a government scholarship). As we shall see, in this area, not "going out" but "inviting in" (*yin jinlai*) is the key consideration.

The "going out" policy is associated most with the Ministry of Commerce, whose profile in China's international involvement has risen steadily in the 1990s and 2000s. As the main ministry (*zhuguan bu*) dealing with foreign economic cooperation, the Ministry of Commerce is at the centre of labour export policy, which is ultimately about its contribution to the Chinese economy. This role was expanded after the restructuring and readjustment of the tasks of ministries in 2009. The Ministry of Commerce already had responsibility over those who were sent abroad through contracting, but since then, it also has been made responsible for managing Chinese individuals working abroad.[14]

Regarding foreign study, however, the Ministry of Education takes the lead; when we include the increasingly important issue of return migration of the highly educated, the Ministry of Human Resources and Social Security, the Ministry of Science and Technology and the Ministry of Public Security (in charge of border exit and entry) play an important role as well. However, here too, the Ministry of Commerce is involved. Many returned "talents" settle in a science and inno-vation park that is managed through committees that fall under the Ministry of Commerce or the Department of Commercial Affairs of the local government.

Policies for both organized labour export and new immigrants tend to come in packages that require cooperation among many different ministries. Adjustments to such a package will then inevitably lead to long-drawn-out re-negotiations between the main ministry in charge (usually the Ministry of Commerce) and each of the other parts of government. If one ministry is slow in making the nec-essary budget adjustments or the like, the entire package is delayed, resulting in slow change and inefficiency.[15]

Labour export on fixed-term contracts through recognized agencies was vigorously promoted in the 2000s as an alternative for unregulated overseas Chinese migration. Labour export has become hugely important in the developing world, however not so much as an alternative to overseas Chinese migration but rather simply as a completely separate flow associated with Chinese investments and projects.

Especially after 2003, labour export (often somewhat euphemistically called "foreign labour cooperation", *duiwai laowu hezuo*) increased rapidly. According to the Ministry of Commerce, in 2010, 346,888 workers were dispatched abroad. The top-five source provinces of these workers were Shandong, Jiangsu, Henan, Guangdong and Hubei. According to data from the State Statistical Bureau, in 2009, 154,801 contracts were signed with a value of US$6.73 billion. Of the contract workers sent abroad since 1978, a full 40 per cent worked in construction, 28 per cent in manufacture, 11 per cent in agriculture, forestry, animal husbandry and fishery, 7 per cent in transport and transportation, 5 per cent in catering and 9 per cent in other sectors of the economy. More than 80 per cent of all contract labour export takes place within Asia, especially Japan and South Korea.

Despite its growing importance, foreign contract employment remains insufficiently regulated. Intermediary agencies specialize merely in what Xiang Biao, following Beaudrillard's concept of "hyperreality", calls *hyperlegality*: the manufacture of simulacra of legality that undermine the intention of the law that have no relation to legal status in reality whatsoever.[16] Agencies are in no position to provide any services or protection to their clients beyond creating the appearance of legality and often are seen as fleecing gullible and inexperienced Chinese workers. More in general, Chinese workers abroad lack any form of Chinese legal protection. In response, in 2012, the Ministry of Commerce promulgated the "Regulations for the administration of foreign labour cooperation".[17] These regulations for the first time provide a clear framework for employment and intermediaries. Earlier State Council regulations from 2008 were principally aimed at Chinese enterprises engaging in contract labour, while in the new regulations, the positive rights of the workers are also mentioned. In article 44, for instance, the new regulations stipulate that the fees of employing companies should conform to China's domestic labour contract law of 2008.

The regulations also stipulate measures against other problems with labour export. Currently, contracts usually start with a government agreement. Then the local Chinese consulate and Chinese enterprises obtain specific information about labour supply and demand, making use of the services of usually state-owned intermediaries that have the right to send contract workers abroad. There is thus insufficient scope for Chinese labour supply and foreign demand to meet freely, and workers often lack training and qualifications for work abroad. There are also no guarantees that workers abroad do not do anything that is, as the regulations put it, "bad for the country" (article 15). To address these issues the Ministry of Commerce plans to provide a free information service to both enterprises and workers, establish an international labour cooperation information and notification system (article 30), and set up a foreign labour cooperation risk assessment and evaluation system (article 31). The state will financially support training programs, and in cooperation with the Ministry of Personnel and Social Security, the Ministry of Commerce will increase supervision of the training programs. Where relevant, local governments at the county level and above should establish an international labour service desk to provide service, as well as encourage and guide worker recruitment (article 34). The 2012 regulations promise work on a crisis management system at the state and local (county and above) level (article 36) and a publicly accessible black list of domestic and international untrustworthy businesses (article 37). Finally, under the heading "legal responsibility", article 40 states that permission to engage in labour cooperation will be cancelled in the case of (1) the organization of labour under a business, travel or study visa; (2) loaning out one's license to other organizations or individuals; or (3) organizing labour related to gambling or prostitution.[18]

Risk assessment and evaluation are particularly acute issues not only for workers but also for Chinese enterprises abroad. Earlier in 2012, the Ministry of Commerce had issued a document proposing a warning and information system for incidents endangering Chinese workers' lives and possessions.[19] The proposal describes different kinds of risks and ways workers abroad should be notified of these risks. The proposal came right after the kidnapping of 29 Chinese workers in Sudan and 24 workers in Egypt (two of 13 such incidents in the last five years), and the subsequent discussion about the fate of Chinese workers abroad in international and domestic media.

1.3.3.   Foreign study and "inviting in"

Studying abroad has become the fastest-growing flow of foreign migration; (former) students account for most of the growth of the Chinese population in many destination countries, especially in the developed world. Study abroad has long ceased to be the privilege of China's most talented youth. Many senior high school graduates will at some point have the opportunity to study abroad for a period of time,[20] while the children of many of China's elite often venture abroad even earlier, being prepared for an application to a foreign elite university in pre-university programmes, private high schools or, in some cases, even earlier than that.

Self-funded study abroad was permitted in the early 1990s; by 2010, 93 per cent of Chinese students abroad were self-financed.[21] Only a minority of these students ever return to China but find employment, obtain permanent residency and ultimately citizenship abroad. Until the early 2000s, this was a matter that raised remarkably few questions in China itself. In fact, the opportunity to study abroad has, for many aspiring Chinese individuals and families, been one of the great gifts of the reform era; restricting this freedom would very likely come at a disproportionately high political price.

However, as the Chinese economy has grown, Chinese students and professionals abroad are increasingly talked about in terms of a brain drain. According to the Ministry of Education, at the end of 2011, the accumulated number of Chinese students abroad was 2,244,100, of whom 818,400 or 36 per cent have returned to China. This is considered very low by policy makers and advisors in China, especially in view of the fact that the higher the educational qualifications attained, the lower the chance that a student returns.[22]

Policy has increasingly emphasized return as part of the "inviting in" of foreign businesses and individuals (*yin jinlai*). In 1987, returning was made a legal requirement for publicly funded students. In 1993, a policy was adopted towards students abroad summarized as "support study overseas, promote return home, maintain freedom of movement" (*zhichi liuxue, guli huiguo, laiqu ziyou*).[23] In 1996, China started actively encouraging students abroad to return with the founding of the China Scholarship Council. Policy documents have been coming out every year – for example, 2007 regulations according to which publicly funded students have to return upon completion of their degree and work in China for a minimum of two years. Failure to do so results in having to pay back the entire scholarship plus a 30 per cent service charge.[24]

Despite the relatively low return percentage, returnees are very prominent among academics and senior administrators in higher education and research institutions, especially the more prestigious and better funded ones. Others are high-tech entrepreneurs or independent professionals; yet others work for large multinationals or government. National and local governments and university administrations strongly encourage students and scholars abroad to return to China to take up academic employment, encouraging them with a range of privileges and perks (salary, housing, research funds) regardless of foreign permanent residence status or even citizenship.

Returnees, or *haigui* in Chinese, have become a policy priority in China. Chinese administrations actively recruit among overseas graduates and scholars and encourage them to set up businesses or contribute their knowledge, skills and patents to partnerships with Chinese businesses. To woo potential investors, governments frequently organize conventions or fairs, creating what Xiang Biao has called an elaborate "ritual economy of 'talent'" (Xiang 2011).

Educated Chinese abroad are increasingly talked about in terms of *brain gain*, a huge talent pool that China will be able to draw on in the years to come. At the Centre, return migration is directly linked with a key strategic issue that preoccupied the new Hu Jintao-Wen Jiabao regime that came to power in 2002. In order to strengthen China and its position in the world, China will have to retain its long-term competitiveness and not get caught into the so-called "middle-income trap". The way to do this is for China to make the transition to technology-intensive economic growth. Attracting or keeping highly educated workers and entrepreneurs, or "talents" (*rencai*) in Chinese government jargon, became central to this (Simon & Cao 2009). In 2010, the government published a long-term talents strategy that in 2011 was incorporated into the Twelfth Five-Year Plan.[25]

It should be emphasized that recruiting educated Chinese abroad is only one aspect of this policy, and a conscious effort is made also to attract "real" (this is the way it is often put in more informal discussions) foreigners to live and work long term in China. Nevertheless, the vast majority of people thus lured back to China continue to have a Chinese background; conversely, ethnic Chinese are much more easily given long-term or permanent residency. For instance, the government's flagship Thousand Talents Programme by August 2011 had already recruited over 1,500 leading scientists and entrepreneurs. More than 70 per cent were foreign nationals, mostly ethnic Chinese.

1.4.   Conclusion

In Europe, and indeed all over the world, Chinese immigration has shot up in the last decades. Europe is a continent where Chinese have resided for many decades. In Europe, universities and other educational institutions hold the promise of valuable knowledge and qualifications that qualitatively raise career prospects and life chances. Europe's is among the most highly developed economies in the world, with not only a huge market for Chinese products and services but also a place for strategic investments in high-value assets and market access and source of state-of-the art technology and skills. More abstractly, Europe is a focus of Chinese modernist longings, a place that long ago achieved a state of modernity that China still yearns for.

Migration from China has become extremely diverse. The Chinese authorities have reacted pragmatically, without making any real attempt to construct a coherent and transparent framework of policies and institutions to deal with emigration, Chinese populations abroad and return migration. Conflicts and confusions among different policy fields and agendas cannot be resolved within the framework of overseas Chinese affairs. Rhetorically, the term "overseas Chinese" continues to be a useful way for Chinese government and emigrants to perform at specific occasions or for certain specific purposes the transnational unity of the Chinese nation, regardless of nationality, ethnicity, residence or class. However, overseas Chinese affairs have remarkably few material implications except when dealing with return visits or return migration of ethnic Chinese, where "overseas Chinese affairs" provides a convenient framework both to fit and to insulate such returnees from Chinese society. The language and institutions of overseas Chinese affairs are ill suited to cater fully to the priorities and expectations of migrants that do not come from any of the designated overseas Chinese areas, in particular high-skilled migrants, such as students, businesspeople, professionals, expatriates or investors. In practice, therefore, they are treated largely separately, not only from each other but also from other new labour migrants, either from old overseas Chinese areas or elsewhere.

The diversity of emigration and the policy agendas that it serves make it hard to generalize about the connections between Chinese outward investment, emigration and Chinese communities abroad. It is probably safe to say that, in China itself, investment and migration are considered separate policy issues. Chinese residents abroad (former students, second-generation overseas Chinese) may find employment with Chinese-invested firms or may even join smaller investments as partners. While this might be useful to these particular firms, it is not a central consideration for Chinese government or business. An important exception are

Chinese skilled and unskilled contract workers employed by Chinese-invested firms or projects: here people quite intentionally follow capital. However, such labour migration is explicitly intended to be temporary and remain separate from local communities of resident Chinese.

In sum, there does not seem to be a coherent and joined-up strategy on the part of the Chinese government to maximize the utility of Chinese emigration to China's long-term goals of continued modernization and a more prominent place in the world. Certain aspects of migration or certain types of migrants are enlisted to serve specific policy objectives, such as technological upgrading of China's economy, a more prominent role of Chinese enterprises abroad or relief of unemployment pressures in certain sectors or areas. Other troublesome aspects of migration have been the target of policy making aimed at minimizing the potential damage that they may do. However, to read into these efforts the orchestration or manipulation of international migration to serve the Chinese government's global strategic objectives would be vastly overstating the point.

Notes

1 This is information from informal conversations with members of foreign visiting delegations or journalists and off-the-record comments in interviews with migrants, but it is hard to corroborate in formal interviews or other sources. Published academic research carefully skirts the issue, only mentioning tacit or active encouragement of emigration or corrupt involvement by local officials; see Chu (2010, ch. 3); Pieke et al. (2004, ch. 2); Soudijn (2006: 69); Zhang (2008).
2 On Japan, see Liu-Farrer (2011).
3 www.ons.gov.uk/ons/publications/re-reference-tables.html?edition=tcm%3A77–286262
4 These figures are from Song (2011). See also Li (2009).
5 In the Dutch data (see note 4 above), roughly one third of Chinese in the Netherlands holds Chinese citizenship. If we extrapolate this on to the Eurostat figure of 670,000 Chinese citizens, we can conclude that there are probably three times as many, i.e. about 2 million people, with China as the country of birth of self and/or parents. To this an unknown but significant number of people must be added who in a UK–style census would classify themselves as Chinese, despite the fact that they or their parents were born outside China. A further unknown is illegal immigrants, who are almost completely beyond the reach of government statistics.
6 European Commission and the Ministry of Education in China, *EU-China Student and Academic Staff Mobility: Present Situation and Future Developments*, April 2011, http://ec.europa.eu/education/external-relation-programmes/doc/china/mobility_en.pdf.
7 Higher Education Statistics Agency, Press release 172 – Non-UK domicile students, 23 February 2012, www.hesa.ac.uk/index.php?option=com_content&task=view&id=2371&Itemid=161.
8 Personal communications to the author from the Chinese embassy in the UK and officials at the British Home Office. See also Cross and Hitchcock (2007).
9 Chen Jia and Ai Yang, "UK Visa Rules May Force Chinese Student Exodus", China Daily, 15 December 2010, www.chinadaily.com.cn/china/2010–12/15/content_11702526.htm; Wang Dongliang, "UK Visa Policy Change to Impact Chinese Students", *People's Daily Online*, 21 March 2012, http://english.peopledaily.com.cn/90883/7765064.html.
10 See also Haiyan Zhang, this volume.

11 The first to formulate this "fragmented authoritarianism" approach to Chinese politics were Lieberthal and Oksenburg (1988).
12 For the text of the 2012 "Zhonghua Renmin Gongheguo chujing rujing guanli fa" ["Exit and entry administration law of the People's Republic of China"], see www.npc.gov.cn/npc/xinwen/2012–07/01/content_1728516.htm. An unofficial translation is available at http://lawandborder.com/?p=1425.
13 Article 13 of the 2012 Exit and Entry Law. Against this background, it seems highly significant that recently Ma Jianguo, vice chairman of Jiangsu Provincial Committee of China Zhi Gong Party, at the annual session of the Chinese People's Political Consultative Conference National Committee, announced that China shall issue special identity documents for overseas Chinese to provide them the same convenience concerning children's education, medical service, home purchases and entrance-exit procedures as domestic citizens to facilitate overseas Chinese returning to the motherland to live and start businesses; "Reforms urged to attract overseas Chinese", *Xinhua News Agency*, 11 March 2012, www.china.org.cn/china/NPC_CPPCC_2012/2012–03/11/content_24865428.htm
14 Interview with Feng Lei, Institute of Finance and Trade Economics, Chinese Academy of Social Sciences, 10 September 2012. The Ministry of Commerce, for instance, hosts the website for the "going out" drive; http://zcq.mofcom.gov.cn/.
15 Interview with Feng Lei, 10 September 2012.
16 Xiang, "Windows", p. 8.
17 For the full text of the 2012 "Duiwai laowu hezuo guanli tiaoli" ["Regulations for the administration of foreign labour cooperation"], see www.gov.cn/zwgk/2012–06/11/content_2157905.htm. The 2008 State Council "Duiwai chengbao gongcheng tiaoli" ["Regulations for projects on foreign contracts"] can be found at www.gov.cn/flfg/2008–07/28/content_1058146.htm.
18 On the considerations that informed the new 2012 regulations, see Zhang (2011). Wu Bin's research on Chinese seafarers echoes the same concerns about abuse, lack of legal protection and arbitrarily high fees (see Wu 2008).
19 "System for advance warning and information notification on safety and risks abroad of foreign investment cooperation" ["Duiwai touzi hezuo jingwai anquan fengxian yujing he xinxi tongbao zhidu"], 15 February 2012, www.mofcom.gov.cn/aarticle/i/jyjl/k/201202/20120207967111.html. This document is a further elaboration of regulations from 2010. On the 2012 kidnappings of Chinese workers abroad, see Peter Ford, "Why Chinese workers are getting kidnapped abroad", *Christian Science Monitor*, 1 February 2012, www.csmonitor.com/World/Asia-Pacific/2012/0201/Why-Chinese-workers-are-getting-kidnapped-abroad; Zhu Dazhi, "The country's influence is large, but Chinese are being kidnapped. What is the logic?" ["Guojia yingxiang da, guoren zao bangjia, shenme luoji?"], 2 February 2012, http://zhudazhi.blog.caixin.com/archives/32774.
20 On this point, see for instance Vanessa Fong, *Paradise Redefined*.
21 Ye Zi, Zhongguo zaiwai liuxuesheng 127 wan ren – cheng shijie zuida shengyuanguo [China's students abroad reach 1,270,000, becoming the world's largest source country], http://news.xinhuanet.com/overseas/2011–04/18/c_121317007.htm.
22 Huiyao Wang, *China's Competition for Global Talents: Strategy, Policy and Recommendations*, Asia Pacific Foundation of Canada, 2012, www.asiapacific.ca/sites/default/files/filefield/researchreportv7.pdf.
23 Cheng Xi, "The evolution of the Chinese Government's policies on selecting and sending students abroad since China's opening up" ["Gaige kaifang yilai Zhongguo zhengfu xuantai liuxueshengde zhengce yange"], *Huaqiao Huaren shi yanjiu*, Vol. 1, p. 43; cited in Barabantseva (2005: 16).
24 Chen Hefang and Feng Jie, "Gaige kaifang yilai woguo gongpai liuxue huiguo zhengce huigu yu sikao" ["Review and reflections on policies regarding China's publicly funded foreign study and return since the reforms"], *Shijie jiaoyu xinxi* Year 2012, No. 2, www.cnki.com.cn/Article/-JYXI201202016.htm.

25 *Guojia zhong-changqi rencai fazhan guihua gangyao (2010–2020)* ["Outline of the national plan for the medium and long-term development of talents (2010–2020)"], 2010, www.gov.cn/jrzg/2010–06/06/content_1621777.htm.

References

Barabantseva, E. (2005) Trans-nationalising Chineseness: Overseas Chinese Policies of the PRC's Central Government, *Asien*, 96, 7–28.

Bohm, A., Fallari, M., Hewett, A., Jones, S., Kemp, N., Meares, D., Pearc, D., & Van Cauter, K. (2004) *Vision 2020: Forecasting International Student Mobility a UK Perspective*. London: The British Council/IDP Australia.

Chu, J. Y. (2010) *Cosmologies of Credit: Transnational Mobility and the Politics of Destination in China*. Durham, NC: Duke University Press.

Cross, J., & Hitchcock, R. (2007) Chinese Students' (or Students from China's) Views of UK HE: Differences, Difficulties and Benefits, and Suggestions for Facilitating Transition, *The East Asian Learner*, 3 (2): November 2007.

Eurostat. (2011) *Migrants in Europe – A Statistical Portrait of the First and Second Generation*. Luxembourg: Eurostat.

Fong, V. L. (2011) *Paradise Redefined: Transnational Chinese Students and the Quest for Flexible Citizenship in the Developed World*. Stanford, CA: Stanford University Press.

Gao, Y. (Ed.) (2010) *Concealed Chains : Labour Exploitation and Chinese Migrants in Europe*, Geneva: International Labour Organization.

Gijsberts, M., Huijnk, W., & Vogels, R. (Eds.) (2011) *Chinese Nederlanders: van horeca naar hogeschool* [*Chinese Dutch: from catering trade to university*]. The Hague: Sociaal en Cultureel Planbureau.

Li, M. (2009) Ouzhou Huaren shehui pouxi: renkou, jingji, diwei yu fenhua [A social analysis of the Chinese in Europe: population, economy, position and composition], *Shijie minzu*, 2009 (5), 47–53.

Lieberthal, K., & Oksenburg, M. (1988) *Policy Making in China: Leaders, Structures, and Processes*. Princeton, NJ: Princeton University Press.

Liu-Farrer, G. (2011) *Labour Migration from China to Japan: International Students, Transnational Migrants*. London: Routledge.

Lynn-Ee Ho, E. (2011) Caught between Two Worlds: Mainland Chinese Return Migration, Hukou Considerations and the Citizenship Dilemma, *Citizenship Studies*, 15 (6–7), 643–58.

Nyíri, P. (1999) *New Chinese Migrants in Europe: The Case of the Chinese Community in Hungary*. Aldershot, UK: Ashgate.

Pieke, F. N. (1987) Four models of China's overseas Chinese policies, *China Information*, 2 (1), 8–16.

Pieke, F. N., & Xiang, B. (2010) Legality and labor: Chinese migratory workers in Britain, *Encounters*, 3, 15–38.

Pieke, F. N., Nyíri, P., Thunø, M., & Ceccagno, A. (2004) *Transnational Chinese: Fujianese Migrants in Europe*. Stanford, CA: Stanford University Press.

Simon, D. F., & Cao. C. (2009) *China's Emerging Technological Edge: Assessing the Role of High-end Talent*. Cambridge: Cambridge University Press.

Song, Q. (2011) Ouzhou de Zhongguo xin yimin: guimo ji tezheng de shehuixue fenxi [New Chinese migrants in Europe: scale, special characteristics and sociological analysis], *Shandong Daxue xuebao*, 2011 (2), 144–50.

Soudijn, M.R.J. (2006) *Chinese Human Smuggling in Transit*. Den Haag: Boom Juridische Uitgevers.

Thunø, M. (1999) Moving Stones from China to Europe: The Dynamics of Emigration from Zhejiang to Europe. In F.N. Pieke & H. Mallee (Eds.) *Internal and International Migration: Chinese Perspectives*. Richmond, VA: Curzon Press, pp. 159–80.

Thunø, M. (2001) Reaching Out and Incorporating Chinese Overseas: The Trans-territorial Scope of the PRC by the End of the 20th Century, *The China Quarterly*, 168, 910–29.

Wang, C., Wong, S.L., & Wenbin, S. (2006) Haigui: A New Area in China's Policy Toward the Chinese Diaspora? *Journal of the Chinese Overseas*, 2 (2), 294–309.

Wang, G. (1993) Greater China and the Chinese overseas, *The China Quarterly*, 136, 926–48.

Watson, J.L. (1977) The Chinese: Hong Kong Villagers in the British Catering Trade. In James L. Watson (Ed.) *Between Two Cultures: Migrants and Minorities in Britain*. Oxford: Basil Blackwell, pp. 181–213.

Wu, B. (2008) *Vulnerability of Chinese Contract Workers Abroad*. Nottingham, UK: University of Nottingham, China Policy Institute.

Xiang, B. (2003) Emigration from China: A Sending Country Perspective, *International Migration*, 41 (3), 22.

Xiang, B. (2011) A Ritual Economy of "Talent": China and Overseas Chinese Professionals, *Journal of Ethnic and Migration Studies*, 37, 821–38.

Zhang, H., Yang, Z., & Van Den Bulcke, D. (2011) *Euro-China Investment Report 2011–2012 – The European Landscape of Chinese Enterprises: An Analysis of Corporate and Entrepreneurial Firms and the Role of the Ethnic Communities*. Antwerp: Antwerp Management School.

Zhang, N. (2011) Renli ziyuan "zou chuqu" fangshi chuangxin [Innovation of methods for human resources "to go out"]. In Feng Lei & Xia Xianliang (Eds.) *Zhongguo zou chuqu fangshi chuangxin yanjiu* [*Research on the innovation of methods for China to go out*]. Beijing: Sheke Wenxian, pp. 120–64.

Zhang, S.X. (2008) *Chinese Human Smuggling Organizations: Families, Social Networks, and Cultural Imperatives*, Stanford: Stanford University Press.

2 The role of migration in shaping China's economic relations with its main partners

Haiyan Zhang

Abstract

This chapter studies the key features and trends of China's international immigration and analyses its impact on the trade and foreign direct investment (FDI) flows between China and its major European partner countries. The main focus is to examine possible interaction among trade, FDI and migration flows and to assess the role of Chinese ethnic communities and migration in facilitating these economic exchanges. The impact of Chinese migration/ethnic communities on host economies, especially with regard to entrepreneurial activities, has been also briefly examined. It is concluded that within the ongoing globalization process, Chinese migrant entrepreneurs emerged as an important source of capital, knowledge, market information and business opportunities and contributed to job creation, innovation and economic growth of host countries.

Introduction

It is well known that overseas Chinese[1] have significantly contributed to the success of China's economic development during the past 30 years, especially during the first stage of the economic liberalization process.[2] They have been the major source of China's inward foreign direct investment, technology, management know-how and expertise about the international markets (Gao 2003; Huang et al. 2008; Smart & Hsu 2004). The contribution of ethnic Chinese communities to the national economic development in Southeast Asian countries has also been very well documented, and their cross-board business and entrepreneurial networks are considered one of the most important factors for regional economic integration in Southeast Asia (Yeung 1999; Yeung & Olds 2000; Zhang & Van Den Bulcke 2000; Zhuang & Wang 2010). Have the ethnic communities and migration flows from China contributed to the international trade and foreign direct investment between China and their recipient countries?[3] The answer to this question is crucial for a better understanding of the role that the Chinese migration and ethnic Chinese communities have played in the trade and investment relations between China and its partner countries.

This chapter studies the key features and trends of China's international immigration and analyses its impact on the trade and FDI flows between China and its major partner countries. The main focus is to examine possible interaction among trade, FDI and migration flows and to assess the role of Chinese ethnic communities and migration in facilitating these economic exchanges. The impact of Chinese migration/ethnic communities on host economies, especially with regard to the labour market, will also be briefly examined. This study consists of four sections. After this introduction, the second section provides a literature review on the interaction among migration, trade and FDI on the one hand and the impact of migrants or international entrepreneurs on the economic development of the host country on the other hand. The third section provides empirical evidence about the economic relations between China and its main partner regions, especially Europe. The migration from China to Europe will be studied, particularly with regard to its changing characteristics during the last decades. The interaction among Chinese migration, trade and FDI flows in Europe and their evolving features will be analysed at regional/key country level. The concluding section will discuss the main findings and their policy implication for host countries.

2.1.   Literature review

The literature review is carried out to answer the main research questions of this study from a theoretical and empirical perspective, such as (1) Is there a co-relation between trade/FDI and migration flows? (2) Is there evidence that the co-relation between Chinese outward foreign direct investment (OFDI)/trade and migration differs because of specific contextual and time factors? (3) Is there evidence of an active role of Chinese migrants and diaspora networks in attracting Chinese FDI and trade flows to recipient countries? (4) What are the channels/mechanisms through which Chinese migrants and diaspora networks ensure this function? (5) What is the impact of Chinese OFDI and its inter-relationship with China's migration/ethnic communities on the economic development of host countries, especially at micro-level? The first two questions deal with the interaction between the trade, FDI and migrant flows at the macro-economic level, while the last three questions focus on the mechanisms through which the migrants and ethnic communities affect the host country at micro-economic level.

2.1.1.   Migration, trade and FDI flows

In a neo-classical trade-theoretic framework, the relationship between migration and trade as well as between migration and FDI is a relationship of substitutability. The trade flows contribute to the equalization of factor price and therefore lowers incentives for factor mobility. On the other hand, the movement of factors reduces price differentials and, therefore, the scope for trade. From the same perspective, the capital is expected to flow to where the type of labour used intensively in production is abundant and, other things being equal, workers will supply their labour services where the highest salary can be obtained. Through such mechanisms, migration and FDI are substitute ways to match workers and employers located in different countries. Seen from the perspective of a given location, the migration and FDI flows move in opposite directions, e.g. immigration and outward FDI or vice versa. However, this neo-classical approach neglects to some extent the potential for migration to favour trade and FDI through a reduction in bilateral transaction costs, as emphasized by recent literature on migration and diaspora networks (Aubry et al. 2012).

The evidence on globalization indicated that international trade has risen dramatically in recent decades, and the growth of FDI and skilled migration is even more pronounced. The linkages among these various dimensions of globalization are rather complementary than a substitution (Aubry et al. 2012), i.e. migration and FDI move in the same direction (Kugler & Rapoport 2006; Navaretti et al. 2007). The studies which focused on the "complementary relation" between the migration and FDI, i.e. the impact of immigration on inward FDI from the home country of these migrants, is based on the effect of agglomeration and networks. Given the fact that migrants participate in the labour force in the destination country, they can both convey information on their home country (including the quality of its workforce and institutions) and develop business networks favouring economic transactions between their home and host countries.

Recent literature suggests that migrants may facilitate the development of social and business networks, which may improve the exchanges between their countries of origin and countries of destination by providing information and matching services that the market and the price system may fail to supply. The community of migrants has been increasingly recognized as an important factor in overcoming informal barriers to international trade, which consist of, e.g. a shortage of information about international trading opportunities, a lack of knowledge on export markets, a weak international legal environment for contract enforcement, etc. (Rauch & Trindade 2002). Two mechanisms have been identified for the business and social networks in general and ethnic Chinese networks in particular to promote international trade and investment. First, the ethnic Chinese networks facilitate information sharing via formal and informal contact. In the case of trade, information sharing helps to match buyers and sellers, while in the case of foreign direct investment, it helps to identify potential investment opportunities. Migrants are well placed to act as middlemen on account of their superior language skills and their knowledge of consumer preferences, business practices, market structure and laws. Second, migrant business networks may help with contract enforcement by way of enforcement of community sanctions, which could reduce opportunistic behaviour such as contract violation (Song 2011).

Empirical studies consistently found a positive association between migration and international trade (Ben 2008; Combes et al. 2005; Girma & Yu 2002; Gould 1994; Head 1998; Rauch 1999, 2001), as well as between migration and FDI (Bhattacharya & Groznik 2005; Buch et al. 2006b; Javorcik et al. 2011, 2006; Kugler & Rapoport 2007). By taking account of the role of expatriate communities, Ben's rigorous analysis showed that a 1 per cent increase in the number of migrants increases trade between their country of residence and country of birth by 0.09 per cent and that this is roughly half the effect that would be estimated if the size of expatriate communities was ignored. Similar analysis of foreign investment suggests that a 1 per cent increase in the number of migrants increases investment between their country of residence and country of birth by around 0.15 per cent. Specific studies on Chinese migrants and ethnic Chinese networks also confirmed a considerable impact on international trade and FDI between China and their countries of destination (Rauch & Trindade 2002; Tong 2005).

The common finding of the growing body of recent studies indicates that the social and business networks of migrants in the host country can help to increase FDI from the country of origin of the migrants by stimulating information flows across international borders and by serving as a contract enforcement mechanism, while the growth in the relative presence of an immigrant community leads to new FDI from those immigrants' native countries (Foad 2012; Javorcik et al. 2011). Foad's study (2012) suggests that the effect is not immediately seen, and in fact the contemporaneous relationship between immigration and FDI may be negative. However, the immigrant network effect on FDI kicks in within a few years and is remarkably persistent. From the point of view of a recipient country, the migration could strengthen the complementarity effect, particularly when considering skilled migrants. The presence of a large migrant community may lead to the setting up of international schools, making a location attractive for foreign firms and their foreign managers. The presence of high-tech foreign companies makes a given location more attractive for foreign engineers also.

The empirical studies also showed that cross-border co-ethnic networks which are created by migrants with their home countries have been increasingly emphasized as determinant factors in the success of some countries in the development of their international business activities. For instance, ethnic Indians working in Silicon Valley facilitated the development of a large ICT service export industry in India by improving business networks and establishing a reputation for Indian ICT workers (Saxenian 2002), while the community of overseas Chinese in Southeast Asia has positively contributed to China's inward internationalization process (Weidenbaum & Hughes 1996). Another study on the interactions between migration and the bilateral FDI of four European countries – Germany, Italy, France and the UK – showed that the stocks of immigrants have a stronger influence on the FDI going to the developing countries.

2.1.2.   *Ethnic communities and international entrepreneurs*

The literature about FDI and migration focuses on the link among ethnic networks and FDI and their respective impact. Especially the effects on the geographical agglomeration of foreign companies, their organisational structural and management practices are dealt with. The theoretical analysis of FDI and multinational enterprises, especially the transaction cost approach, suggests that the choice of setting up a production unit or service facility abroad ("hierarchy" or internalization) instead of international trade ("market") should allow reduction of transaction costs which are usually related to collecting information, negotiating contracts and solving conflicts, at least when they are sufficient to compensate for the coordination costs that go together with FDI activities via subsidiaries (Casson 1995). These information costs are crucial for understanding and carrying out the international expansion of companies, because they are related not only to the investment decision as such but also to the implementation of that decision. The information costs particularly concern "uncodified" and "undiffused" knowledge, which is often embedded in the social structure, related to the cultural context that constitutes informal barriers to international trade and investment (Griffiths et al. 1998). The access to this information/knowledge not only yields a reduction of the risks involved in the internationalization process but also provides a vehicle for acquiring internal and external resources and opportunities for combining them (Eriksson et al. 1997). Therefore, the propensity or the ability of a firm to "transplant" its value-added activities abroad via FDI is largely determined by the firm's perception of and capability to overcome information/ knowledge costs that are present abroad.

A social network can be considered a set of linkages that either directly or indirectly connects entrepreneurs to their social groups that are generally based on e.g. affection, friendship, kinship, geographical proximity, cultural similarity, education, etc. The new institutional approach has recognized that the social network of entrepreneurs may boost the economic efficiency of firms in business relationships and allow them to solve the co-ordination problems in a better way. The social networks of entrepreneurs have therefore been considered in the literature as a source of competitiveness of firms, because they can provide entrepreneurs with information, business opportunities and resources in term of social capital (Burt 1992), knowledge (Sohn 1994) and the government's favourable attitude and policy (Boddewyn 1988). The resources provided by a social network are different from the "traditional" tangible assets, because they are intangible and jointly developed and owned by network members, who tend to share the same cultural value and business philosophy and practices.

Among social networks of entrepreneurs, the groups of migrants in a particular foreign market or region, i.e. the ethnic network, can be considered as a vehicle to promote international business activities, e.g. foreign trade and FDI. The ethnic network is therefore able to stimulate FDI by providing foreign investors with important information about the host market, local government regulations and potential business partners. This crucial information may otherwise be difficult or costly to obtain (Gould 1994; Rauch 2001; Rauch & Casella 2001; Tong 2005).

In addition to access to low-cost/free information and resources, the cultural similarity and common business philosophy and practices among members of an ethnic network may help the entrepreneurs in the initial steps to enter into a co-operative arrangement, while high trust can sustain an equilibrium of honesty and openness to avoid opportunistic behaviour and to encourage partners to share their tangible and intangible assets. Because an ethnic network can provide community enforcement of sanctions to deter violations of contracts in a weak international legal environment (Greif 1993; Rauch & Trindade 2002), it can be considered not only a way to ensure the contract enforcement with lower costs and higher effectiveness but also a mechanism to facilitate coordination and trust in international business transactions. Yet trust itself is not costless, as it has to be developed over time as social bonds strengthen through shared norms and/or similar values (Larson 1992).

A number of empirical studies show that not only the overseas Chinese and Indians have facilitated FDI between the host countries and the country of origin but that also many other ethnic groups living outside their countries of origin have caused such effects. A study (Buch et al. 2006a) on state-level German data showed that FDI and migrants have a tendency to agglomerate in specific regions: the stocks of inward FDI into Germany are higher in those states with a large foreign population. It was found that especially this presence of FDI tends to be highest in states where migrants from the same country of origin are living. A study on the link between FDI and migrants in the United States (Javorcik et al. 2011) established that the volume of U.S. FDI abroad is positively correlated with the stock of migrants from the partner country present in the United States. These data further point out that the relationship between FDI and migration is stronger for migrants with a tertiary education. Thus several studies confirmed that ethnic networks serve as an important channel of information about business conditions and opportunities abroad and may create additional FDI flows. In addition to the FDI–creation effect, the ethnic networks substitute to some extent for the lack of cultural proximity between home and host countries and provide incentives for firms and migrants to locate in specific countries or regions, showing a positive effect on agglomeration of foreign direct investment in the host nations.

Among cross-border co-ethnic networks, the overseas Chinese have drawn most attention from scholars, journalists and policy decision makers because of their vigorous networking activity and their commercial successes in Southeast Asia. Research in Southeast Asian economies has identified that networks of migrants are powerful determinants not only in the economic success of ethnic Chinese entrepreneurs in their countries of residence (Brown 1995; Redding 1990, 1995, 1996) but also in their internationalization process (Kao 1993; Yeung & Olds 2000). The ethnic network of overseas Chinese is also believed to have played a crucial role in promoting FDI. The main evidence of the literature is that the ethnic Chinese networks are significant facilitators of cross-border investments between their home and host countries. Tong's study (2005) clearly showed that the strength of ethnic Chinese networks between country pairs, approximated by the product of the numbers of ethnic Chinese in both countries, is positively correlated with the cumulative amount of their reciprocal FDI. This finding is not limited to countries in Southeast Asia but is also applicable to other country pairs included in his study, regardless of whether the investment originated from industrial countries or developing economies.

Studies on Chinese migrant entrepreneurs in Eastern European countries have shown that they have not only created new business activities in the host countries through vertical integration with their country of origin, i.e. mainland China, but also mobilized resource through ethnic ties with Chinese business communities in other countries. The cross-border cooperation between migrant entrepreneurs from local Chinese ethnic communities and overseas Chinese networks in other countries has resulted in the geographical agglomeration or co-location of Chinese small and medium-sized firms in Central and Eastern Europe (Zhang et al. 2011, 2012).

The international ethnic entrepreneurship has been a field with growing interest for both academicians and policy makers (Chand & Ghorbani 2011; Dai et al. 2011; Ibrahim & Galt 2011; Ilhan-Nas et al. 2011; OECD 2010). Recent studies introduced a new concept, i.e. "transnationalism", to analyse the international migration and suggested the success of ethnic entrepreneurs depends on their contacts and associates in another country, primarily their home country (Rusinovic 2008). The resources of ethnic communities, such as kinship, friendship and community ties, are considered drivers for international migrant entrepreneurs to establish and operate their businesses. These factors contribute to the formation, maintenance and success of ethnic entrepreneurs (Teixeira 2001).

The transnational entrepreneurs present a large proportion of the self-employed persons in the ethnic communities, and they are identified as "the discovery, enactment, and exploitation of opportunities across national borders to create future goods and services" (Ilhan-Nas et al. 2011; Keupp & Gassman 2009). The ability of certain ethnic groups to create a self-sustaining entrepreneurial class is the basis for the development and vitality of two key mechanisms – ethnic vertical integration and resource mobilization through ethnic ties – which, through a self-sustaining and cumulative process, produce multiplier effects on business creation (Raijman & Tienda 2003). Over time, there is a shift from low– to high–value-added business involving ethnic business communities, showing higher potential significance of immigrant entrepreneurs for the national and, in particular, the local economies in the countries of settlement (Kloosterman & Rath 2010).

The network concept has been frequently used to explain the typical organizational structures as well as the internationalization process of Chinese multinational enterprises (Zhang & Van Den Bulcke 2000). There seems to be general agreement in the literature that the corporate governance and business systems of Chinese enterprises are greatly affected by the social and personal relations of their entrepreneurs (Whitley 1990, 1991, 1994). Hence, a better understanding of how the ethnic network of Chinese entrepreneurs might assist in reducing transaction costs and substitute for deficiencies in their resource-based ownership advantages is a relevant research topic. An important concern in research on the internationalization process, strategic setting, control and organization is also to find out how and to what extent these social and personal networks affect organizational and management practices of Chinese enterprises in building successful cross-border inter- and intra-firm linkages.

2.2. China's migration, trade and FDI

Over the last three decades, China has become an increasingly important part of the global community. In 2012, the total of China's international trade of goods reached US$3,867 billion, which ranked China the largest exporter and second most important importer (after the United States) in the World. China's international trade accelerated during the last decade as a result of its adhesion to the WTO, although the recent figure showed that its export growth slowed down – especially to Western European countries – due to the global financial crisis which started in 2008. China has also been one of the most important host countries for multinational companies. During 2007 through 2012, the annual inward FDI flow to China reached more than US$100 billion, which has significantly increased during the last two years, despite negative growth in 2009 as a result of the global financial crisis. The total inward FDI stock of China reached US$833 billion by the end of 2012, which made China the most important recipient of foreign direct investment among the developing countries. During the middle of the first decade of the twenty-first century, China also emerged as one of the most important sources of FDI. The annual outward FDI flow from China reached about US$50 billion during recent years, while its total stock amounted to US$532 billion by the end of 2012, which reached 64 per cent of its total inward FDI stock (UNCTAD 2013). Besides Asia (including Hong Kong and Taiwan), which accounted for more than half of China's global trade flows and three fifths of its total outward FDI stock, the United States and Europe are two most important trade and investment partners for China. America (including Latin America) accounted for one fifth of China's total imports and exports in 2010, while Europe had a similar share of 19 per cent. In terms of capital movement, the total Chinese outward FDI stock in the United States reached US$17 billion by the end of 2012, while it amounted to US$37 billion in Europe. These two continents accounted for 3 and 7 per cent of total Chinese OFDI, respectively (MOFCOM 2013).

The globalization of the Chinese economy generated not only trade and FDI flows but also international migration. The interaction among goods, capital and people has not only significantly changed China's global position but also changed its relationship with other partners. Table 2.1 provided an overview of changing position of China in global migration over the last three decades. As compared to the rapid growth of trade and FDI, the migrant flows from China have also increased significantly, although its growth rate has been less important. According to the Department of Economic and Social Affairs of the United Nations (2012), the stock of Chinese emigrants nearly doubled during the last three decades, i.e. from 4.3 million in 1990 to 8.4 million in 2010.[4]

During the last three decades, Chinese migration has accelerated, i.e. the stock of Chinese migrants increased by 37.7 per cent during 1990 to 2000 and by 44 per cent during 2000 to 2010. The most important destination of Chinese migrants is Asia, which accounted for 52.6 per cent of the total stock of Chinese migrants by the end of 2010. Yet the share of Asia has declined over the last three decades, as this proportion was 72 per cent in 1990 and 58 per cent in 2000. Within the Asian continent, Eastern Asia took a dominant share (i.e. 40 per cent), while the top three destinations, i.e. Hong Kong, Japan and Singapore, accounted, respectively, for 26.4, 6.9 and 4.8 per cent of total Chinese migrants. As compared to Asia, North America has increasingly become a very important host region for Chinese migrants. The region hosts about one third of total Chinese migrants, i.e. 30.8 per cent in 2010, while the relative proportion was only 18.5 and 25 in 1990 and 2000. The United States and Canada hosted, respectively, 23.3 and 7.5 per cent of total migrants from China by the end of 2010. The importance of Europe has

Destination	Number of migrants and geographical distribution						Changes over time (%)	
	1990	%	2000	%	2010	%	1990–2000	2000–2010
WORLD	**4,252,389**	**100.00**	**5,854,387**	**100.00**	**8,432,427**	**100.00**	**37.67**	**44.04**
More developed regions	1,267,042	29.80	2,451,968	41.88	4,429,960	52.53	93.52	80.67
Less developed regions	2,985,347	70.20	3,402,419	58.12	4,002,467	47.47	13.97	17.64
AFRICA	**17,319**	**0.41**	**41,570**	**0.71**	**54,568**	**0.65**	**140.03**	**31.27**
Eastern Africa	5,192	0.12	24,067	0.41	26,140	0.31	363.54	8.61
Middle Africa	449	0.01	472	0.01	627	0.01	5.12	32.84
Northern Africa	2,564	0.06	3,664	0.06	4,766	0.06	42.90	30.08
Southern Africa	7,751	0.18	11,223	0.19	20,057	0.24	44.79	78.71
Western Africa	1,363	0.03	2,144	0.04	2,978	0.04	57.30	38.90
ASIA	**3,062,115**	**72.01**	**3,608,324**	**61.63**	**4,436,736**	**52.62**	**17.84**	**22.96**
Central Asia	4,687	0.11	4,446	0.08	7,291	0.09	(5.14)	63.99
Eastern Asia	2,335,783	54.93	2,776,069	47.42	3,381,327	40.10	18.85	21.80
South-Eastern Asia	552,780	13.00	642,304	10.97	846,311	10.04	16.20	31.76
Southern Asia	166,354	3.91	166,959	2.85	185,888	2.20	0.36	11.34
Western Asia	2,511	0.06	18,546	0.32	15,919	0.19	638.59	(14.16)
EUROPE	**234,739**	**5.52**	**412,229**	**7.04**	**886,882**	**10.52**	**75.61**	**115.14**
Eastern Europe	75,460	1.77	71,860	1.23	81,424	0.97	(4.77)	13.31
Northern Europe	31,957	0.75	78,921	1.35	187,832	2.23	146.96	138.00
Southern Europe	40,744	0.96	100,765	1.72	360,335	4.27	147.31	257.60
Western Europe	86,578	2.04	160,683	2.74	257,291	3.05	85.59	60.12
LATIN AMERICA AND THE CARIBBEAN	**49,102**	**1.15**	**66,599**	**1.14**	**85,421**	**1.01**	**35.63**	**28.26**
Caribbean	5,706	0.13	7,818	0.13	10,826	0.13	37.01	38.48
Central America	11,486	0.27	15,989	0.27	25,136	0.30	39.20	57.21
South America	31,910	0.75	42,792	0.73	49,459	0.59	34.10	15.58
NORTH AMERICA	**785,099**	**18.46**	**1,482,641**	**25.33**	**2,594,324**	**30.77**	**88.85**	**74.98**
OCEANIA	**104,015**	**2.45**	**243,024**	**4.15**	**374,496**	**4.44**	**133.64**	**54.10**
Australia and New Zealand	96,821	2.28	221,498	3.78	363,458	4.31	128.77	64.09
Melanesia	77	–	101	–	122	–	–	20.79
Micronesia	6,289	0.15	20,336	0.35	9,669	0.11	223.36	(52.45)
Polynesia	828	0.02	1,089	0.02	1,247	0.01	31.52	14.51

Source: United Nations, Department of Economic and Social Affairs (2012)

also increased, as its share in the stock of Chinese migrants doubled during the last three decades, i.e. from 5.5 per cent in 1990 to 10.5 per cent in 2010. The most rapidly growing destinations of Chinese migrants in Europe are Northern Europe, with growth of 147 per cent between 1990 and 2000 and 138 per cent during 2000 and 2010, as a result of rapid increase of Chinese migrants to the UK (see further). Chinese migration to Australia and New Zealand also experienced rapid growth, especially during 1990 to 2000. These two countries accounted for 4.3 per cent of Chinese migrants. Chinese migration to Africa is still at a very low level, as it accounts only for 0.65 per cent in the total Chinese migrant population. Moreover, this share has likely decreased over the last decades, from 0.71 per cent in 2000. The rapid growth of Chinese migration to Africa occurred in 1990 to 2000, especially in Eastern and sub-Saharan regions. Overall, the most rapid growth of Chinese migration occurred in developed regions, i.e. North America and Europe, which have become the two most important trade and investment partners of China during the last three decades, while Chinese migrants are likely less favourable for African countries and other less developed economies as their destination.

2.2.1.   *Chinese migrants in Europe*

A more comprehensive dataset about the evolution of overseas Chinese by Taiwan's Overseas Compatriot Affairs Commission confirmed the trends from the UN migration data. Over the last 50 years, Chinese migrant flows substantially changed (Figure 2.1). Europe and America became the most favourable destinations of Chinese migrants in the 1980s, while Asia remained the most important host region. The fluctuation of Chinese migration in Africa is quite important as a result of rapid change of economic and political situation and the attitude of the host government towards Chinese migrants in some African countries.

Europe hosted a total of 887,000 Chinese migrants by the end of 2010. The largest European host countries for Chinese migrants are Italy (196,000), Spain (144,000), Germany (136,000), the UK (116,000), Russia (61,000), France (47,000) and the Netherlands (38,000).[5] Southern Europe is the most important destination of Chinese migrants in Europe, accounting for 40 per cent of the total stock of Chinese migrants in the European continent, followed by Western Europe (29 per cent), Northern Europe (21 per cent) and Eastern Europe (9 per cent). The most important host countries in Eastern Europe, excluding Russia, are the Czech Republic, Hungary, Slovakia, Bulgaria and Romania. Yet the share of Eastern Europe in China's total migrants in Europe has substantially declined over the last three decades, i.e. from 32 per cent in 1990 to 17 per cent in 2000 and 9.2 per cent in 2010. The migration from China to Western European countries has also decreased, i.e. from 37 per cent of the total Chinese migrants in Europe in 1990 to 29 per cent in 2010, especially France, of which the share declined from 17.8 to 5.3 per cent. Yet the share of Germany doubled during the same period, i.e. from 7.9 per cent to 15.3 per cent, as a result of its strong trade and investment links with China. As compared to Eastern and Western Europe, Northern Europe has rapidly become a favourable destination of Chinese migrants, as its share in the total Chinese migrant stock in Europe increased from 13.6 to 21.2 per cent during the period of 1990 through 2010, while the largest destination of Chinese migrants in this sub-region is the UK, which recorded a growth rate of 118 per cent during 1990 to 2000 and 126 per cent during 2000 to 2010. Chinese students constitute a substantial part of the migration from China to the UK, which has become the most important destination for Chinese students in Europe. Chinese migrants to Southern Europe also increased rapidly, especially during the last decade. The total number of Chinese emigrants in this region went up by 258 per cent between 2000 and 2010, while the share of this sub-region in the stock of Chinese migrants in Europe increased from 24.4 to 40.6 per cent during this period. Two large economies of the region, i.e. Italy and Spain, experienced the most rapid growth of Chinese migrants. The total number of migrants from China to Spain, for instance, increased by 50 times between 1990 and 2010, i.e. from 2,800 to 144 thousand. A large part of Chinese migrants in these two countries are entrepreneurs and workers who have been involved in manufacturing and trading activities in the textile industry (e.g. clothes, bags and footwear), such as in the Prato area.

Migration from China to Europe dates back to the early nineteenth century or even earlier. The first Chinese community was established in Liverpool in the late 1850s by migrants mainly from the port city of Tianjin and Shanghai, when Alfred Holt and Company employed a large number of Chinese seamen while establishing the Blue Funnel Shipping Line to import cotton, silk and tea from China (Christiansen 2003). However, migration from China to Europe proceeded at a rather slow tempo till the Second World War. Only from the 1960s onwards did Europe experience several waves of Chinese immigrants with a strong rate of growth (Figure 2.1). During the last 50 years, Chinese immigration to Europe

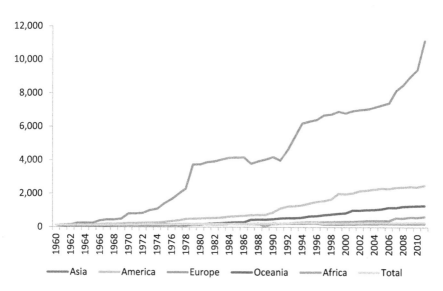

Figure 2.1 Changing geographical patterns of Chinese migrant flows (index 1960 = 100), 1960–2011

Source: Taiwan's Overseas Compatriot Affairs Commission (2011)

increased by 7.9 per cent annually (CAGR) as compared to only 1.7 per cent for the total number of Chinese migrants in the world. As a result, the number of overseas Chinese living in Europe rose from 14,000 in 1960 to 1.32 million in 2010, excluding Russia (Taiwan's Overseas Compatriot Affairs Commission 2011).

During the previous century, the first wave of Chinese migrants to Europe started in the 1960s. At that time they arrived mainly from former British, French and Dutch colonies as refugees, e.g. French Indochina and Dutch Indonesia, because in these countries they were to various degrees exposed to post-colonial nationalism and either expelled or forced to assimilate. The number of Chinese migrants from these Asian countries went up in the 1970s, when different conflicts occurred, especially in Vietnam, Laos and Cambodia. Besides this main migration stream, a limited number of Chinese specialized cooks and other workers were recruited from Southeast Asia, especially in the New Territories of Hong Kong and Macau, to work in the expanding Chinese catering sector in Europe in the 1960s and 1970s. Before the 1980s, Chinese migrants were spread out in several Western European countries, mainly in the UK, France and the Netherlands, and their economic activities were mainly concentrated in ethnic niche sectors or markets, such as Chinese restaurants, retail trade of ethnic products and services to Chinese communities. These early migrants formed a quite homogenous group, as most of them were unskilled and came from the rural areas of Zhejiang and Guangdong provinces on the one hand and from Hong Kong, Macau and Taiwan and other Asian neighbouring countries on the other hand (Christiansen 2003; Guerassimoff 2003a, 2003b). Several factors contributed to the expansion of the Chinese community in Europe during the last decades. First, shortly after the open-door policy was launched by Deng Xiaoping in 1978, the Chinese government liberalized emigration, which had been prohibited since the early 1950s. The relatives of migrants living in China and returned migrants became politically rehabilitated and were by law granted special social, economic and political privileges (Thunø 2001, 2003). Permission was given to relatives of migrants to leave the country in order to reunite with their family members abroad. As a result of the Chinese government's decision to allow outward mobility and to incorporate them into the domestic development process as sources of capital and new technology, emigration from China to Europe increased rapidly, especially the so-called "chain migration" from a number of Chinese cities, e.g. Wenzhou and Qintian in Zhejiang province, which, prior to 1949, had already established emigration links to Europe (Benton & Pieke 1998).

Second, besides migrants from traditional Chinese emigration areas by way of family reunification schemes, a new wave of entrepreneurial migrants emerged in the 1990s who often had no connection to the historical, rural-based chains of migration as compared to the earlier Chinese migrant population in Western Europe. These newcomers entered Central and Eastern European countries because of the existence of a visa-free treaty between China and some of these countries, such as Hungary (Nyíri 2003), during 1988 to 1992. As a result of the introduction of a more strict migration policy and crackdown on illegal migration after 1992, most of the Chinese migrants moved from one country to another in the region. These "newcomers" even went to Southern Europe, especially Italy, via illegal networks (Ceccagno 2003).

Third, the most remarkable feature of the recent trends in Chinese migration to Europe has been the substantial growth of skilled migrants, including students enrolled in European universities, academic, technical and professional persons (Zhang 2003). China is now the largest home country of outbound students. By the end of 2010, a total number of about 1.27 million Chinese students left China to study abroad. The main country of destination for Chinese students is the United States, which absorbs more than half of the total Chinese students abroad, while the UK, France and Germany are the most important host countries in Europe. The opening up of the labour market to foreign high-skilled persons and changes in related immigration policies in European countries in recent years may even accelerate skilled migration from China and later on play a positive role in the promotion of economic cooperation and cultural exchanges between China and Europe. The arrival of students and highly skilled professionals has not only resulted in the expansion of economic, scientific and technological cooperation, as well as cultural and educational exchanges and cooperation between China and the rest of the world, but also injected "new blood" into China's ethnic communities abroad.

Fourth, as a result of the transformation of the Chinese economic system and continuous impressive performance of the Chinese economy, the private sector in China has expanded tremendously, together with the emergence of a large number of private entrepreneurs. Because Chinese private enterprises, especially small and medium-sized enterprises (SMEs), have for a long time been discriminated against by the Chinese government, e.g. with regard to their access to the state owned banking sector, to government loans and subsidies and to policy support in general, a number of these companies turned to overseas markets to secure their private business on the one hand and to look for new business opportunities on the other hand.

Fifth, the increase of Chinese direct investment has created new migration flows of managers, employees and workers and their family members. Although the expatriate community of Chinese-owned enterprises, especially of state-owned enterprises, is quite different from the ethnic community of traditional migrants – meaning that they often co-exist in a parallel way – these Chinese expatriates have re-enforced the presence of Chinese migrants in Europe and created additional links between the overseas Chinese community and their home country.

In summary, the presence of the ethnic Chinese community in Europe substantially increased during the last 50 years and is still growing rapidly. With the arrival of new migrants, especially international entrepreneurs, students and highly skilled professionals and expatriate managers of Chinese multinational companies, the characteristics of the Chinese ethnic community in Europe is evolving. This might have a significant impact on the economic relationship between China and Europe on the one hand and the migrant policy of the host European countries on the other hand.

FDI and trade data at the country level reveal that the importance of a particular nation in the total Chinese migrants and its relative share in total Chinese FDI stock and trade in Europe is positively linked, i.e. a country with a higher proportion of Chinese migrants in Europe has attracted larger Chinese FDI stock (Table 2.2). The top ten host countries of Chinese migrant in the EU received 90 per cent of total Chinese migrant population in Europe, while their shares in China's outward FDI and trade are, respectively, 54 and 80 per cent. The positive relation between the number of overseas Chinese living in the host countries and the amount of Chinese FDI may to some extent reflect the contribution of the ethnic community in attracting Chinese capital to the service and manufacturing industries. At the country level, for instance, Russia received about 7 per cent of the total Chinese migrants in Europe and hosts 18 per cent of Chinese FDI stock, while the relative proportion for the UK is 13 per cent and 9 per cent. Yet the largest host country of Chinese outward FDI in Europe is Luxembourg. It received about 37 per cent of Chinese total investment stock but hosts a very small proportion of Chinese migrants, i.e. less than 0.01 per cent. It is likely that Luxembourg, as an established financial centre with an advantageous fiscal system, is used by Chinese investors as a platform for holding companies, not a manufacturing or service location for Chinese companies as such. Also, a Bank of China branch in Luxembourg has been established for more than 20 years. The positive relation between immigration and investment has also been observed in Germany, Sweden and Hungary. Yet some other European countries, such as France, Italy, Spain

Table 2.2 Top destinations of Chinese migrants and their impact on China's trade and FDI in Europe, 2010

	No. of migrants		China's outward FDI		Bilateral trade	
	Number	%	Stock (US$ billion)	%	Value (US$ billion)	%
Italy	195,744	22.07	0.22	1.42	45.15	9.41
Spain	143,996	16.24	0.25	1.59	24.42	5.09
Germany	135,807	15.31	1.50	9.55	142.30	29.66
UK	116,053	13.09	1.36	8.66	50.07	10.44
Russian Federation	61,971	6.99	2.79	17.74	–	–
France	47,246	5.33	0.24	1.53	44.97	9.37
Netherlands	38,317	4.32	0.49	3.10	56.18	11.71
Sweden	25,760	2.90	1.48	9.41	11.62	2.42
Ireland	18,509	2.09	0.14	0.89	5.41	1.13
Portugal	15,795	1.78	0.02	0.14	3.27	0.68
Subtotal	799,198	90.11	8.49	54.03	383.38	79.90
Europe total	886,882	100.00	15.71	100.00	479.80	100.00

Source: MOFCOM (2012) and United Nations, Department of Economic and Social Affairs (2012), UNCTAD (2012)

and the Netherlands, although they host a relatively high proportion of Chinese migrants, do not receive a high proportion of Chinese FDI.

A recent study of Chinese OFDI in Europe (Zhang et al. 2011, 2012) on the basis of the Amadeus database clearly showed a number of interactions between ethnic Chinese business communities in Europe and Chinese direct investors at corporate level. First, the availability of ethnic businesses and entrepreneurial networks and strong cultural ties and historic links with the home country are likely to present locational advantages, especially for small and medium-sized firms when they enter and operate in a foreign business environment. These firms trended to co-locate with firms from the same home country in European cities where there is a high concentration of overseas Chinese. These locational advantages are particularly useful for firms entering new markets. This is even more so for emerging multinational companies, which usually lack the firm-specific advantages that are necessary to successfully cope with the cultural and institutional distance that separates them from developed countries in Europe. The potential of locating in an established ethnic business community may be an important determinant of the location decision for small emerging multinational enterprises. Therefore, it is reasonable to indicate that the Chinese immigrant entrepreneurs to European countries could become an important new source of FDI and a catalyser to create business clusters by attracting new investment. In Central and Eastern Europe, Chinese migrants are concentrated in certain parts of a capital cities, e.g. in the rust belts of the 8th and 10th districts of Budapest, to benefit from good communication and transport infrastructure on the one hand and easy access to information and suppliers from China on the other hand. The Amadeus dataset showed that 97 per cent of Chinese-owned enterprises in Hungary are located in the Budapest area, while this proportion is 89 per cent in Romania for Bucharest, 86 per cent in Russia in Moscow and 82 per cent in Bulgaria for Sophia. By contrast, Chinese-owned companies in Western Europe are less agglomerated in capital cities, e.g. only 42 per cent of Chinese companies in the UK are located in London, while this share is even lower for Germany. The agglomeration of Chinese companies in wholesale or distribution activities resulted in a number of large Chinese communities in the capital cities of some Eastern and Central European countries, while the emergence of overseas Chinese population has in return attracted new investors. This self-enforcement can be considered an on-going process for the geographical concentration of Chinese FDI and migrant entrepreneurs. Yet this agglomeration trend is still quite "volatile", as it depends on the immigration policy of host countries and their business environment. Over the years, the original "open air" and rather primitive markets for Chinese products in Central and Eastern European countries have been gradually replaced by trade and exhibition centres, which were established by Chinese entrepreneurs, sometimes with supports from the host country and Chinese governments. These centres are specialized in the wholesale of Chinese products, with showrooms and office space for Chinese and local distributors and wholesalers. Their target markets are upgrading from low-end to branded products.

Second, the study also showed that the migrant entrepreneurs from China played a role as business partners in formulating joint ventures with individuals and companies from China and their participation in the management of these businesses. Actually, a total number of 1,304 overseas Chinese individuals and companies are partners in Chinese joint ventures in Europe. Overseas Chinese play an important role by introducing Chinese investors to their residence countries and by participating in the investment of joint ventures to share their financial resources and market knowledge. It is also interesting to find that overseas Chinese from third countries also participate in establishing joint ventures. This type of cross-border cooperation between Chinese and overseas Chinese partners demonstrates the relevance of Chinese ethnic networks in the internationalization process of Chinese corporate companies or family enterprises as a self-supporting or mutual-enhancement mechanism. Overseas Chinese quite often facilitate or bridge the gaps between Chinese investors and foreign investors from both local and third countries.

Third, overseas Chinese also participate in the management of Chinese companies in Europe. According to the Amadeus database, two thirds of 426 overseas Chinese board members also function as executive directors. About two fifths of these overseas Chinese executives come from European host countries, i.e. they belong to local Chinese communities, while the other three fifths are from third countries, especially Hong Kong and Taiwan. The participation of local overseas Chinese in the management of small and privately owned Chinese companies might the result not only from their contribution as shareholders but also as entrepreneurs. The role of overseas Chinese in large and medium-sized companies, especially in high-tech manufacturing subsidiaries, might be determined by other motivations or needs. For the high-tech companies, which often result from the takeover of existing firms, the post-acquisition management could be a huge challenge with regard to, for example, the integration of the acquired companies into the value chain of the acquiring companies, especially when the cultural distance is high. The role of overseas Chinese companies and professional managers from greater China can be important, as they have a longer experience in doing business in European or international markets as compared to companies from mainland China. Therefore, their familiarity with Western multinational companies and markets on the one hand and their cultural proximity with Chinese companies on the other hand provides them with unique position as "intermediary" to bridge the differences between Chinese and European partners. This was already the role of many overseas Chinese companies, especially from greater China, when Western companies started to invest in mainland China.

2.2.2.   *Impact on local employment*

It is evident that FDI and trade activities may generate new jobs. According to MOFCOM's data (MOFCOM 2012), Chinese multinational companies created 1.22 million jobs abroad by the end of 2011, of which 888,000 employed foreign employees. According to the same report, 1,600 Chinese companies had 50,000 employees in the 27 EU member countries in 2011. Yet the concerns of local business communities and politicians of some host countries about Chinese investors have been often related to their negative impact on the local labour market. In Africa, although migrant entrepreneurs from China are not able or willing to enter the established wage labour market to compete with local labour, they rarely create new jobs because of the limited size of their business or their reliance on migrant workers from China through social networks. Moreover, Chinese migrant entrepreneurs have been often considered unfair competitors towards local businesses, while the decline of local traditional industries could result in job losses (Ma 2008; Park 2009).

The similar concerns about unfair competition from Chinese migrant entrepreneurs have also been observed in some Southern and Eastern European regions, e.g. in Prato, Elche and Budapest, when Chinese migrants have developed some manufacturing clusters in labour-intensive industries (e.g. garments and fashion clothing, shoes, bags, etc.). The agglomeration of Chinese migrants and their business activities on the one hand and the lack of linkages with local business communities often created tensions between the ethnic Chinese entrepreneurs and local businesspeople (Johanson et al. 2009). This often resulted in the introduction of a stricter immigration policy and enforcement of labour regulations by the host governments. The change to a more regulated business environment and especially the emergence of certain mistrust and sometimes a hostile atmosphere in the local business community may even result in the relocation of migrant entrepreneurs and business activities, as happened in some cities. For instance, after violent protests erupted at Elche in Spain against Chinese importers and distributors in the shoe business, the Chinese business community moved to Fuenlabrada in Madrid, and a new distribution centre of Chinese footwear and clothing was established with about 700 companies active in wholesale (*Financial Times* 2011). Yet from a long-term perspective, the increasing integration of Chinese migrant entrepreneurs into local business communities and their upgrade from low-end market to higher–value-added activities might inevitably contribute to job creation in the local market.

2.3. Conclusion

The literature review and empirical data confirmed that the Chinese migrant flows have significantly increased during the last decades as a result of intensified trade and FDI relationship between China and the rest of the world. As compared to traditional migration flows, recent migrants from China are quite distinctive because they are mainly composed of entrepreneurs and high-skilled (potential) labourers. It is widely recognized that entrepreneurship contributes to job creation, innovation and economic growth. Within the ongoing globalization process, Chinese migrant entrepreneurs emerged as an important source of capital, knowledge, market information and business opportunities, especially in developing economies. The international investment of Chinese individuals and family businesses, often combined with migration purposes, has also become more and more important in developed countries. Although their investment is often small and concentrated in international trade activities, their contribution to the economy of their host countries cannot be neglected, as they have created new business opportunities with China for the local economy and companies. However, this role of international entrepreneurs was not always sufficiently taken into consideration by most host governments and local business communities. Moreover, given the fact that Chinese migrant entrepreneurs and family business used to operate with low operating costs to target the low-end market on the basis of their business model in China, their operations in Central and Eastern Europe as well as in other countries have been considered "dumping" Chinese cheap goods into local markets, destroying local businesses through unfair pricing competition. This has been a major concern of some European host countries (e.g. Hungary, Italy and Spain) and about growing Chinese business communities in their territories.

The surge of Chinese students in Western countries and their potential impact on the local labour market revealed another new development of the migration flows from China. The well-trained Chinese high-skilled labourers, especially new graduates from Western universities, have become a new human resources (HR) source in the local labour market. They may bring new competence to the local and multinational companies by bridging the cultural and other differences and facilitating businesses dealing with China. Yet the immigration policy and labour regulation of host countries are still quite restrictive for foreign professionals and workers.

The results of this study have a number of policy implications. First, the immigration policy and labour regulations facing the arrival and growth of this new type or unconventional migrants, e.g. international entrepreneurs and high skilled labourers from China, need to be re-assessed, taking into consideration of the positive contribution of these new type of migrants not only to the local economy of host countries but especially to the trade and investment relationship between the host country and their country of origin. Second, since the geographical agglomeration of Chinese investors, especially the migrant entrepreneurs, appears to be quite strong we suggest that regional authorities might create special facilities and welcome packages for these international entrepreneurs. Yet the concentration of Chinese entrepreneurial companies in some African countries and capital cities in Eastern Europe resulted from the earlier migration flows from China, and their economic contribution to the local economy were not yet fully acknowledged by relevant authorities. How to turn this preliminary agglomeration of migrant communities into effective service and industrial clusters with strong links to the local economy has been and is still a challenge for the host governments at the regional and national levels. Third, given the fact that the ethnic business communities have become important players in prompting transnational entrepreneurship and cross-border business activities, such as trade and FDI, promoting cooperation with local ethnic business communities gives ethnic entrepreneurs a head start for participating in transnational economic activities in general and in developing cross-border economic activities in particular. Therefore, promoting international entrepreneurship and linking up with local ethnic business communities need to be important dimensions of the policy mix for the host governments to create positive effects from these growing business communities.

Notes

1 In this study, "overseas Chinese" refers to ethnic Chinese residing outside of China, Taiwan and Hong Kong, regardless of citizenship.
2 During the first decade of China's opening to the world, China received US$9546.5 million of foreign direct investments (FDI), of which US$9254.16 million came from the Chinese overseas, and US$292.34 million came directly from the Southeast Asian Chinese (Zhuang & Wang 2010).
3 The definitions of migrants vary among different data sources and between datasets and law. Among different possibilities, migrants may be defined as foreign born, foreign nationals or people who have moved to the recipient country for a year or more. In this study, Chines migrants are defined as Chinese nationals who move into a foreign country to stay temporarily (sometimes for as little as a year) or to settle for the long term. The *Chinese migrants* are considered "flow of individuals" during a given year, while the *Chinese ethnic community* is the accumulated number or "stock" of migrants and their decedents who already reside in the recipient country. These two terms are commonly used interchangeably in this study, although their definitions are quite distinctive.
4 According to Taiwan's Overseas Compatriot Affairs Commission (2012), the total number of overseas Chinese living outside of Mainland China, Hong Kong and Taiwan reached 40.31 million by the end of 2011. This data coverage and methodology as well as the definition of migrants in this estimate are clearly different from those of the UN.
5 These data are quite different form the estimates of Taiwan's Overseas Compatriot Affairs Commission, which indicated that Europe hosts about 2 million overseas Chinese, including those from Taiwan and Hong Kong.

References

Aubry, A., Kugler, M., & Rapoport, H. (2012) *Migration, FDI and the Margins of Trade.* Ph.D. Workshop 2012–2013, Department of Economics, Bar-Ilan University. Economics and Business Administration Building.

Ben, D. (2008) *Migration, Trade and Investment.* Staff Working Paper. Government of the Commonwealth of Australia – Productivity Commission.

Benton, G., & Pieke, F. (Eds.) (1998) *The Chinese in Europe.* London: Macmillan Press.

Bhattacharya, U., & Groznik, P. (2005) *Melting Pot or Salad Bowl: Some Evidence from US Investment Abroad.* 2003 European Finance Association annual meeting.

Boddewyn, J.J. (1988) Political Aspects of MNE Theory, *Journal of International Business Studies,* 341–64.

Brown, R.A. (Ed.) (1995) *Chinese Business Enterprise in Asia.* London: Routledge.

Buch, C.M., Kleinert, J., & Toubal, F. (2006a) Where Enterprises Lead, People Follow? Links between Migration and FDI in Germany, *European Economic Review,* 50, 2017–36.

Buch, C.M., Kleinert, J., & Toubal, F. (2006b) Where Enterprises Lead, People Follow? Links between Migration and FDI in Germany, *European Economic Review, Elsevier,* 50, 2017–36.

Burt, R.S. (1992) *Structural Holes: The Social Structure of Competition.* Cambridge, MA: Harvard University Press.

Casson, M. (1995) *The Organisation of International Business: Studies in the Economics of Trust*. Aldershot: Edward Elgar.

Ceccagno, A. (2003) New Chinese Migrants in Italy, *International Migration*, 41, 187–213.

Chand, M., & Ghorbani, M. (2011) National Culture, Networks and Ethnic Entrepreneurship: A Comparison of the Indian and Chinese Immigrants in the US, *International Business Review*, 20, 593–606.

Christiansen, F. (2003) *Chinatown, Europe: An Exploration of Overseas Chinese Identity in the 1990s*. London: Routledge.

Combes, P.-P., Lafourcade, M., & Mayer, T. (2005) The Trade-Creating Effects of Business and Social Networks: Evidence from France, *Journal of International Economics*, 66, 1–29.

Dai, F., Wang, K.Y.W., & Teo, S.T.T. (2011) Chinese Immigrants in Network Marketing Business in Western Host Country Context, *International Business Review*, 20, 659–69.

Eriksson, K., Johanson, J., Majkgard, A., & Sharma, D. (1997) Experiential Knowledge and Cost in the Internationalization Process, *Journal of International Business Studies*, 28, 337–60.

Financial Times. (2011, 21 January). A growing phenomenon. www.ft.com/cms/s/0/8f76d39e-2599-11e0-8258-00144feab49a.html#slide0

Foad, H. (2012) FDI and Immigration: A Regional Analysis, *Annals of Regional Science*, 49, 237–59.

Gao, T. (2003) Ethnic Chinese Networks and International Investment: Evidence from Inward FDI in China, *Journal of Asian Economics*, 14, 611–29.

Girma, S., & Yu, Z. (2002) The Link Between Immigration and Trade: Evidence from the UK, *Review of World Economics*, 138, 115–30.

Gould, D.M. (1994) Immigrant Links to the Home Country: Empirical Implications for U.S. Bilateral Trade Flows, *Review of Economics and Statistics*, 76, 302–16.

Greif, A. (1993) Contract Enforceability and Economic Institutions in Early Trade: The Maghribi Traders' Coalition, *American Economic Review, American Economic Association*, 83, 525–48.

Griffiths, D., Boisot, M., & Mole, V. (1998) Strategies for Managing Knowledge Assets: A Tale of Two Companies, *Technovation*, 18, 529–39.

Guerassimoff, C. (2003a) Migrations chinoises en Europe, *Migrations-Sociétés*, 15, 21–28.

Guerassimoff, C. (2003b) The New Chinese Migrants in France, *International Migration*, 41, 135–54.

Head, K., & Ries, J. (1998) Immigration and Trade Creation: Econometric Evidence from Canada, *Canadian Journal of Economics*, 31, 47–62.

Huang, Y., Jin, L., & Qian, Y. (2008) *Does Ethnicity Pay? Evidence from Overseas Chinese FDI in China*. MIT Sloan Research Paper No. 4690–08.

Ibrahim, G., & Galt, V. (2011) Explaining Ethnic Entrepreneurship: An Evolutionary Economics Approach, *International Business Review*, 20, 607–13.

Ilhan-Nas, T., Sahin, K., & Cilingir, Z. (2011) International Ethnic Entrepreneurship: Antecedents, Outcomes and Environmental Context, *International Business Review*, 20, 614–26.

Javorcik, B., Özden, Ç., Spatareanu, M., & Neagu, C. (2006) *Migrant Networks and Foreign Direct Investment*. Washington, DC: World Bank Working Paper Series.

Javorcik, B.S., Özden, Ç., Spatareanu, M., & Neagu, C. (2011) Migrant Network and Foreign Direct Investment, *Journal of Development Economics*, 94, 231–41.

Johanson, G., Smyth, R., & French, R. (Eds.) (2009) *Living Outside the Walls: The Chinese in Prato*. Newcastle upon Tyne: Cambridge Scholars.

Kao, J. (1993) The Worldwide Web of Chinese Business, *Harvard Business Review*, 71 (2), 24–36.

Keupp, M. M., & Gassman, O. (2009) The Past and Future of International Entrepreneurship: A Review and Suggestions for Developing the Field, *Journal of Management*, 35, 600–33.

Kloosterman, R., & Rath, J. (2010) Shifting Landscapes of Immigrant Entrepreneurship. In OECD (Ed.) *Open for Business: Migrant Entrepreneurship in OECD Countries*. Paris, OECD, pp. 101–123.

Kugler, M., & Rapoport, H. (2006). Migration and FDI: complements or substitutes. ESF-CEPR conference on "Outsourcing and migration in a European context". Rome.

Kugler, M., & Rapoport, H. (2007) International Labour and Capital Flows: Complements or Substitutes? *Economics Letters*, 94, 155–62.

Larson, A. (1992) Network Dyads in Entrepreneurial Settings: A Study of the Governance of Exchange Relationships, *Administrative Science Quarterly*, 37, 76–104.

Ma, M. (2008) Chinese Migration and China's Foreign Policy, *Journal of Chinese Overseas*, 4, 94.

MOFCOM. (2012) *2011 Statistical Bulletin of Chinas Outward Foreign Direct Investment*. Beijing: Ministry of Commerce of People's Republic of China, National Bureau of Statistics of People's Republic of China and State Administration of Foreign Exchange.

MOFCOM. (2013) *2012 Statistical Bulletin of Chinas Outward Foreign Direct Investment*. Beijing: Ministry of Commerce of People's Republic of China, National Bureau of Statistics of People's Republic of China and State Administration of Foreign Exchange.

Navaretti, G. B., de Simone, G., & Sembenelli, A. (2007) *Migration and Foreign Direct Investment: A Review of the Literature*. Paper prepared for the research project "Migrazione e mobilità di impresa: determinanti e ricadute sul territorio" carried out by Centro Studi Luca d'Agliano within the framework of the Fondazione CRT/Progetto Alfieri project.

Nyíri, P. (2003) Chinese Migration to Eastern Europe, *International Migration*, 41, 239–65.

OECD. (2010) *Open for Business: Migrant Entrepreneurship in OECD Countries*. Paris: Author.

Park, Y. J. (2009) *Chinese Migration in Africa*. China in Africa Project. Johannesburg: SAIIA.

Raijman, R., & Tienda, M. (2003) Ethnic Foundations of Economic Transactions: Mexican and Korean Immigrant Entrepreneurs in Chicago, *Ethnic and Racial Studies*, 26, 783–801.

Rauch, J. (1999) Networks versus Markets in International Trade, *Journal of International Economics*, 48, 7–35.

Rauch, J. (2001) Business and Social Networks in International Trade, *Journal of Economic Literature*, 39, 1177–203.

Rauch, J., & Trindade, V. (2002) Ethnic Chinese Networks in International Trade, *Review of Economics and Statistics*, 84, 116–30.

Rauch, J. E., & Casella, A. (Eds.) (2001) *Networks and Markets*. New York: Russell Sage Foundation.

Redding, G. (1990) *The Spirit of Chinese Capitalism*. Berlin: De Gruyter.

Redding, G. (1995) Overseas Chinese Networks: Understanding the Enigma, *Long Range Planning*, 28, 61–69.

Redding, S. G. (1996) Weak Organization and Strong Linkages: Managerial Ideology and Chinese Family Business Networks. In Hamilton, G. G. (Ed.) *Asian Business Networks*. Berlin: Walter de Gruyter, pp. 27–42.

Rusinovic, K. (2008) Transnational Embeddedness: Transnational Activities and Networks among First- and Second-Generation Immigrant Entrepreneurs in the Netherlands, *Journal of Ethnic and Migration Studies*, 34, 431–51.

Saxenian, A. (2002) *Local and Global Networks of Immigrant Professionals in Silicon Valley*. San Francisco: Public Policy Institute of California.

Smart, A., & Hsu, J.-Y. (2004) The Chinese Diaspora, Foreign Investment and Economic Development in China, *Review of International Affairs*, 3, 544–66.

Sohn, D.J.H. (1994) Social Knowledge as a Control System: A Proposition and Evidence from the Japanese FDI Behaviour, *Journal of International Business Studies*, 295–324.

Song, H. (2011). Chinese Private Direct Investment and Overseas Chinese Network in Africa. *China & World Economy*, 19 (4), 109–126.

Taiwan's Overseas Compatriot Affairs Commission. (2011) *2010 Annual Overseas Chinese Affairs Report*. Taipei: Author.

Teixeira, C. (2001) Community Resources and Opportunities in Ethnic Economies: A Case Study of Portuguese and Black Entrepreneurs in Toronto, *Urban Studies*, 38, 2055–78.

Thunø, M. (2001) Reaching Out and Incorporating Chinese Overseas: The Trans-Territorial Scope of the PRC by the End of the 20th Century, *China Quarterly*, 168, 910–29.

Thunø, M. (2003) Channels of Entry and Preferred Destinations: The Circumvention of Denmark by Chinese Immigrants, *International Migration*, 41, 99–133.

Tong, S.Y. (2005) Ethnic Networks in FDI and the Impact of Institutional Development, *Review of Development Economics*, 9, 563–80.

UNCTAD. (2012) *World Investment Report, 2012: Towards a new generation of investment policies*. Geneva: Author.

UNCTAD (2013). World Investment Report 2013: Global Value Chains: Investment and Trade For Development. New York: United Nations.

Weidenbaum, M., & Hughes, S. (1996) *The Bamboo Network*. New York: Free Press.

Whitley, R.D. (1990) Eastern Asian Enterprise Structures and the Comparative Analysis of Forms of Business Organisation, *Organisation Studies*, 11, 47–74.

Whitley, R.D. (1991) The Social Construction of Business Systems in East Asia, *Organisation Studies*, 12, 1–28.

Whitley, R.D. (1994) *Business Systems in East Asia: Firms, Markets and Societies*. London: Sage.

Yeung, H.W.-C. (1999) The Internationalization of Ethnic Chinese Business Firms from Southeast Asia: Strategies, Processes and Competitive Advantage, *International Journal of Urban and Regional Research*, 23, 103–27.

Yeung, H.W.-C., & Olds, K. (Eds.) (2000) *Globalization of Chinese Business Firms*. London: Macmillan.

Zhang, G. (2003) Migration of Highly Skilled Chinese to Europe: Trends and Perspective, *International Migration*, 41, 73–97.

Zhang, H., & Van Den Bulcke, D. (2000) Internationalisation of Ethnic Chinese-Owned Enterprises: A Network Approach. In Yeung, H.W., & Olds, K. (Eds.) *The Globalisation of Chinese Business Firms*. London: Macmillan, pp. 126–149.

Zhang, H., Yang, Z., & Van Den Bulcke, D. (2011) *The European Landscape of Chinese Enterprises: An Analysis of Corporate and Entrepreneurial Firms and the Role of the Ethnic Communities*. Antwerp: Antwerp Management School.

Zhang, H., Yang, Z., & Van Den Bulcke, D. (2012) Geographical Agglomeration of Indian and Chinese Multinationals in Europe: A Comparative Analysis, *Science Technology & Society*, 17(3), 385–408.

Zhuang, G., & Wang, W. (2010) Migration and Trade: The Role of Overseas Chinese in Economic Relations between China and Southeast Asia, *International Journal of China Studies*, 1, 174–93.

3 Chinese immigrant businesses in the industrial district of Prato and their interpretation

Gabi Dei Ottati

Abstract

After decades of economic growth based on the wool industry, during the 1990s, the Prato industrial district experienced the influx of Chinese immigrants who, in little more than a decade, gave rise to a business system of international relevance specialized in *pronto moda*. The chapter focuses on the different interpretations of this phenomenon and in particular on the complex of causes that can explain the exceptional development of Chinese business activity in Prato, unparalleled elsewhere; finally, extending the analysis to the present day, the chapter examines the possible role of the Chinese immigrants in promoting new local development.

Introduction

Setting up a business is a goal that has been increasingly pursued over recent decades by immigrants in the developed economies, by virtue of a number of economic, social, technological and political-institutional changes. This phenomenon has affected Italy as well, although somewhat later than in other countries, and within no more than a few years, it has become a phenomenon of some magnitude, now accounting for roughly 10 per cent of all businesses registered at the Italian Chambers of Commerce (Unioncamere 2012: 346).

In general, immigrants and their enterprises are not uniformly distributed either throughout a territory or in a given range of economic activities. Rather, they tend to be concentrated in certain locations and sectors, which differ on the basis of the immigrants' place of origin and the characters of the context in which the immigrants settle. In Italy, immigrant firms are concentrated in third-sector activities if they are located in the great urban areas, whereas they focus on manufacturing activities if they are located in industrial districts.[1]

As is known, Italy has a production structure which is substantially different from that of the other industrialized countries. Not only does Italy show a widespread tendency towards small and medium-sized businesses,[2] but it is also characterized by an industrial specialization in the production of goods for the person and the home. These specificities of Italian industry can be explained partly by the relative decline of large firms after their growth in the 1950s and 1960s and, above all, by the rise of industrial districts.[3] The industrial district is a particular form of socio-economic organization in which small and medium-sized businesses, most often specialized in a particular production sector and related activities, tend to cluster together in given areas. The numerous small and medium-sized firms constituting these agglomerations are linked by a division of labour that is integrated through a "localized thickening" of economic and social relations. That is to say, there is a notable level of exchange (market) relations among these businesses, but exchange typically takes place between persons belonging to the same social group, whose members share implicit rules of reciprocal cooperation (community). The resulting dense web of both market and community relations allows integration of the activities undertaken by the many businesses that make up the district. This feature, in turn, enables the individual firms to benefit from the advantage of external economies due to the large size and overall variety of the agglomerations.[4] The importance of industrial districts in the Italian economy also accounts for the specialization of Italian exports, which began to be particularly marked as from the 1970s, when Italy experienced and then maintained an active commercial balance in the sector of goods for the person (textiles, apparel, footwear, leather goods, jewellery) and for the home (furnishings, ceramic tiles, small electrical appliances). Therefore, these sectors, together with instrumental mechanics, constitute the essence of the so-called Made in Italy, i.e. the products with regard to which Italy has acquired a significant position in international trade (Fortis & Carminati 2009; Porter 1990).

In recent times, the Italian industrial districts, above all those specialized in products for the person, have seen a considerable spread of firms run by Chinese immigrants. Thus in 2007, out of the total of micro-firms in the sector of textiles, apparel and leather goods located in Italian industrial districts, Chinese-run firms constituted no less than 31 per cent (Lombardi et al. 2011).[5] Among these industrial districts, the area of Prato is perhaps the best known on account of its long-standing textiles tradition and the spectacularly successful development of the industrial district of regenerated wool during the second half of the twentieth century.[6] But over the last few years, Prato has attracted the attention of scholars and media not so much for its textile industry as for the exceptional growth of entrepreneurial activity among Chinese immigrants: indeed, this has become one of the distinguishing features of this area. Thus, over a period of little more than 10 years, written assessments of this phenomenon – excluding the numerous articles in Italian and foreign newspapers – have burgeoned, to the point of now amounting to more than 50 titles distributed among scientific journals, books and contributions to anthologies or readers, or research reports. Taken together, this has produced a vast literature on the subject of Chinese immigration in Prato; moreover, this literature is also extremely varied with regard to the research method and interpretation, making it difficult to reach an in-depth and genuinely scientific comprehension of the phenomenon.

Taking this literature as our starting point, the main aim of this chapter is to offer new perspectives that can contribute to building up a more comprehensive interpretation of the businesses set up by Chinese immigrants in Prato.

The chapter is organized as follows. Section 3.1 outlines the first arrivals of Chinese immigrants in the district of Prato and the multiplication of sewing workshops in the 1990s. In section 3.2, attention focuses on the development of fast fashion in Prato at the beginning of the new millennium. Section 3.3 focuses on several different interpretations of this developmental phase. Section 3.4 offers some final conclusions.

3.1. The spread of Chinese sewing workshops in the final decade of the twentieth century

In the wake of the reform policies enacted by the Chinese government as from 1978, the migration of Chinese subjects once again gathered momentum, with particularly marked migratory flows from the south-eastern coastal provinces of China towards Europe. This new flow was favoured by the presence in Europe of groups of Chinese immigrants who had arrived somewhat earlier, in the first half of the twentieth century, from the same geographic areas as the new migrants (Li 2010). Many were from the province of Zhejiang, in particular the city of Wenzhou (Wu 2009), and Italy soon became one of the most attractive European countries for this new migratory flow, with the number of residents in Italy of Chinese nationality rising from roughly 16,000 in 1994 to almost 87,000 in 2004 and then to 210,000 by 2011.[7]

The greater attraction of Italy as compared to other European countries can be explained in terms of economic considerations and migratory policy. On the latter point, since Italy had a long history of emigration of its own citizens, policies for immigration control had never been enacted. But as early as the 1980s, this led to the presence of a substantial number of irregular immigrants. In the attempt to overcome the resulting difficulties, the policy of recurrent amnesties was adopted; for example, during the 1990s, there were no fewer than three (1990, 1995, 1998). From the point of view of the new immigrants, regularization of their position was indispensable not only in order to avail themselves of certain rights but also so as to become self-employed and set up businesses of their own; consequently, the amnesty policy constituted an incentive to the flow of Chinese immigrants into Italy. Furthermore, the structure of the Italian economy, characterized, as described, by innumerable small and medium-sized manufacturing businesses, particularly in the industrial districts, represented an ideal context, allowing the new Chinese migrants to achieve their main aspiration: that of setting up their own small businesses consisting of subcontractor workshops in the production of goods for the person and the home – thus replicating the standard forms of production in the areas of origin of the majority of these immigrants.[8]

In short, the growth of Chinese immigration went hand in hand with the rapid development of Chinese entrepreneurship. The micro-enterprises set up by Chinese immigrants and registered at an Italian Chamber of Commerce numbered about 8,300 in 2000, but by 2005, this number had risen to almost 22,000, reaching more than 39,000 by 2011.[9] During the 1990s, most of these very small businesses consisted of subcontractor workshops in the manufacture of goods for the person, but in the new millennium, the proportion of businesses involved in manufacturing gradually began to decrease in favour of commercial activities.[10]

In Prato, the first immigrants began to arrive in the late 1980s, after moving to the town from the locality of Campi Bisenzio (a municipality situated between Florence and Prato), where there already existed a settlement of Chinese immigrants originating from Wenzhou (Tassinari 1994). As they had done in Campi Bisenzio, the Chinese immigrants in Prato set up small subcontractor businesses, but not as subcontractors of firms that produced fabric and yarn. Rather, they set up as subcontractors of knitwear production and also of the still relatively small number of garment manufacturers, as the latter were experiencing difficulty in finding cottage-industry workers for the sewing and making-up stages of garment making, on account of the change in women's and young people's expectations regarding working conditions and career prospects.

This circumstance, together with the availability of space for workshops and small factories[11] as well as the mechanism of migratory chains typical of these migrants (Tassinari 1994: 116), soon resulted in a multiplication of Chinese workshops in the area in question. Thus it was not long before a very significant number of Chinese workshops had been set up in Prato, and Chinese immigration became a non-marginal phenomenon. By 1994, within just a few years after the first arrivals, the residents of Chinese origin in the municipality of Prato already numbered almost 2000, with almost 300 businesses (Table 3.1). It was at this point that the Local Council of the Municipality of Prato set up an Immigration Research and Service Centre, focusing specifically on Chinese immigrants.

The analyses performed by the researchers of the Centre gave statistical documentation of the rapid growth of Chinese immigration in Prato, which within just a decade from its outset had seen its numbers surge to 9,000 regular presences and more than 1,200 businesses (Rastrelli 2001: 27). The researchers at the Centre soon warned against interpreting this entrepreneurial development exclusively in terms of ethnical and cultural factors involving the migrants. Instead, Rastrelli's study underlined that it was necessary to take into account the actual conditions

Table 3.1 Province of Prato: number of businesses owned by Chinese immigrants: 1992–2001

Year	Total	% variation	Clothing businesses	% of clothing business on total	% variation (Clothing only)
1992	211	—	210	99.53	—
1994	289	36.97	283	97.92	34.76
1996	375	29.76	351	93.60	24.03
1997	479	27.73	448	93.53	27.64
1998	862	79.96	766	88.86	70.98
1999	1,158	34.34	1,016	87.74	32.64
2000	1,288	11.23	1,098	85.25	8.07
2001	1,499	16.38	1,201	80.12	9.38

Source: Prato Chamber of Commerce

under which immigrants form part of the working context of the host society (Ras-trelli 2001: 29–30). The researchers' approach was thus based on what is known, in the literature on migrant entrepreneurship, as the "interactive model", which takes into consideration the relations between factors on the supply side (migrant characters) and on the demand side (structure of opportunities in the immigra-tion context; Waldinger, Aldrich, & Ward 1990). These first studies showed that the presence of Chinese immigrants in Prato had given rise to the formation of an ethnic economy in the sense that the workers in their businesses were exclu-sively Chinese; but on the other hand, the study also highlighted that the work-ing conditions in the Chinese workshops responded to the demands of the Italian firms that were their clients. Therefore, even the widespread irregularities (tax evasion, non-compliance with social security payments, use of the workplace as a living area) noted in the Chinese businesses could not be attributed exclusively to the socio-economic model characteristic of these immigrants. Rather, it was also a function of the type of relations built up with the clients in the local market (Rastrelli 2001: 30).[12]

Within this local market, since the businesses run by Chinese immigrants were subcontractors of Prato apparel and knitwear firms that had "a fairly substantial market power" (Guercini 2002: 63) with respect to the Chinese subcontractors, the self-employed work by such subcontractors was interpreted as a "delocaliza-tion *in loco*" (Ceccagno 2003: 38–9). This enabled the Italian clients to reduce their costs and production times and to be confident, at least temporarily, of being able to face the increasingly stiff competition on the market induced by the glo-balization of the economy. Furthermore, recourse to workshops run by Chinese immigrants also compensated for the difficulties arising from the generation change that was affecting both the employed and self-employed labour supply in the manufacturing sector.

Additional research was undertaken, again at the behest of the local authori-ties,[13] in order to acquire in-depth information on firms run by Chinese immi-grants. In particular, cross-checking the data on Chinese families resident in Prato against the data on the owners of Chinese businesses registered at the local Cham-ber of Commerce confirmed the centrality of the role of the extended family and of the networks of social relations, showing that these factors were important in achieving the entrepreneurial projects these immigrants set up (Marsden 2002). Moreover, an analysis of some Chinese firms that had already been operating in Prato for some time in the garment-making sector and were already fairly well structured showed that in 1998, these firms were still operating only as subcon-tractors, mainly for local clients, and that their evolution consisted, at most, in supplying more than one stage of the manufacturing process (e.g. sewing and ironing; Guercini 2002).

In sum, these initial studies pinpointed a number of the significant aspects of Chinese entrepreneurship in Prato that would play a major role in its later devel-opment. First, in Prato – unlike the situation in Campi and in other Italian dis-tricts – the Chinese immigrants and the businesses they set up did not become a part of the main industry of the district (textiles). Rather, they made a significant contribution to the development of a new sector: fast fashion (Colombi 2002: 7).

Second, a surprising similarity was noted between the production organisation of the new Chinese workshops and that of the textile craftsmen in the early days of the Prato industrial district, in the 1950s and 1960s (Colombi 2002: 16–7).

3.2. The rise of a Chinese fast fashion system in the first decade of the twenty-first century

As illustrated in the previous section, the multiplication of Chinese subcontractor workshops was crucial for the development of the apparel industry in Prato and, above all, for the particular manner of organising production that goes by the name of "fast fashion" (*pronto moda*). Fast fashion is an apparel-production system that was beginning to be adopted in the 1990s, partly as a result of a change in consumer demand, which was becoming increasingly variable and fragmented, and partly also on account of changes that were taking place on the international level concerning the relations between distribution and production in the textile-apparel value chain (Gereffi & Memedovic 2003). Essentially, in fast fashion, the time frames of the stages of design, production and distribution are so tightly scheduled within a very limited space of time that they tend to overlap, in contrast to the so-called "programmed" procedure (adopted by the few clothing manufacturers existing in Prato in the early 1990s), in which the stages are extended over a period of several months.

By the end of the 1990s, the Chinese immigrants in Prato constituted a substantial presence in the overall population. Moreover, they owned a fairly large number of firms, concentrated in the fast fashion sector of the apparel industry (Table 3.1).

It was at this point that some Chinese entrepreneurs who, having been present in Prato for a longer period of time, having acquired more extensive knowledge of production and had built up a network of relations in the local context, decided to make an entrepreneurial leap, transforming themselves from subcontractors to final entrepreneurs. That is to say, they moved from the garment sewing stage to that of designing models and then on to the marketing of fast fashion garments. This transformation, initially undertaken by a limited number of Chinese entrepreneurs in Prato, spread rapidly, and the quantity of fast fashion firms in Prato[14] multiplied in the first decade of the new century, precisely when the local textile system, which had long been the core element of the economy – indeed, of the very identity – of the city of Prato itself[15] was undergoing an unprecedented crisis (Table 3.2 and Figure 3.1). The value of the textile exports (excluded clothing items) in the Province of Prato between 2001 and 2008 declined by more than 40 per cent (Table 3.3), and the number of firms and workers in the Prato textile sector decreased year by year.[16] This constant shrinkage of the number of local Italian workers, firms and investments, together with the use of imported semi-finished products and partial delocalization designed to make it easier to beat off the increasingly stiff competition, drastically reduced the size and variety of the Prato textile system, thereby also changing the quantity and quality of

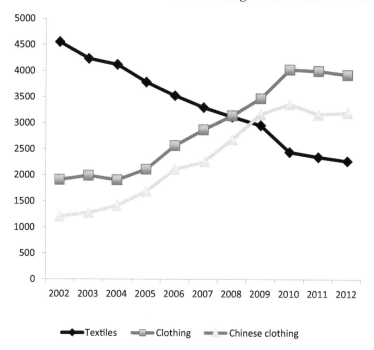

Figure 3.1 Textiles and apparel businesses (total vs. run by Chinese entrepreneurs) in the Province of Prato: 2002–2012

Source: Chamber of Commerce of Prato

Table 3.2 Textiles and apparel businesses (total vs. run by Chinese entrepreneurs) in the Province of Prato: 2002–2012

Sectors	2002	2003	2004	2005	2006	2007	2008	2009	2010	2011	2012
Textiles	4,554	4,235	4,122	3,787	3,526	3,300	3,121	2,959	2,448	2,353	2,274
Apparel	1,910	1,991	1,905	2,113	2,571	2,875	3,144	3,476	4,029	4,003	3,928
Chinese Apparel firms	1,210	1,278	1,412	1,688	2,110	2,254	2,690	3,174	3,364	3,165	3,200

Source: Chamber of Commerce of Prato

relations among enterprises. Not only did the traditional web of relations begin to fade, but the blend of competition and cooperation that had hitherto been the hallmark of such relations became increasingly difficult to maintain and reproduce: competition began to prevail over cooperation, above all in subcontractor relations, with consequent erosion of trust within the system.[17]

Table 3.3 Province of Prato: exports of the textiles and apparel sector between 2001 and 2012

	Absolute values (thousands of euros)			Absolute variations		% variations	
	2001	*2008*	*2012*	*2001–08*	*2008–12*	*2001–08*	*2008–12*
VALUES AT CURRENT PRICES							
Textile fibre yarn	228,936	142,911	181,826	−86,025	38,914	−37.6%	27.2%
Fabric	1,558,336	897,443	713,407	−660,892	−184,036	−42.4%	−20.5%
Other textiles	407,109	265,669	287,833	−141,440	22,165	−34.7%	8.3%
Apparel	212,516	254,299	403,814	41,783	149,515	19.7%	58.8%
Fur clothing	1,303	5,679	6,351	4,376	672	335.9%	11.8%
Knitwear	215,098	131,486	132,507	−83,612	1,020	−38.9%	0.8%
TOTAL	**2,623,297**	**1,697,487**	**1,725,737**	**−925,810**	**28,250**	**−35.3%**	**1.7%**

Source: IRPET on Istat data

Such changes in the number of businesses belonging to the original Prato textiles system and also affecting relations within this system made it increasingly difficult to benefit from the production and spread of the kind of external economies which are actually internal to the overall agglomeration. This further exacerbated the downwards spiral, as such economies are fundamental for the efficiency and vitality of the organizational form constituting the industrial district (Dei Ottati 2009b).[18]

In short, the crisis affecting the textiles district was not due to the presence of Chinese immigrants but rather was primarily the result of difficulty in adapting to the kind of competition characterising the new international context (globalization of the markets with the entry of new producer countries and change in relations between distribution and production in the textile and apparel value chain). However, the distinction between the successful trend of Chinese fast fashion in contrast to the decline of the Prato textile system led to a change in the local population's attitude towards the Chinese immigrants: "from a resource to an emergency" (*La Nazione*, Prato, 4 April 2002). This, in turn, triggered tensions and difficulties in relations between the native community and the Chinese immigrants.[19]

3.3. Some interpretations of the Chinese businesses in Prato

As already mentioned, the multiplication of firms run by Chinese immigrants in Prato has sparked an array of studies and a variety of interpretations.[20] Before outlining our own interpretation (section 3.3.3.), two different readings of the situation will be described, which offer contrasting views of the present and future impact of this phenomenon on the local economy and society.

3.3.1.   *A multi-ethnic industrial district as adaptation to changes induced by globalization*

It was pointed out earlier that the interpretation which holds that the Chinese businesses played a role functional to the competitiveness of Italian businesses arose very early, with the first investigations into Chinese-run businesses when the latter were still subcontractors of Italian firms. This approach to the question was prompted by the realization that the pace of work and the working conditions accepted by the Chinese immigrants allowed production costs and time to be reduced to levels that would have been unthinkable with an exclusively Italian workforce (Ceccagno 2003).

That these immigrants were functional to the local economy was further confirmed when Prato became "the only place in Italy" (Ceccagno 2012: 45) where Chinese migrants became self-employed fast fashion producers. With the transformation from mere subcontractors to final entrepreneurs in the quick fashion sector, the Chinese immigrants would transform the district of Prato into a new and dynamic centre of fashion, capable of attracting clients from the whole of Europe and even beyond (Ceccagno 2009: 55).

Thus, according to this interpretation, Chinese fast fashion provided an impetus that spurred the Prato textile system to remodel its production in order to adapt to the new demand for medium-low–level textiles of the kind used in Chinese fast fashion (Ceccagno 2009: 64–5). As further support for the argument that the Chinese immigrants have contributed to adapting the Prato district to the changed context of globalization, it is also claimed that Chinese fast fashion has not only given a new boost to the Prato textile sector, inasmuch as the Chinese businesses bought textiles from local firms, but it has also created job opportunities for Italians as well as for Chinese immigrants. This is because Italian workers are typically employed in fast fashion as fashion designers, pattern makers and commercial representatives but also as accountants and secretaries (Ceccagno 2009: 61).[21] Therefore, this line of analysis seems to suggest, by creating a fast fashion centre that rapidly built up an international reputation, the Chinese businesses effectively revitalized the Prato district. For instance, it has been stated that

> This town (Prato) used to be a textile district that specialized in the production and export of textiles. While the core production of the district is still textiles, in the last few years, thanks also to the presence of Chinese workshops and final firms producing garments, the local chain of production has expanded to include the last phase of manufacturing, so much so that the area of Prato can now be described as a fashion district.
>
> (Ceccagno 2009: 69)[22]

Similarly, in a subsequent article, the author adds that "Migrants' contribution to the remaking and competitive repositioning of cities is often downplayed, distorted and denied. In the case of Prato, the contribution of Chinese migrants to reframing the city's socio-economic landscape is contested and rejected by the main stakeholders" (Ceccagno 2012: 59).

3.3.2.   *A parallel Chinese district as a threat to the local economy*

A perspective that can be defined as diametrically opposite to the foregoing assertion emerges from a reading of the publication by Silvia Pieraccini (Pieraccini 2008, 2010), bearing the significant title *L'assedio cinese* [*The Chinese Siege*]. The work traces the evolution of Chinese immigration to Prato starting from the early 1990s, when apparel was an absolutely marginal sector of the Prato district and the Chinese mainly devoted themselves to sewing tops such as T-shirts and garments as outworkers for small local clothing firms. Pieraccini's retrospective overview then underlines the change of direction that came about at the turn of the century, when the Chinese subcontractors made an entrepreneurial "leap", setting up the first fast fashion ladies-wear production firms that sold directly on the market (Pieraccini 2008: 3–5). Another argument put forward in the book is that in the wake of this "leap", the Chinese workers in Prato, for whom "illegality was absolutely routine" (Pieraccini 2008: 26–30; 2010: 44–50), were able to achieve rapid progress in the fast fashion sector and had extended their range of businesses to include complementary activities such as garment dyeing or the importing of textiles from China. In short, the author suggests that the Chinese immigrants had, as it were, given rise to "a parallel district" overlaid on the historical productions of the area: a production system that was not contributing to lengthening the textile production chain downstream; additionally, the author contends that the Chinese system was overturning the image of quality that Prato had established over the years, replacing it with a shabby imitation based on low-quality products and flouted rules (Pieraccini 2008: 7).

Evidence corroborating this critical view emerges, according to the author, from the fact that the fabric utilized by the Chinese fast fashion producers to manufacture their garments was not made by Prato firms, except in marginal cases;[23] rather, it was imported from China. This claim is indirectly confirmed by the strong increase in imports of textile products from China precisely at the beginning of the third millennium.[24] A further observation put forward in this context is that the statistics on imports do not give an accurate picture of the extent of the phenomenon because, it is alleged, a substantial quantity of textiles are smuggled into the country (Pieraccini 2010: 41).

The types of widespread illegality mentioned in the survey also include tax evasion, which in the author's view is fairly elevated and is also favoured by a production cycle which is so short (barely 2–3 days) that it often leaves no trace. Furthermore, tax evasion also tends to be accompanied by the even more severe failure to comply with the employer's duty to pay the required social security contributions on behalf of workers; and this breach of the law often occurs not only in cases pertaining to informal workers acting as invisible subcontractors in the garment-making industry and not covered by any contractual relation, but even with regard to workers who do have a proper contract (Pieraccini 2008: 27–8; 2010: 44–6). More generally, the phenomenon of tax evasion, often confirmed during inspections carried out in the Chinese workshops by the official authorities,[25] is further exacerbated by the utilization of workers who have no valid entry permit or work permit. It has been claimed that the number of clandestine workers has increased markedly with the rise of Chinese fast fashion, to the point that estimates made on the basis of the number of Chinese garment workshops registered at the Chamber of Commerce compared with the average number of sewing machines found in laboratories suggest a presence of "roughly 30,000 [Chinese] clandestine workers" (Pieraccini 2010: 47).[26]

In addition to the widespread illegality and the large quantity of fabric imported from China, the sense of alarm among the local population that has been sparked by the presence of these immigrants has been further enflamed by the large amounts of money transferred from Prato to China in the form of immigrants' remittances. Examination of the data has shown that such remittances rose markedly between 2005 and 2009, to the point that by the latter date, they exceeded 464 million euros, thus representing roughly a quarter of total remittances from Italy to China (Figure 3.2).

Such a marked increase in remittances from Prato to China, achieved within such a short space of time, is suggestive of an explanation of this monetary flow that goes beyond the mere fast fashion and commercial activities undertaken by the Chinese in Prato. One of the hypotheses put forward alludes to the possible presence of *money transfer operators* in Prato, acting as money collectors on

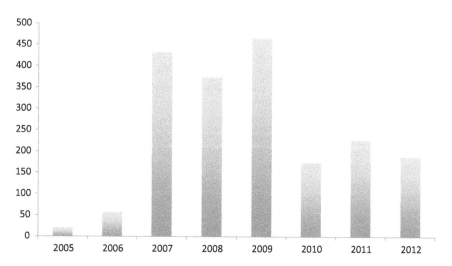

Figure 3.2 Province of Prato: Remittances to China from 2005 to 2012 (millions of euros)

Source: Bank of Italy statistics of remittances

behalf of Chinese migrants who may have been resident locally but conceivably even elsewhere, in some other part of Italy or perhaps in other parts of Europe (Pieraccini 2008). An even more plausible explanation is that the remittances were a means used by the Chinese fast fashion operators to pay for imported fabric (Pieraccini 2010: 99) but also for real estate and other investments in China.[27]

Silvia Pieraccini's book concludes with several queries on the Chinese presence and the future of Prato, in which one perceives the fear of a prospect of decline and blight.

3.3.3. *Chinese businesses in Prato: from a "social cushion" alleviating the repercussions of the textile crisis to a "resource" for a new local development*

The third interpretation we wish to propose here is contained in a recent article by the present author (Dei Ottati 2014). It seeks to take into account the various economic and social aspects of the two populations involved, partly also as a means of singling out appropriate measures and action that can help to overcome the current economic and social difficulties facing the two communities. The author's interest in this field of research stems not only from the fact that Prato was long regarded as an exemplary case of development in the Italy of the industrial districts (Becattini 2001) but also from her lifelong dedication to the study of Prato's economy.

The concept put forward in this third interpretation is that during the earliest phase, the immigrants from China settled in the district of Prato as subcontractors of the local knitwear and apparel firms in a manner that was functional to the needs of the latter, while at the same time it gave the immigrants themselves an opportunity to make a dream come true, a dream that had underpinned their migratory project from the very outset: namely the aim of setting themselves up as self-employed with their own small businesses. This early phase was then followed by a markedly different second stage, in which the scenario of an integration subordinated to the local economy gave way to a substantial degree of separateness from the economic framework of the local area.

The transition to this second stage came about when, roughly a decade after the arrival of the first Chinese migrants in Prato, the number of Chinese-run businesses had risen to a quite substantial proportion of the overall firms present in the area, and some of these firms began to undergo a transformation from subcontractors to fast fashion businesses run by immigrants themselves. This evolution had two effects: first, it generated a further growth in the number of Chinese businesses and immigrants in Prato; second and most notably, it also changed the quality and quantity of relations among Chinese firms and, above all, between these and the local Prato firms. On the one hand, the relations among the Chinese firms themselves intensified and were favoured by the division of labour among such businesses, becoming increasingly intertwined with social relations; on the other, relations between the local Prato firms and the Chinese immigrant-owned firms became more and more strained and the frequency of relations declined sharply, because the Chinese subcontractor firms worked primarily for Chinese final firms. As a result, Prato came to have a veritable Chinese fast fashion production system, whose main links with the local economy essentially consisted of income transfer by the Chinese for purposes of consumption and, above all, for renting or purchasing properties which they could use for their production activity but also as living quarters at the same time, according to a widespread practice in their country of origin.

This interpretation does not coincide with the picture outlined in section 3.3.1., because the present author does not espouse the view that the development of firms run by Chinese immigrants in Prato helped the Prato economy to adapt to the ongoing changes in international competition. But at the same time, this author's interpretation also differs from the ideas put forward in section 3.3.2., because it does not hold that the presence of illegality in Chinese workshops is sufficient to account for the rise of an entrepreneurial phenomenon that has no parallel in Italy. In effect, although businesses owned and run by Chinese immigrants are by no means infrequent in the Italian fashion districts, only in Prato do they number in the thousands rather than the few hundred or so recorded in other districts (Intesa Sanpaolo 2010: 112). Furthermore and most significantly, some of these businesses have evolved from being subcontractors to being final firms specialized in the designing and marketing of apparel.

Another point which should be mentioned is that unfortunately, the utilization of irregular immigrants is not a feature exclusive to Prato or among Chinese immigrants. It is also found in other localities and among various ethnic groups (Fasani 2009). Furthermore, the informal economy is not a characteristic limited to Chinese businesses in Prato: it is a widespread practice found throughout numerous ethnic communities[28] and is well-known in many economic contexts, especially in Italy and, above all, in the less developed regions.[29] And even with regard to Prato, a recent study has found that illegality cannot be associated exclusively with Chinese firms (Barbu et al. 2013: 14).[30] Accordingly, we argue that the amazing development and success of Chinese entrepreneurial activity in Prato should be partly attributed to other factors in addition to illegality. Among such factors, four have been singled out, distinct from one another yet revealing subtle connections.

(1) These Chinese businesses were set up in a sector (fast fashion) that was marginal within the Prato economy but which was undergoing growth due to changes in the demand for apparel products. More specifically, the apparel sector was experiencing increasing fragmentation and variability of consumer demand, and this tendency prompted wholesalers and retailers to work with far smaller quantities and shorter and shorter delivery times. As a result, their demand for fast fashion apparel increased.[31]

(2) Chinese entrepreneurs who had been immigrated in Prato for a longer period of time and thus had built a network of relations in the local context were able to set up their own final firms and thereby access the markets directly. This functional *upgrading* was possible not only because of the entrepreneurial spirit

of individuals who had acquired greater experience but also because of their location in the Prato district, given that Prato, by virtue of its textile tradition, has a worldwide reputation and consequently is a hub for buyers and operators in fashion. Thus the very fact of being located in Prato facilitated Chinese entrepreneurs' direct access to the fast fashion market. However, in order to operate successfully in fast fashion, it is crucial to be able to make an instant identification of favoured high-end styles and rapidly design a collection replicating such styles. This requires creative and design skills that Chinese entrepreneurs did not possess, as such skills require a solid background in fashion design and cannot be immediately learned. Prato, with its reservoir of qualified Italian designers and prototype makers, offered the crucial advantage of filling the gap in the skills that are essential for starting a fast fashion business. This explains why, from the very outset, Chinese fast fashion final firms hired Italians as fashion designers and pattern makers and also hired Italian accountants, because the complex Italian accountancy laws called for in-depth and up-to-date knowledge of the specific subject matter.

(3) Another explanatory factor underlying the spectacular development of Chinese fast fashion in Prato lies in the formation of a production system composed of thousands of Chinese businesses held together by the bonds of a dense web of economic and social relations. This system, already mentioned earlier in the context of the "localised thickening" of relations among small businesses in the early days of the industrial district in Italy, began to take shape more concretely after the establishment of Chinese final firms. With the advent of the final firms, the division of labour among the firms intensified: regular immigrant workers who had acquired sufficient know-how started up their own sub-contracting workshops with the aid of the money accumulated by working as employees in co-ethnic firms and informal credit from family members and friends, who were also generally employed as workers in the new firms. In turn, sub-contractors who had acquired sufficient experience started to become final firms and to employ sub-contracting firms belonging to some relative or friend.[32] As a result, not only did the agglomeration of enterprises grow considerably in the number and variety of activities carried out (Table 3.4) but also, most importantly, the relations among such firms multiplied and presented a distinctive feature: namely, the economic relations within this network took place mainly among people from the same family or the same town, who were united by membership in the same social group and therefore by a bond of solidarity and compliance with a common set of implicit rules of behaviour.[33]

These features of the Chinese productive system gave rise to an increasing "thickening" of both economic and social relations within and among immigrants' firms, forming a dense web, invisible but resilient, which led to close integration among the activities carried out by the many firms of the system. Consequently, the circulation of information, finished and half-finished products, work and money among firms and persons was notably facilitated, so that the production scale upon which economic efficiency depends became that of the whole system

Table 3.4 Businesses run by Chinese in the Province of Prato by sector: 2001, 2005, 2010, 2012

SECTORS	2001	2005	2010	2012
Textiles	68	163	243	264
Apparel	1,201	1,688	3,364	3,200
Leather goods	26	45	92	116
Furniture	9	/	44	34
Other manufacturing activity	/	58	49	58
Wholesale import/export trade	50	197	406	468
Retail trade	76	147	269	255
Other commercial activities	/	/	6	6
Catering and housing	15	22	141	161
Bars	9	11	/	/
Transport and travel agencies	/	6	8	7
Information and Communication	/	22	/	/
Real estate businesses	8	33	76	82
Building industry	/	13	26	24
Credit and insurance	/	/	10	13
IT services	/	6	21	19
Professional and technical services	/	6	29	43
Other services	/	/	36	49
Other	37	24	20	31
TOTAL	**1,499**	**2,441**	**4,840**	**4,830**

Source: Chamber of Commerce of Prato

instead of that of the single firm. And since the scale of the system was large, its businesses, although individually small, were integrated with one another, enabling them to compete with larger enterprises.[34]

(4) As is known and has been documented (Marsden & Caserta 2010: 16–7), the migrants maintained strong relations with relatives and friends who had stayed in China or had emigrated elsewhere. This feature, taken together with the simultaneous emergence of China as an economic power, favoured the rise of transnational entrepreneurs in Prato as well. Even though this further transformation may initially have affected no more than a few hundred migrants, it is a phenomenon that can have a significant impact. In a more general perspective, immigrants who become importers of fabric or clothing accessories made in China or those who invest in businesses located in their place of origin, by virtue of the relations they have both in the sending and receiving areas, can forge a link between the potential demand for consumption goods in the host country with that of supply in the immigrants' place of origin and, on occasion, vice versa. Such a connection tends to promote export-led growth in the sending area.[35]

Several significant considerations spring from the growing importance of the transnational aspect. In particular, when transnational relations of this kind reach a sizeable number and frequency, they establish connections not merely between individual firms but between the overall economy of the sending area and the production system of which the immigrant entrepreneurs form part in their place of immigration. Thus the "thickening" of economic, social and institutional relations nourished by the businesses of transnational entrepreneurs appears to extend the circulation of information, goods, labour and capital from the system in the host country to the economy and society in the sending area. Such an interpretation seems to be confirmed by the evidence of the large amount of money sent from Prato to China, especially from 2007 to 2009, in the form of remittances (Figure 3.2): our hypothesis is that this flow of money is largely attributable to imports from China and investments in China.

Moreover, the economic relations of Chinese emigrants – known in China as "overseas Chinese" – with their homeland are also fostered by a number of other factors. Clearly, the economic growth in China creates many business opportunities for overseas Chinese. Additionally, though by no means of secondary importance, a significant role is played by the favourable conditions (in terms of access to credit, land and property and simplified bureaucratic procedures) for investments granted to overseas Chinese by the Chinese government, especially at local level in high-emigration areas. In effect, the economic connections between place of immigration and place of origin are nurtured not simply through the transactions established by individual entrepreneurs but also through institutional ties established by business associations of overseas Chinese abroad and provincial or municipal governments in China. For instance, in Wenzhou, the local government has founded the Association of Overseas Wenzhouese, which actively promotes investments and donations for building local infrastructures and financing social services.[36] This extension allows the firms that engage in such activity and also, to a certain degree, the system of which they form part, to benefit from the advantages of transnational relations that are far from negligible in the new global economy.

This interpretation is fundamentally in agreement, albeit based on different considerations, with the view presented in section 3.3.2., where it is suggested that the Chinese fast fashion system in Prato has so far mainly fulfilled a function as a "social cushion" alleviating the negative economic effects arising from the crisis in the textiles system, but without contributing to adaptation of the local economy to the radically changed context of the third millennium. Evidence in this direction comes from the realization that the protracted crisis affecting the old textiles district shows no sign of abating (Figure 3.1 and Table 3.2).[37]

Given the changed context, both within Prato and in the overall external area, what the regeneration of local development truly requires is a profound renewal of its economic, social and institutional foundations. However, on account of the now considerable economic and social weight of the presence of Chinese immigrants in Prato, renewal is not conceivable without the integration of at least a significant part of these immigrants. And on closer examination, a move towards genuine integration, long regarded as desirable but seemingly rendered more difficult rather than easier as the years went by, at the time of writing (2014) seems more feasible than in the past and advantageous for both the populations (of businesses and people) involved.

Looking at the question from the perspective of the Chinese immigrants themselves, the transformation of a substantial number of these Chinese immigrants from subcontractors to owners of final firms and more generally the shift towards tertiary activities and international trade (Table 3.4) is making the economic success of these immigrants increasingly dependent on their transnational relations and commercial flair and on their ability to supply products that are competitive not so much in terms of price but of quality and stylistic content. Interviews with Chinese entrepreneurs conducted in the course of an ongoing study have shown that the most successful Chinese firms are often those that have transnational relations. This is the case, for example, of a firm that imports apparel accessories, which is run by two partners, one of whom lives in Prato, where he deals with sales and identifies fashion trends, while the other lives in China, where he searches for the most suitable firms to manufacture the accessories that will be imported into Italy. Another case is that of an apparel importer who has already been in Italy for quite some time but not in Prato; he recently left the importing business and moved to Prato, where he opened a menswear final firm: for a part of his production, this entrepreneur makes use of subcontractors located in China, where he has a trusted assistant who deals with the internationalised production. An even more striking example of the value of relations with the country of origin is given by a well-known Chino-Pratese entrepreneur who owns two apparel firms: one in Prato, which deals with designing the apparel and the associated sales, and one in China, run by a relative of his, where the actual production takes place. This entrepreneur, working collaboratively with a Prato businessman, has succeeded in carrying out a project of setting up a Permanent Exhibition Centre devoted to Made in Italy products (above all apparel, but also other products) called "Principi d'Italia" (*Princes of Italy*) in the Chinese province of Anhui. The Chino-Pratese entrepreneur acts as an intermediary between the Italian firms (a hundred or so) that seek to access the Chinese market and the Chinese firms aiming to buy Italian products, for which demand is rising in China. The intermediation functions on the basis of a commission paid by both the sellers and the buyers. The Chino-Pratese entrepreneur's relations with the Chinese local authorities played a fundamental part in setting up the Permanent Exhibition Centre, to the point that the local authorities authorized the opening of a customs office within the Exhibition Centre.

Another important aspect is that many of the Chinese immigrants in Prato have been established in the town for a considerable length of time; they live in Prato with their families, and it is in Prato that they have fulfilled their aspiration to achieve economic mobility. Above all, their children have been brought up in Prato and have attended Italian schools: these young people now have a background, a lifestyle and expectations that are different not only from those of their parents but also from those of others of their age who live in China. These offspring of Chinese immigrants are a non-negligible part of the young population of Prato,[38] and they are to all extents and purposes "young people from Prato", although it is difficult, in the current situation, to imagine that they truly feel they are "Pratese".

Turning now to the overall picture of the Prato textile district, over the last decade, its production system has severely declined, both as regards the number of firms and also the relations among such firms. Therefore, there is a need for a new entrepreneurial spirit and greater cohesion in order to inject new verve into the system. First of all, the changes that have taken place in the relations between production and distribution within the textiles-apparel value chain (Gereffi & Memedovic 2003) seem to indicate that in order to revive profitability, there is a need for greater integration with activities downstream of textile production and, in particular, integration with fashion product design and distribution to the final consumer, since these are the steps in the value chain where the greater part of value is concentrated.[39] Second, the need to contain production costs, as well as the shortage of a native workforce (in Prato as in other developed societies) willing to work in manufacturing, inevitably make it necessary to move towards a partial internationalization of production, but without lowering quality and constant product innovation, as these constitute the indispensable features required to beat the competition of low-labour-cost countries.

Overall, these considerations suggest that intensification of economic and social relations between the native Prato population and the Chinese immigrants would be advantageous for both. In effect, an increase in relations with Prato producers would help Chinese entrepreneurs to shift towards high-end products, and this in turn would prompt Chinese businessmen to purchase Prato textiles and, more generally, to increase their relations with Italian operators. Conversely, greater relations with the Chinese entrepreneurs of Prato would help the Prato textiles producers to integrate downstream with apparel manufacturing (a goal often declared to be desirable, but so far, little has been achieved). Furthermore, by interacting with Chinese entrepreneurs who have the language and cultural background as well as knowledge of the social and institutional relations needed to do business in China, Prato producers would find it easier to internationalize part of the manufacturing activities and, above all, marketing activities. This would help small and medium-sized Prato businesses to seize the opportunities offered by globalization, inasmuch as subjects lacking not only adequate financial capital but, in particular, the appropriate social capital would otherwise encounter considerable difficulty in achieving such an objective. Finally, the role of bridge builders, enabling the manufacturing and market areas of the emergent regions of Asia to be linked to the potential new Prato system, would be advantageous not only for the people of Prato itself but also for the Chinese immigrants who, by extending their relations beyond the ethnical networks, would multiply the growth opportunities both for their own businesses and also for those of the regions that are brought into communication with one another.[40]

3.4. Concluding remarks

After the foregoing observations on the advantages deriving from genuine integration between the people of Prato and the Chinese immigrants, it is helpful to underline why these objectives may perhaps be easier to achieve today than in the past, if the subjects involved are aware of the potential and act accordingly.

It was noted earlier that two aspects – on the one hand the crisis which, since the beginning of this century, has affected the Prato textiles system and, on the other, the rapid development of Chinese fast fashion – have led to considerable tensions between the local population of Prato and the Chinese immigrants. As shown by an investigation conducted in 2009 among Chinese entrepreneurs in Prato, this has led to considerable apprehension and widespread uncertainty among the Chinese immigrants, so much that three quarters of the Chinese entrepreneurs interviewed declared that they were unsure whether they and their families would stay in Prato in the future or whether they would return to China or possibly move elsewhere (Marsden & Caserta 2010: 39). In this regard, it is worth noting that in another investigation conducted only a few years earlier, more than 71 per cent of the Chinese entrepreneurs who were interviewed expressed the conviction that they would stay in Prato (Santini, Rabino, & Zanni 2011: 42).

According to more recent research, this uncertainty, combined with the persistence of the economic crisis in Italy as compared to the development in the country of origin, appears to have increased the likelihood that part of the Chinese entrepreneurial community could abandon the area of Prato (Fabbri 2011). Indeed, this appears to some extent to be already taking place. Not only is Prato no longer felt to be attractive to Chinese migrants, but even those who are already well established have apparently ceased to invest in the area and have begun to leave.[41]

But if a large number of Chinese entrepreneurs was to decide to return to their country of origin or to move elsewhere, there can be little doubt that the overall repercussions for the town of Prato would be counterproductive. It cannot be ignored that even though the development of Chinese fast fashion in Prato arose rather separately from the rest of the local economy, it has nevertheless brought many new entrepreneurs and workers to Prato. The development of Chinese fast fashion, together with the multiplication of Chinese businesses, has meant that investments in such businesses have also increased. Although data on Chinese immigrants' investments and international trade are not available, it appears that so far, the financial and commercial flows have mainly favoured China. As shown in the third interpretation presented earlier, this outcome is due above all to the fact that the Prato Chinese system is characterized by greater integration with the Chinese homeland rather than with the local economy: but if the Chinese business sector in Prato were also integrated with local Prato enterprises, the result could be completely different. In contrast, the adverse effect of a possible exodus from Prato of the Chinese entrepreneurs would make itself felt not only in terms of the decrease in income transfers (rental or purchase of business premises), which, as mentioned earlier, have in the past few years acted as a "social cushion" alleviating the negative economic effect of the textiles crisis: it would mean above all the disappearance of a new and fundamental spirit of initiative and entrepreneurial energy that is crucial for revival of the local economy and society, especially in the new context of the global economy.

However, an objection can be raised against this perspective, in the sense that the attempts made by the local institutions, above all at the beginning, to promote integration between Chinese immigrants and the local population of Prato have failed precisely also because of the social and economic lack of openness held to be typical of the community of Chinese immigrants. But in this context, it should be noted that even immigration, just like the economy and society in general, changes over time.

On the issue of the Chinese community's unwillingness to open up to the local society's way of life, the cited 2009 investigation noted that many of the Chinese entrepreneurs who were interviewed expressed the desire for greater participation in local affairs and Italian citizenship for their children (Marsden & Caserta 2010: 38–9). Such demands are suggestive of these people's proposal to settle permanently in their chosen migratory area. The transition from temporary to permanent immigration is fundamental because it changes the expectations and behaviour of the subjects involved: whereas temporary immigrants' main aim is to make as much money as possible in the shortest possible time so as to go back to their home country as soon as possible, where they will be wealthy and respected, permanent immigrants seek to build a better life and a good future for themselves and their family in their new place of residence. Hence, the permanent immigrants are eager to integrate, to take part in the society where they are now living, and thus also to abide by the rules of their new place of residence. And if one adds to this the presence of thousands of young Chinese who were born or have grown up in Prato and who can be recognised as Chinese only by their facial features, then it can easily be understood why today, many Chinese immigrants would like to integrate with the local society, if only they are given the chance to do so.

Finally, even the lack of economic openness, as noted, is not destined to last forever. Recent and still ongoing research bears witness to an evolutionary process taking place within the Chinese businesses in Prato. First, Chinese economic activities are undergoing a process of diversification, as mentioned several times in this chapter, with a significant growth of the service sector. Second, the multiplication of fast fashion final firms and the gradual move of some among them towards better-quality products that command a higher price also has the effect of encouraging such firms to establish a wider range of relations with Italians as employees, consultants, agents and suppliers, mainly in Prato. Although at present this evolution involves only a minority of Chinese firms of Prato, it is nevertheless indicative of an ongoing trend that is significant precisely because it demonstrates that integration, if consciously pursued, is possible.

The social and economic evolution currently taking place among those Chinese entrepreneurs of Prato who arrived some time ago and have thus been working in the area for a considerable period of time suggests that the time is now right for there to be a more genuine process of social and economic integration between the local population of Prato and the Chinese immigrants, with a more concrete chance of being brought about.[42] This may provide the opportunity to move on from the early phase of subservient economic integration devoid of social integration and from the subsequent phase of relative separateness in the economic and social sphere.

Once awareness of this scenario has been acquired and there is realisation of the reciprocal advantages it can bring with it, then what is needed is to foster the greatest possible intensification of relations between the two populations so that they can intermingle. It should not be overlooked that the people of Prato have a long tradition in the art of "mixing". But this time, unlike in previous circumstances, the raw materials to be mixed are not the different textile fibres but the variety (of abilities, culture, ideas) of the people who constitute the real raw material of all development.

Notes

1 On immigrant entrepreneurs in some Italian industrial districts, see Barberis (2008). On the localization of businesses run by Chinese immigrants in Italy, see Lombardi et al. (2011).

2 In Italy at the beginning of the 1990s, the percentage of workers employed in firms with fewer than 50 employees was 52.5 per cent, whereas in Germany and France the percentages were, respectively, 21.7 per cent and 25.8 per cent (Brusco and Paba 1997: 268).

3 On the evolution of large firms and industrial districts in the postwar development of Italy, see Becattini and Coltorti (2006); Becattini and Dei Ottati (2006).

4 On the industrial district as a form of organisation, see Becattini, Bellandi, Dei Ottati, & Sforzi (2003). On industrial districts in the Italian economy, see Pyke, Becattini, Sengenberger (1990); Cossentino, Pyke, & Sengenberger (1996).

5 On the spread of Chinese businesses in Italian industrial districts specialised in clothing, textiles and leather goods, see also Intesa Sanpaolo (2010: 111–16).

6 On the postwar development of the Prato textiles district, see Becattini (2001); Dei Ottati (2003).

7 The figures reported are official ISTAT data referring to Chinese residents in Italy. It is worth noting that these figures are lower than the number of permits to stay (regular Chinese immigrants) and, of course, they do not consider the irregular migrants.

8 On the provenance and the characters of the area of origin of the new Chinese immigrants in Italy, see Wu (2009).

9 Micro-enterprises are those having fewer than 10 persons employed. The figures refer to such enterprises because they are the only ones for which it is possible to establish the nationality of the entrepreneur. In the case of Chinese immigrant enterprises, this type of firm constitutes more than 90 per cent of the total; therefore, their number is a good proxy of the actual size of the phenomenon.

10 On Chinese entrepreneurs in Italy, see Bàculo (2006); Marsden (2011).

11 During the carded woollen crisis of the second half of the 1980s, many small textiles firms of Prato had gone out of business (Dei Ottati 1996), and thus in the so-called industry-city (the current Chinatown of Prato), large numbers of small industrial premises and sheds had been left empty, and their owners were only too happy to rent them out.

12 On the question of the intricate links between the Chinese informal economy and the Italian formal economy, Becucci states, "the insertion of Chinese citizens into the Italian economy through ethnic entrepreneurial activity . . . is only apparently separate from the more broad-ranging production processes that characterize post-Fordist industrial organization. If anything, labour-intensive Chinese businesses are situated . . . within that grey area of interconnection between the formal and informal economy. It is in this framework that one notes some of the most widespread illicit phenomenologies in which Chinese citizens in Italy are involved" (Becucci 2008: 73).

13 On the action undertaken by the Prato institutions with regard to immigration, see Campomori (2005).

14   While in 2000, the fast fashion final firms set up by Chinese could be counted on the fingers of one hand, by 2001, they already numbered about fifty and by 2003 a hundred or so (Ceccagno 2004: 41). According to a recent study, in 2012, the number of Chinese fast fashion final firms had risen to 700 to 800 (IRES 2012: 48).

15   On Prato identity and its crisis, see Bracci (2011).

16   In the Province of Prato, the number of textile establishments fell from 4,976 in 2001 to 2,926 in 2009, while the number of textile workers dropped from 32,218 to 18,431 (Istat data: 2001 Industrial Census and 2009 ASIA). On the Prato textile crisis in the new millennium, see Dei Ottati (2009a).

17   On the erosion of trust between subcontractors and clients in the district of Prato at the beginning of the third millennium, see Dei Ottati (2005).

18   The change affecting relations within the Prato textiles district, which is – in the view of some scholars – attributable to a weakening of community relations and the ensuing predominance of impersonal (purely market-based) relations is viewed as a possible explanation for the establishment of a numerous and economically significant Chinese community without either integration or, at least initially, notable conflicts (Bracci 2009).

19   On the way in which the explosion of the textile crisis in the third millennium has transformed relations between the local population of Prato and the Chinese immigrants, whereas previously such relations were basically conflict free, see Fabbri (2011).

20   Studies on immigrant entrepreneurship are usually distinguished according to the different approaches formulated by migration sociology. In this regard, see Ambrosini (2011: 107–36).

21   Despite the absence of data on the number of Italians working for Chinese firms, as will be described in greater detail in section 3.3.3, Chinese fast fashion firms are generally lacking in certain skills (language ability and technical competence) and, therefore, initially at least, they need to use qualified Italian staff such as fashion designers, accountants and sales personnel, because the Chinese workers have an inadequate background in such areas.

22   The same interpretation is confirmed in Ceccagno (2012, p. 46).

23   The low level of relations between Prato textiles enterprises and Chinese fast fashion businesses is also documented in the investigation conducted in 2006 on 50 Chinese businesses in Prato by the Tuscan Regional Watchdog on the craft industry. See Santini, Rabino, & Zanni (2011, p. 45).

24   Imports of textile products from China in the Province of Prato rose from a value of 61.6 million euros in 2002 to 103.9 million euros in 2008, representing 10 per cent and 26 per cent of total textile imports of the Province in 2002 and 2008, respectively (data from CCIAA Prato). Even though textile product imports also involved raw textiles which were then finished by the Prato textile enterprises, there seems to be little doubt that a substantial portion of these imports were used in Chinese fast fashion.

25   To combat the widespread illegality in the numerous Chinese businesses, an agreement (called "Pact for Safe Prato") was drawn up in 2007 among the Local Council of Prato, the Prefecture, the Province of Prato and the Region of Tuscany, on the basis of which a special fund was set up to increase the local police force in order to strengthen the monitoring of Chinese businesses. Spot checks numbered 158 in 2008, rising to 233 in 2009 and 320 in 2010. In particular, in 2010, the spot checks led to the seizure of 144 buildings and 6,259 pieces of machinery, while the fines imposed for the various breaches of the law amounted to more than 228,000 euros (Municipality of Prato, Council Office for Town Safety and Municipal Police).

26   On the basis of the official ISTAT statistics (registry of firms), the number of people employed in Chinese firms in the Province of Prato in 2010 was 11,694. Aware that the official data are rather unreliable due to the existence of informal labour, various different estimates of the number of irregular Chinese workers in the Province of Prato were drawn up, utilizing two types of data: not only the data on the number of irregular

workers detected during the spot checks carried out by the municipal police in agreement with other institutions and authorities, which resulted in an estimated figure of 5,847 irregular workers, but also the data emerging from metered water consumption in Chinese businesses, which led to an estimate of 8,771 irregular workers (IRPET 2013: 50–52).

27 These explanations, in particular the second and the third, are confirmed by the interviews conducted as part of the research that led to the interpretation put forward in section 3.3.3.

28 For an example of informal economic activities practiced by Islamic immigrants in the Netherlands, see Kloosterman et al. (1999).

29 According to Istat (Italian Statistical Institute) estimates, in Italy in 2009, the number of irregular workers amounted to 2,600,000, representing 10.5 per cent of the overall employed persons. Moreover, in 2008, the units of irregular work in Italy were on average 11.9 per cent of the total, but with strong variations among the regions, ranging from a minimum of 8.5 per cent in Emilia Romagna to a maximum of 26.6 per cent in Calabria (www.istat.it).

30 Confidential information obtained by the Prato Office of the General Command of the Inland Revenue Police indicates that out of 1,500 spot checks carried out between 2009 and 2011, of which 400 were on Chinese businesses, a presumed total of 133 cases of tax evasion were detected, of which 46 concerned Chinese businesses, for a total undeclared income of 323 million euros, of which 83 million was attributed to Chinese entrepreneurs. The same source also found that the number of total tax evaders (no declared income) amounted to 81, 10 of which were Chinese, and that the irregular workers numbered 483, of which 265 were Chinese (Barbu, Dunford and Liu 2013: 14). These data show that although illegality was widespread among the Chinese businesses, it was by no means absent in the rest of the local economy.

31 On the importance of operating in an expanding market for upward mobility of immigrant entrepreneurs, see Kloosterman (2010: 35–6).

32 According to a study on Chinese enterprises in Prato, it can be said that "extension of family networks corresponds often with an extension of the business activities taken forward with various companies by various members of the family. About two thirds of entrepreneurs interviewed . . . stated that there are other business people in the family who run one or more companies" (Marsden & Caserta 2010: 17).

33 On the importance of the implicit rules of competition and cooperation that form the basis of the functioning of industrial district, see Brusco (1999); Dei Ottati (1991).

34 On the crucial importance of the "thickening" of relations – which are both of competition and cooperation – for the emergence of the industrial district model of organization, see Becattini (1990); Brusco (1995).

35 For evidence of export-led growth in Wenzhou, the area of origin of most of the Chinese entrepreneurs in Prato, see Wu (2009).

36 On the contribution of overseas Chinese to Wenzhou development, see Zhang and Smyth (2009).

37 This interpretation is also put forward by Marina Faccioli, who states that the GDP of Prato "is, for the most part, produced and sustained by income transfer from the Chinese immigrants to the local population of Prato, above all in business transactions pertaining to the use of buildings" (Faccioli 2010: 88).

38 As of 31 December 2012, the residents of Chinese nationality in the Municipality of Prato below the age of 18 years numbered and represented 14 per cent of the total of residents in this age band (Municipality of Prato, Statistics Office).

39 In the knitwear-apparel district of Carpi, for example, the total turnover of the area decreased throughout the 1990s but began to increase once more in the third millennium as a result of the choice made by some new entrepreneurs that invested in fashion design, distribution and advertising. See Barberis, Bigarelli, Dei Ottati (2012: 73).

40 On the role of immigrant entrepreneurs acting as a bridge between Silicon Valley and the emergent regions of Asia, see Saxenian (1999); Saxenian and Sabel (2009).
41 A recent study on the Chinese labour market in Prato states, "Prato is no longer as attractive as it was until not long ago, because China itself now offers countless opportunities and therefore many Chinese prefer to stay in the homeland". A little bit farther on in the same study, one finds the observation that in Prato today "it is very difficult to find a job. And even if people (i.e. the Chinese) do find a job, the pay is low and so they tend to leave . . . Many of them go back to China because there's a very strong thrust toward development in China" (IRES 2012: 51). In this regard, see also Ceccagno (2012).
42 In this regard, it is helpful to recall, as pointed out by Colombi as early as 2002 (Colombi 2002: 16–7) and more recently by Calvin Chen – a Chinese American scholar who made a three-year study of the Chinese immigrants in Prato and even lived among them for a certain period of time – that some surprising similarities between the local Prato population and the Chinese immigrants in Prato can be noted. Thus Chen observes that "The Chinese were not only in the right place at the right time, but also seemed in many ways, tailored-made for an industrial system that privileged small-batch, family-based production" (Chen 2011: 32).

References

Ambrosini, M. (2011) *Sociologia delle migrazioni*. Bologna: Il Mulino.
Bàculo, L. (2006) Gli italiani in Cina, i cinesi in Italia, *QA-Rivista dell'Associazione Rossi-Doria*, 3, 63–98.
Barberis, E. (2008) *Imprenditori immigrati. Tra inserimento sociale e partecipazione allo sviluppo*. Rome: Ediesse.
Barberis, E., Bigarelli, D., & Dei Ottati, G. (2012) Distretti industriali e imprese di immigrati cinesi: rischi e opportunità con particolare riferimento a Carpi e Prato. In Bellandi, M., & Caloffi, A. (Eds.) *Innovazione e trasformazione industriale, la prospettiva dei sistemi di produzione locale italiani*. Bologna: Il Mullino, pp. 43–62.
Barbu, M., Dunford M., & Liu, W. (2013) Employment, Entrepreneurship, and Citizenship in the Globalised Economy: The Chinese in Prato, *Environment and Planning A*, 45, 1–22.
Becattini, G. (1990) The Marshallian Industrial District as a Socio-Economic Notion. In Pyke, F., Becattini, G. & W. Sengenberger (Eds.) *Industrial Districts and Inter-Firm Co-operation in Italy*. Geneva: International Institute for Labour Studies, pp. 37–51.
Becattini, G. (2001) *The Caterpillar and the Butterfly. An Exemplary Case of Development in the Italy of the Industrial Districts*. Florence: Felice Le Monnier.
Becattini, G., Bellandi, M., Dei Ottati, G., & Sforzi, F. (2003) *From Industrial Districts to Local Development. An Itinerary of Research*. Cheltenham: Edward Elgar.
Becattini, G., & Coltorti, F. (2006) Areas of Large Enterprises and Industrial Districts in the Development of Post-War Italy: A Preliminary Survey, *European Planning Studies*, 14 (8), 1105–38.
Becattini, G., & Dei Ottati, G. (2006) The Performance of Italian Industrial Districts and Large Enterprises Areas in the 1990s, *European Planning Studies*, 14 (8), 1139–62.
Becucci, S. (2008) Immigrazione cinese e mercato del lavoro in Italia. Un caso di interconnessione funzionale fra economia formale e informale, *Studi sulla questione criminale*, 3 (3), 61–73.
Bracci, F. (2009) Migranti cinesi e contesto locale: il distretto pratese e la transizione fredda, *Sviluppo locale*, 13 (31), 91–111.

Bracci, F. (2011) Oltre la pratesità: due indagini su identità ed appartenenze nel contesto pratese. In *Oltre la "pratesità". L'immigrazione nella provincia di Prato. VII rapporto anno 2010*. Prato: Province of Prato, Osservatorio provinciale sull'immigrazione, pp. 55–243.

Brusco, S. (1995) Local Productive Systems and New Industrial Policy in Italy. In Bagnasco, A., & Sabel, C. (Eds.) *Small and Medium Size Enterprises*. London: Pinter, pp. 51–68.

Brusco, S. (1999) The Rules of the Game in Industrial Districts. In Grandori, A. (Ed.) *Interfirm Networks: Organization and Industrial Competitiveness*. London: Routledge, pp. 17–40.

Brusco, S., & Paba, S. (1997) Per una storia dei distretti industriali italiani dal secondo dopoguerra agli anni novanta. In Barca, F. (Ed.) *Storia del capitalismo italiano dal dopoguerra a oggi*. Rome: Donzelli editore, pp. 265–333.

Campomori, F. (2005) Come integrare l'immigrato? Modelli locali di intervento a Prato, Vicenza e Caserta. In Caponio, T., & Colombo, A. (Eds.) *Migrazioni globali, integrazioni locali*. Bologna: Il Mulino, pp. 235–65.

Ceccagno, A. (Ed.) (2003) *Migranti a Prato: Il distretto tessile multietnico*. Centro di ricerca e servizi per l'immigrazione del Comune di Prato. Milan: Franco Angeli.

Ceccagno, A. (2004) *Giovani migranti cinesi: la seconda generazione a Prato*. Milan: Franco Angeli.

Ceccagno, A. (2009) Chinese Migrants as Apparel Manufacturers in an Era of Perishable Global Fashion: New Fashion Scenarios in Prato. In Johanson, G., Smyth, R., & French, R. (Eds.) *Living Outside the Walls: The Chinese in Prato*. Newcastle upon Tyne: Cambridge Scholars, pp. 42–74.

Ceccagno, A. (2012) The Hidden Crisis: The Prato Industrial District and the Once Thriving Chinese Garment Industry, *Revue européenne des migrations internationales*, 28 (4), 43–65.

Chen, C. (2011) Made in Italy (by the Chinese): Economic Restructuring and the Politics of Migration. *Inter Asia Papers*, 20. Barcelona: Instituto de Estudios Internationales e Interculturales, Universitat Autonoma de Barcelona.

Colombi, M. (2002) Migranti e imprenditori: una ricerca sull'imprenditoria cinese a Prato. In Colombi, M. (Ed.) *L'imprenditoria cinese nel distretto industriale di Prato*. Florence: Olschki, pp. 1–17.

Cossentino, F., Pyke F., & Sengenberger, W. (Eds.) (1996) *Local and Regional Response to Global Pressure: The Case of Italy and Its Industrial Districts*. Geneva: International Institute for Labour Studies.

Dei Ottati, G. (1991) The Economic Bases of Diffuse Industrialization, *International Studies of Management & Organization*, 21 (1), 53–74.

Dei Ottati, G. (1996) Economic Changes in the District of Prato in the 1980s: Towards a More Conscious and Organized Industrial District, *European Planning Studies*, 4 (1), 35–52.

Dei Ottati, G. (2003) Exit, Voice and the Evolution of Industrial Districts: The Case of the Post–World War II Economic Development of Prato, *Cambridge Journal of Economics*, 27 (4) 501–522.

Dei Ottati, G. (2005) Global Competition and Entrepreneurial Behaviour in Industrial Districts: Trust Relations in an Italian Industrial District. In Hoehmann, H. H., & F. Welter (Eds.) *Trust and Entrepreneurship. A West-East Perspective*. Cheltenham: Edward Elgar, pp. 255–71.

Dei Ottati, G. (2009a) An Industrial District Facing the Challenges of Globalization: Prato Today, *European Planning Studies*, 17 (12), 1817–1835.

Dei Ottati, G. (2009b) Semi-Automatic and Deliberate Actions in the Evolution of Industrial Districts. In Becattini, G., Bellandi, M., & De Propis, L. (Eds.) *A Handbook of Industrial Districts*. Cheltenham: Edward Elgar, pp. 204–15.

Dei Ottati, G. (2014) A Transnational Fast Fashion Industrial District: An Analysis of the Chinese Businesses in Prato, *Cambridge Journal of Economics*, 38 (5), 1247–1274.

Fabbri, M. (2011) *Imprenditori cinesi nel settore delle confezioni e dell'abbigliamento a Prato*. In CNEL, *Il profilo nazionale degli immigrati imprenditori in Italia*. Rome: Consiglio Nazionale Economia e Lavoro, pp. 113–35.

Faccioli, M. (2010) Nuove filiere economiche e culturali nella riproposizione del distretto di Prato, *Geotema*, 35 (6), 83–8.

Fasani, F. (2009) *Undocumented Migration. Counting the Uncountable*. Data and trends across Europe. Country report. Italy: European Commission.

Fortis, M., & Carminati, M. (2009) Sectors of Excellence in the Italian Industrial Districts, in Becattini, G., Bellandi, M., & De Propis, L. (Eds.) *A Handbook of Industrial Districts*. Cheltenham: Edward Elgar, pp. 417–28.

Gereffi, G., & Memedovic, O. (2003) *The Global Apparel Value Chain: What Prospects for Upgrading by Developing Countries*. Vienna: UNIDO.

Guercini, S. (2002) Profilo del vertice, processi di sviluppo e politiche di mercato dell'impresa cinese a Prato. In Colombi, M. (Ed.) *L'imprenditoria cinese nel distretto industriale di Prato*. Florence: Olschki, pp. 35–70.

Intesa Sanpaolo-Servizio Studi e Ricerche. (2010, December) *Economia e Finanza dei Distretti Industriali*. Rapporto n. 3.

IRES (Istituto di Ricerche Economiche e Sociali). (2012) *Mi chiamo Chen e lavoro a Prato, 2008–2012: imprese e dipendenti cinesi nel territorio provinciale*. Province of Prato, mimeo.

IRPET (Istituto Regionale per la Programmazione Economica della Toscana). (2013) *Prato: il ruolo economico della comunità cinese*. Florence: IRPET.

Kloosterman, R.C. (2010) Matching Opportunities With Resources: A Framework for Analysing (Migrant) Entrepreneurship from a Mixed Embeddedness Perspective, *Entrepreneurship & Regional Development*, 22 (1), 25–45.

Kloosterman, R., van der Leun, J., & Rath, J. (1999) Mixed Embeddedness: (In)formal Economic Activities and Immigrant Businesses in the Netherlands, *International Journal of Urban and Regional Research*, 23 (2), 252–266.

Li, M. (2010) An Overview of the Migration Mechanism Between China and Europe. In Gao, Y. (Ed.) *Concealed Chains. Labour Exploitation and Chinese Migrants in Europe*. Geneva: International Labour Office, pp. 19–32.

Lombardi, S., Lorenzini, F., Sforzi, F., & Verrecchia, F. (2011, 30 August–2 September) *Chinese Entrepreneurs in Context*. Paper presented to the ERSA (European Regional Sciences Association) Congress, Barcelona.

Marsden, A. (2002) Il ruolo della famiglia nello sviluppo dell'imprenditoria cinese a Prato. In Colombi, M. (Ed.) *L'imprenditoria cinese nel distretto industriale di Prato*. Florence: Olschki, pp. 71–103.

Marsden, A. (2011) Imprenditoria cinese in Italia e processi di integrazione sociale, *Quaderni di sociologia*, 55 (57), 7–21.

Marsden, A., & Caserta, D. (2010) *Storie e progetti imprenditoriali dei cinesi a Prato*. Prato: Camera di commercio.

Pieraccini, S. (2008) *L'assedio cinese: il distretto parallelo del pronto moda di Prato.* Milano: Il sole 24 ore.

Pieraccini, S. (2010) *L'assedio cinese: il distretto senza regole degli abiti low cost di Prato* (2nd updated ed.). Milan: Il sole 24 ore.

Porter, M. (1990) *The Competitive Advantage of Nations.* New York: Free Press.

Pyke, F., Becattini, G., & Sengenberger, W. (Eds.) (1990) *Industrial Districts and Inter-Firm Co-Operation in Italy.* Geneva: International Institute for Labour Studies.

Rastrelli, E. (2001) L'immigrazione cinese a Prato. In Rastrelli, E. (Ed.) *Atti del convegno Dinamiche europee della diaspora cinese: prospettive per Prato.* Province of Prato, 18 May 2001, pp. 27–35.

Santini, C., Rabino, S., & Zanni, L. (2011) Chinese Immigrants Socio-Economic Enclave in an Italian Industrial District: The Case of Prato, *World Review of Entrepreneurship, Management and Sustainable Development,* 7 (1), 30–51.

Saxenian, A. (1999) *Silicon Valley's New Immigrant Entrepreneurs.* San Francisco: Public Policy Institute of California.

Saxenian, A., & Sabel, C. (2009) The New Argonauts: Global Search and Local Institution Building. In Becattini, G., Bellandi, M., & De Propis, L. (Eds.) *A Handbook of Industrial Districts.* Cheltenham: Edward Elgar, pp. 229–42.

Tassinari, A. (1994) L'immigrazione cinese in Toscana. In Campani, G., Carchedi, F., & Tassinari, A. (Eds.) *L'immigrazione silenziosa. Le comunità cinesi in Italia.* Turin: Edizioni della Fondazione Giovanni Agnelli, pp. 105–25.

Unioncamere. (2012) *Rapporto Unioncamere 2012. L'economia reale dal punto di osservazione delle camere di commercio.* Rome: Unioncamere.

Waldinger, R., Aldrich, H., & Ward, R. (1990) Opportunities, Group Characteristics and Strategies. In Waldinger, R., Aldrich, H., & Ward, R. (Eds.) *Ethnic Entrepreneurs. Immigrant Business in Industrial Societies.* Newbury Park, CA: Sage, pp. 13–48.

Wu, B. (2009) International Migration and Wenzhou's Development. In Johanson, G., Smyth, R., & French, R. (Eds.) *Living Outside the Walls: The Chinese in Prato.* Newcastle upon Tyne: Cambridge Scholars, pp. 238–60.

Zhang, X., & Smyth, R. (2009) The Contribution of Donations of Overseas Chinese to Wenzhou. In Johanson, G., Smyth, R., & French, R. (Eds.) *Living Outside the Walls: The Chinese in Prato.* Newcastle upon Tyne: Cambridge Scholars, pp. 261–73.

4 The transformation of the Chinese business community in Portugal in the context of crisis and of China's "go global"[1]

Annette Bongardt and Miguel Santos Neves

Abstract

This chapter assesses the transformation of the Chinese business community in Portugal as a result of the interaction between China's "go global" policy and the impact of the 2008/2009 global crisis. It analyses the small business community's coping strategies, the impact of recent Chinese large direct investments and changes to Portuguese immigration laws. It concludes that the small business community adopted pro-active coping strategies and reassessed its insertion patterns in the local and global economy. With the large-scale business segment, a dualistic community structure emerged. The community became more heterogeneous and complex, less cohesive and more internationalised beyond the single European market.

Introduction

The Chinese overseas community and especially its business communities have emerged as a strategic informal factor in China's integration in the global economy and as a fundamental dimension of China's soft power. They are performing three functions that are different but complementary: namely they act as catalysts of economic flows and entry points for Chinese exports, as producers and providers of economic intelligence and as informal "ambassadors" for the paradiplomacy of Chinese provinces and cities. The environment in which these communities operate has, however, undergone significant change over recent years, notably as a result of China's "go global" strategy and its growing weight in the global economy and of the impact of the 2008 to 2009 global economic and financial crisis. At the European Union (EU) level, increasing economic inter-linkages with China have given rise to trade and investment-related tensions, made more acute by the crisis context.[2] Prior to the crisis the EU used to be no chief destination for Chinese inward investment, but since 2010, there has been both a qualitative and a quantitative change. The EU has become a prime destination for Chinese direct investment, especially for large Chinese enterprises. This fact has in turn added scale and complexity to the existing local overseas Chinese business communities, Portugal being a case in point.

This chapter aims to contribute to the literature on the Chinese diaspora by shedding light on the dynamics of the Chinese business community in Portugal in the context of the recent crises (the global 2008–2009 economic and financial crisis, aggravated in Portugal by the sovereign debt crisis) and its interaction with the intensification of China's "go global" policy. It sets out to analyse the process and outcome of the transformation that the community underwent in the changed context, focussing on the three fundamental factors with an impact on the transformation of the Chinese overseas community in Portugal: first, the existing community's coping strategies in the face of the crisis and its involvement with China's "go global"; second, the impact of recent large-scale Chinese direct investments, driven by China's globalisation strategy, which take advantage of crisis-induced investment opportunities; and, last but not least, the consequences of the (similarly crisis-induced) changes to Portuguese immigration policy, which facilitate migration inflows and promote inward investments.

The chapter is organized as follows: section 2 frames the discussion by providing some background information on the Chinese community in Portugal. Section 3 focuses on the dynamics in the established small-scale Chinese business community in Portugal, analysing the different coping strategies that Chinese businesses have adopted in the crisis context. It considers the short- or long-term nature of actions taken as well as the factors that condition the choice of strategy, taking into account both crisis-related and other factors. The section is based on fieldwork on the small-scale Chinese family firms typically found in Portugal.

Section 4 looks at the recent and novel phenomenon of large Chinese direct investments in Portugal. It considers whether and to what extent direct inward investments by Chinese large firms lead to a transformation of the local Chinese business community, notably in terms of its structure and cohesiveness. It evaluates the kind of linkages and the potential impact of those large investments on the typically rather small-scale businesses of Chinese entrepreneurs in Portugal (e.g. in terms of supply chain relations or attraction of other small or medium-scale Chinese investments with a complementary logic) and on Chinese immigration flows.

Section 5 looks into the impact of the crisis-induced changes to Portuguese immigration policy on the Chinese business community, set against the continuing inflow of Chinese entrepreneurs into Portugal despite a declining Portuguese economy, marked by stagnation and more recently by recession. It considers to what extent the existing diaspora has contributed to attracting new investment inflows.

Section 6 presents the main conclusions and highlights challenges for the European Union that arise from China's global strategy.

4.1. The Chinese community in Portugal

Chinese migration flows to Portugal have been increasing continuously since the late 1990s. According to official government statistics (Portuguese Border police – *Serviço de Estrangeiros e Fronteiras (SEF)* 2005, 2009, 2013), the increase in inflows has led to an almost sixfold rise in stocks, from 3,062 immigrants from China in 1999 to 17,447 in 2012; representatives of the Chinese community present estimates that are higher.[3] This outcome can be seen to result from a complex interplay of various factors, notably the saturation of ethnic markets in Northern Europe, prompting re-emigration towards Southern European countries (Beltrán 2000), a new wave of immigration from Mainland China and the evolution of Portuguese immigration policy, namely the legalization of irregular immigrants in 2001 and 2004.

The recent evolution of the Chinese community is characterised by a trend of rather stable inflows and an increase in total numbers in the face of economic crisis (global financial and economic and subsequent Portuguese sovereign debt crisis), which stands in sharp contrast with the other immigrant communities in Portugal. While the inflows of Chinese to Portugal have about stabilized and total numbers have increased, Portugal has seen a general decline in the numbers of immigrants (from 451,742 in 2009 to 414,610 in 2012), accompanied by a decline in the total numbers of all the other main immigrant communities. The weight of the Chinese community in the total immigrant population has increased from 3.2 per cent in 2009 to 4.2 per cent in 2012 as a result.[4]

Chinese immigrants came to Portugal in three different periods and driven by different motivations, which gave rise to a rather heterogeneous Chinese business community in Portugal (see Bongardt & Neves 2006 for a more detailed analysis). The community is composed of three main sub-groups who arrived in three successive waves. First, Chinese businessmen from Mozambique, who came to Portugal after decolonisation in the mid-1970s looking for safety, being well integrated in the Portuguese culture, as most of them possessed Portuguese nationality. Their ties with China were mainly with Guangdong Province. Second, a smaller group from Hong Kong and Macao came in the early 1990s before the handover of the territories to the People's Republic of China (PRC), looking for an "insurance policy", i.e., an alternative location for their business as a risk-reduction strategy in the face of uncertainty about the "one country, two systems" regime's future. These immigrants in general had a reasonable level of international experience. Third, the Chinese from Mainland China, dominated by immigrants from Zhejiang province (both from Wenzhou and Qingtian), mostly arrived in Portugal from the late 1990s onwards, in the context of China's increasing integration in the global economy. This group, motivated chiefly by economic opportunity, took advantage of the *guanxi* network within Europe, especially with communities in Spain, Italy and France, thereby making use of the scale and opportunities of the single European market, although they lacked any previous international experience.

In 2009,[5] the geographical distribution of Chinese migrants in Portugal displayed a concentration in four main districts, namely Lisbon (37.2 per cent), Porto (13.6 per cent), Faro (9 per cent) and Setúbal (7.9 per cent), which together amount to 67.7 per cent of the total. This figure represents a reduction in comparison with 2005, when those districts jointly accounted for 79.8 per cent, whereas in 2000, they had accounted for 82 per cent. Over the years, the relative importance of the

Portuguese capital, Lisbon, declined from 58.3 per cent in 2000 to 37.2 per cent in 2009, while the other districts remain about stable. The figures therefore suggest a geographical diversification out of Lisbon in the pre-crisis period, which can be explained by intensifying competition in the ethnic economy with the expansion of the community.

The Chinese community is characterized by a young age profile, which is also below the overall age structure of immigrants in Portugal.[6] Four fifths of its members are aged under 39 years, and more than two thirds are in the "active age" group (20–64 years). In 2005, the 0 to 19 age group accounted for 28.2 per cent of total Chinese immigrants, the age group of between 20 and 39 years for 51.6 per cent, the 40 to 64 years age group for 16.4 per cent and the age group above 65 years for 2 per cent.

As for the size of the Chinese business community and in the absence of official statistics on the numbers of entrepreneurs and firms in the community, one can only refer to estimates. Based on information provided by Chinese business associations, estimates indicate a minimum of 4,000 Chinese shops, 300 restaurants and 500 warehouses in Portugal in 2009;[7] in 2012, a reduction by 20 to 25 per cent is said to have occurred in the number of shops/restaurants/warehouses, which brought the total number down to 3,800.[8] As for entrepreneurs, the only available official data regard the requests for residence status, where a distinction is made between the self-employed and workers. In 2005, one in six Chinese applicants indicated the status of entrepreneur (SEF 2005: 69). A conservative estimate of 2,000 to 2,500 entrepreneurs looks credible, taking into account that many entrepreneurs have more than one shop/facility.

The business community operates predominantly in the service sector, especially in retail and wholesale trade. In 2006, the sector accounted for more than 75 per cent and presented a high level of internationalisation in the pre-crisis period, especially as far as trade and investment links with China are concerned (Bongardt & Neves 2006).

The composition of the community, thus far characterised by small family-run businesses, has recently started to undergo change as a result of both the impact of economic crisis and China's globalisation strategy. It has resulted in restructuring of existing businesses but also in the emergence of the new phenomenon of Chinese large-scale direct investment in Portugal. On top of that, recent changes in Portuguese immigration policy, which envisage attracting foreign investment, have so far been mostly made use of by Chinese nationals. The dynamics and interplay of those changes will be discussed in what follows.

4.2. The dynamics of the Chinese small business community in the crisis context

4.2.1. Methodology of the fieldwork

The fieldwork involved the collection of primary data through a questionnaire directed at Chinese businessmen in Portugal,[9] applied between July and September

2013 by a team of researchers.[10] The questionnaire was modelled and followed up on a previous questionnaire tested and applied in 2005 on the Chinese business community in Portugal (see Bongardt & Neves 2006), to which new questions were added to obtain information on entrepreneurs' responses to the crisis and on the possible development of links with large Chinese firms investing in Portugal. The 2006 study served as a reference for the pre-crisis situation. A series of interviews were conducted with the main Chinese business associations with a view to ensuring the representativeness of the sample in regional and in sectoral terms. The questionnaire was prepared in Portuguese and Chinese language (bilingual) in order to facilitate access to interviewees and promote trust and confidence and thereby encourage responses. Respondents were assured of anonymity with respect to the treatment of filled-in questionnaires, which was well received and seen to promote cooperation. The same applies to the inclusion of a native Chinese speaker in the team, a fact that moreover facilitated additional interview evidence beyond the questionnaire. The questionnaire to the Chinese small business community in Portugal was composed of six sections with a different focus, featuring mostly closed questions.[11]

The team of researchers applied the questionnaires *in loco* to Chinese businessmen in different regions in Portugal, namely in the Greater Lisbon area, in Coimbra, in Setúbal and in Porto and Northern Portugal.[12] The choice of these districts followed on the one hand the pattern of geographical distribution of Chinese immigrants that is reflected in official statistics and, on the other, the indications both of Chinese business associations in Portugal and the results of the authors' previous research.[13] The sample of Chinese entrepreneurs was chosen in a non-intentional way.

A second set of data was obtained through semi-structured interviews (30). The interviewees were chosen in function of their specific and wider knowledge of the reality and evolution of Chinese businesses in Portugal. They included representatives of Chinese business associations, namely the three main associations (*Associação dos Comerciantes e Industriais Luso-Chinesa* [Greater Lisbon]; *Liga dos Chineses em Portugal* [Porto and Northern region]; and *Associação Luso-Chinesa em Portugal* [South]), but also accountancy firms that provide services to a large number of Chinese businesses or the director of the main Chinese newspaper in Portugal (*Sino*). In addition, 20 of the entrepreneurs (all of whom respondents to the questionnaire) were selected for more in-depth interviews on the basis of different criteria, such as the complexity of their response strategy to the crisis or new kinds of ties with China. They were chosen due to their specific and wider knowledge of the reality and evolution of Chinese businesses in Portugal.

The fieldwork aimed at about 80 questionnaires. Of those, after analysis of the responses, 64 questionnaires were validated and made up the survey sample. The qualitative information that resulted from the interviews with Chinese businessmen and associations provided important indications as to the consistency of findings and complemented statistical data, allowing for a synthesis of quantitative and qualitative information. The results of the statistical analysis were compared with the authors' previous research on the topic (Bongardt & Neves 2006).[14]

4.2.2. Profiles of the entrepreneur and the business

This section analyses the principal features of Chinese entrepreneurs in Portugal and their businesses as shaped by the crisis context and compares them with their pre-crisis situation (analysed in Bongardt & Neves 2006).

The vast majority of Chinese entrepreneurs in the present sample (93.7 per cent) come from Mainland China, with only a minority originating in other places in Asia (i.e. Hong Kong, Taiwan and Southeast Asia). In turn, more than three quarters of those Mainland Chinese businessmen (76.6 per cent) originate in Zhejiang province, with other provinces (Shandong, Shanghai, Fujian, Sichuan) being of little importance. The predominance of Zhejiang province as a region of origin is consistent with pre-crisis data (74 per cent, see ibid.: 29–30), showing that the crisis did not affect patterns. The relevance of Zhejiang immigration networks explains why the majority of respondents indicate that family ties were the main factor for having chosen Portugal. The relevance of Zhejiang province is in line with the patterns observed in other Southern European countries (such as Italy, where more than 70 per cent of immigrants originate from Zhejiang province with special relevance of the city of Wenzhou, as is the case of Prato and Spain, where the majority originates from the city of Qingtian; Beltrán 2000; Latham & Wu 2013). It reflects both the specialisation of Zhejiang in emigration to Europe and the importance of well-developed immigration networks for facilitating new immigration flows.

As for the length of stay in Portugal, there has been a shift when compared to 2006 results, since the predominant length of stay has changed from less than 10 years in 2006 to more than 10 years. The majority of Chinese entrepreneurs (56.3 per cent) have been in Portugal for more than a decade (see Table 4.1). The findings suggest a certain stability in the Chinese community, to the extent that longer stays in Portugal reflect both the passing of time since the 2006 survey

Table 4.1 Profile of the entrepreneur

	Absolute Frequency	*Percentage*
Length of Stay (years)		
< 5	15	23.4
5–9	12	18.8
10–14	17	26.6
+15	19	29.7
Origin		
Mainland China	60	**93.7**
of which: Zhejiang	49	76.6
of which: other provinces	10	15.6
Asia	3	**4.7**
N/A	1	
Total sample	64	100

Source: Interview evidence, July–September 2013

and the absence of a crisis-induced exodus. It is also worth noting that short-term stays (less than five years) have remained stable at the same level (almost a quarter) when compared to pre-crisis levels, which suggests that immigration flows have not been interrupted in the crisis. In fact, according to official immigration data, Chinese immigration flows have slightly diminished since 2009 but have remained at a relatively high level (immigration from China ranking fifth in Portuguese immigration flows in 2012); still, stocks have increased notwithstanding the crisis (SEF 2013).

The survey allowed for crossing datasets on a Chinese person's length of stay in Portugal and the number of years it took him or her to set up a business (in a total of 40 cases). Recent Chinese immigrants appear to be quicker at starting their own businesses, with time lags less than one year, than immigrations with longer stays. While the data are compatible with the well-known cycle of immigration according to which the immigrant starts working for a Chinese business and, after acquiring the necessary knowledge and savings, he/she starts his/her own business, it suggests that the duration of the cycle has shortened with recent immigration inflows, probably due to immigrants' different profiles and motivations.

The survey data depict firm size patterns in line with those observed before the crisis. The indicators that could be obtained regard the number of employees and the number of establishments per firm, as businessmen were most reluctant to disclose information on sales volumes. All firms in the sample are in the small and medium-sized enterprise (SME) category. About 90 per cent of those can be qualified as micro-enterprises considering that the most common combination found in Chinese businesses is a business with a single establishment (71.4 per cent) with fewer than five employees (73 per cent). Interview evidence revealed differences

Table 4.2 Profile of the business

	Absolute Frequency	*Percentage %*
Number of establishments		
1	45	71.4
2–3	15	23.8
4–5	2	3.2
Number of Employees		
< 5	46	73
5–10	13	20.6
11–20	3	4.8
Location		
Lisbon	37	57.8
Setúbal	12	18.8
Oporto	6	9.4
Coimbra	5	7.8
Other	4	6.3
Total Sample	64	100

Source: Interview evidence, July–September 2013

between entrepreneurs within the micro segment, as larger entrepreneurs tend to own firms with several establishments (allowing for some geographical diversification) or several micro-firms in different sectors (sectoral diversification) as a risk-reduction strategy. Although the micro-enterprise pattern did not change in relation to the pre-crisis period, the interviews captured a less visible change, namely downsizing within the micro segment.

With respect to the localisation of the business, the sample covered the principal centres of Chinese immigration in Portugal, with the majority of businesses being located in the three main locations of Greater Lisbon (57.8 per cent), Setúbal (18.8 per cent) and Porto (9.4). As for the sector of activity, in our sample, all businesses (64) were in the service sector, a finding in line with 2006 results, which had yielded a predominant weight of the service sector. In the present sample, within the service sector, most businesses are in the retail trade sub-sector (84.3 per cent), followed by restaurants (15.6 per cent), wholesale trade (4.7 per cent) and tourism (1.6 per cent). Businessmen tend to be active in just one single sub-sector. Only in 6.3 per cent of the cases the businessman was involved in more than one sub-sector. The results thereby confirm the pre-crisis dominance of retail and wholesale trade and the decline in the relevance of the restaurant sub-sector (the present sample includes several cases of a change of business from restaurants to retail trade).

4.2.3. *Chinese small entrepreneurs' coping strategies in the crisis*

Chinese small-scale enterprises, as small businesses in Portugal in general, have been strongly affected by the decline in Portuguese domestic demand in the crisis context. The Portuguese economy shrank in 2009 (−2.9 per cent), recovering in 2010 (growth of 1.9 per cent) to enter into recession in 2011. Over the period 2011 to 2013, Portuguese GDP contracted (−6 per cent; Bank of Portugal 2013), mainly driven by a sharp decline both in domestic consumption and an even greater one in investment, whereas exports of goods and services performed relatively well (expanding by 5.7 per cent in 2013).[15]

The main hypothesis underlying the study was that one would find diverse responses by Chinese businessmen in the face of adverse market conditions and that some would be rather pro-active.[16] Survey results basically confirm this hypothesis, evidencing a wide range of coping strategies, with pro-active ones accounting for a remarkable share of the total.

Looking at the Chinese entrepreneurs' responses to the crisis, one can discern two basic responses: a passive one, where no more fundamental action is taken and a pro-active one, meaning a search for ways to reverse the decline in the business.

While about 39 per cent of businessmen assumed a passive stance,[17] it stands out that a majority of businessmen (58 per cent) took a more pro-active stance, adopting a variety of strategies.

The group of Chinese entrepreneurs with a passive stance essentially attempts to survive during the crisis, accepting a decline in profits and margins while

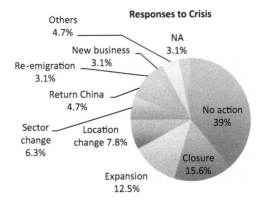

Figure 4.1 Chinese entrepreneurs' strategic responses in the face of the crisis
Source: Questionnaire evidence (period July–September 2013)

competitors close down, hoping to recover in the aftermath of the crisis. To that effect, businessmen tried to cut costs while maintaining their business along the same lines, for instance by reducing the number of employees, extending opening hours and increasing the time owners spend in the establishment.[18] The survey evidence allowed for capturing change within the micro category, not visible in the statistics, by evidencing that the crisis triggered some downsizing within a specific group of micro-sized firms.

The dominance of pro-active strategies in the sample (which exceeded initial expectations) raises the question as to the factors that account for this result.

The more pro-active group may be divided into two sub-groups: one group (15.6 per cent) that decided to shut down operations and a second group (42.4 per cent) that recurred to more complex, differentiated strategies to survive and prosper. Different patterns emerge from an analysis of the sample, which notably regard expansion of the business, starting a business, changing sector and changing geographical location.

4.2.3.1.   Business closure, re-emigration and return to China

Business closure needs to be put in a context reaching beyond the crisis, related to the Chinese entrepreneurs' prevailing business model. Since the early years of 2000, there had been a rapid increase in the numbers of Chinese restaurants and bazaar-type shops in Portugal. Towards the end of the decade this fact had generated some saturation and decline in the business due to what was felt to be "excessive competition" by some of the businessmen. The crisis was therefore not the only factor but rather one that added to already existing strong competitive pressures facing the predominant business model, which cumulatively led to the mentioned estimated 20 to 25 per cent reduction in the number of shops.

The sub-group of businessmen that decided to close down operations is qualified as pro-active because entrepreneurs took drastic action to extinguish their business. The businessmen either (re)entered the labour market or, in other cases, acted in order to rebuild their business abroad, through re-emigration to another country or by returning to China[19] to open a business.

The shutting-down option was found to root in essentially two motivations for the Chinese businesses. First, to what may be characterized as "closure by necessity": the business is not viable, losses have been accumulated or are anticipated, and the business is seen as not capable of generating the necessary income for the family. In this case, the businessman tends to return to the labour market and work for another (mostly Chinese) business. Second, "closure due to opportunity": the main drive is the existence of a better business alternative, mostly but not exclusively abroad. With respect to this option, supplementary questionnaire interview evidence yielded that closing down does not necessarily imply cutting ties with Portugal. This fact was illustrated by the two cases of re-emigration (to France and to Brazil) and the three cases of return to China in our sample. Interview evidence also captured another phenomenon, which involves a different kind of temporary circular emigration, related to Chinese businessmen who have been investing in Portuguese-speaking countries, notably Angola and Brazil. In doing so, they have kept residence and some business in Portugal so as not to lose residence rights.

Some cases of return to China look particularly interesting. One case is a Chinese businessman in the wine import/export business who, after negative results of his operation in Portugal, decided to move to China, where he opened three shops (one in Zhejiang, one in Shanxi and a third one in Beijing) to sell exclusively Portuguese wines. The case represents an emerging new tendency among Chinese businessmen of setting up wine shops in Zhejiang to sell Portuguese wines; it conveys a rational strategy to explore the strong personal and institutional ties that Chinese businessmen maintain with their province of origin. In another case, a businessman, who had been involved in traditional Chinese bazaar-type shops and restaurants in Lisbon and in Almada (just south of Lisbon), decided to diversify into the wine sector, setting up several shops in 2011, among them one in downtown Lisbon and another one in Shanghai, also specialized in Portuguese wines.[20] In addition, the businessman has been collaborating with a Portuguese producer in order to adapt the characteristics of the product to Chinese taste (dry wines).

In sum, in the midst of the Portuguese crisis some Chinese businessmen started to export and directly sell Portuguese wine in China, with an offer adapted to Chinese taste and in line with the pattern of demand of the rising Chinese middle class for prestige goods. Doing that, the businessmen maintained a direct link with the Portuguese economy, employing their knowledge and *guanxi* to sell Portuguese goods (and thereby promote Portuguese exports).

4.2.3.2. Differentiated strategies: expansion, change of location, change of sector and opening a new business

The other sub-group of Chinese businessmen adopting pro-active strategies remained in Portugal and was involved in some restructuring of their business.

Rather than recurring to mere cost cutting (a more passive strategy), they reacted by means of a range of differentiated strategies. Contrary to what might be expected at times of crisis, the strategy that was most often adopted, in almost a third of the cases, was expansion of the business (12.5 per cent). Expansion comprised expanding establishments and opening new ones. In many cases, it followed a rationale of diversifying and of acting by anticipation.

Several factors work in support of the expansion strategy. First, financing based on family sources, which constitutes the dominant source for Chinese small business entrepreneurs, as evidenced by the survey results (93.5 per cent),[21] means not only that there is very little dependency on the banking system but also that there are resources available for small businesses in a context of credit squeeze and high interest rates. Second, the existence of business deals in or with China, a growing economy, is likely to yield positive results and make resources available to finance expansion. It is noteworthy that 40 per cent of the businessmen who were involved in expansion of their business had economic deals with China in the form of either trade (import-export, such as exports of marble blocks to China) or direct investment. Third, the need for risk reduction, insofar as expansion is also driven by the objective of diversification into other sectors. This has been a consistent strategy of Chinese businessmen to manage and reduce risk, as already highlighted in the authors' 2006 study.

Henceforth, a couple of cases will be presented that illustrate the Chinese entrepreneurs' search for viable market niches and for taking well-pondered risks in difficult sectors. The case of a businessman operating in the fruit and vegetables sub-sector, who already had a successful shop in Lisbon (Arroios) before the crisis, decided to open a second one in Algés (adjacent to Lisbon) in 2011 to explore business opportunities that had arisen in the crisis. The opportunity consists in selling mature fruit and vegetable produce with fast shelf rotation at low prices at a site just in front of a large supermarket outlet (Pingo Doce supermarket chain) in Algés. According to the businessman,[22] many clients switched to his shop for their fruit and vegetable needs, given that prices are lower across the board but also that produce and prices are more differentiated. An interview conducted with clients on the spot confirmed that prices are perceived as lower and quality higher as compared with the next-door supermarket, which is seen as being the result of shorter and more regional supply chains. It is noteworthy that this type of Chinese fruit and vegetable shop only sells Portuguese produce, in contrast to conventional supermarkets that source more internationally. Two factors were seen to determine the businessman's capacity to compete with the supermarket chain: on the one hand, wholesalers sell the kind of produce (mature produce) at a discount to retailers; on the other hand, the businessman had established business ties with local producers that supplied him without intermediaries, which opens up the possibility of a mutually advantageous commercial relation of higher producer prices and lower retail costs.

This strategy is also noteworthy insofar as it constitutes a first move out of the ethnic economy.[23] Thus far, the businesses in which Chinese entrepreneurs have been generally active have been characterized by a strong Chinese presence all along the supply chain, with a high degree of dependency on *guanxi* networks. A Chinese shop or restaurant would typically source mainly from China or from other Chinese entrepreneurs and wholesalers in Portugal or in other EU countries. In the case of the new fruits and vegetables business, however, there is a pre-dominance of local Portuguese suppliers (wholesalers or producers), which has led to a greater degree of interaction with the Portuguese business fabric. Along the same lines, it is worth noting that the Chinese bazaar type shops started to include Portuguese products and that changes in the restaurant sector, namely new "Japanese" restaurants owned by Chinese entrepreneurs (which implies sourcing fresh fish locally) or the case of the businessman who shifted from Chinese food to doner kebab, all point to a diversification of sourcing that extends beyond the ethnic community. Hence, one of the interesting consequences of the crisis is that it has brought about a greater degree of integration of the Chinese small business community with the host economy, which to some extent runs counter to expecta-tions given the Portuguese economy's recession. At the same time, this finding is consistent with the mentioned results that indicate that the ties that Chinese businessmen in Portugal maintain with the Chinese economy have declined when comparing 2006 and 2013 survey results. The effects of the economic crisis in Portugal are likely to be the main factor behind this change.

Another case is characterized not by the expansion of a well-functioning busi-ness but rather by expansion aimed at diversification of the business into a more promising area once the initial business was getting into difficulties.[24] The busi-nessman in question had a bazaar-type shop in Lisbon and decided to open a new fruit and vegetable shop in Algés in 2011 to diversify into a more promising sector while maintaining the initial business. In other cases, "expansion with diversifica-tion" aimed at taking advantage of new business opportunities, such as the case of a travel agency in the centre of Lisbon, which expanded in 2011 by setting up a new branch in Porto, or the case of a businessman operating in the restaurant and bazaar-type shop sector, who expanded into a travel agency in 2012.[25] In both cases, the businessmen were responding to the increasing flows of Chinese tourists to Europe visiting Portugal for short spells, in general two days, within packages that include Spain and Italy.

Another facet of expansion regards the establishment's dimension. Two cases are illustrative:[26] a Chinese bazaar-type shop in the centre of Cascais (seaside town about 30 km from Lisbon), which expanded its shop area and increased its product range (notably by garments and shoes), and another one that augmented its shop area threefold and became one of the largest shops in the city centre (sell-ing garments of all kinds, from bathing suits to evening dresses).

A somewhat related phenomenon observed in downtown Lisbon (possibly applicable to other main Portuguese cities) is that many traditional establish-ments, owned by Portuguese retailers and closed down in the crisis, were taken over by Chinese businessmen. According to interview evidence, this started in 2010, when many Chinese shops were opened, and has recently stabilized, with some of these new shops already closing down. Some of these were linked to an expansion of wholesalers' businesses (e.g. garments, suitcases, shoes), which entered the retail sector, thereby augmenting their channels of distribution and counteracting lower demand in the crisis by adding direct sales.

The strategy of changing the business's geographical area was adopted by 7.8 per cent of respondents in the sample. In all cases, this implied changing the business from smaller towns (Torres Vedras, Portalegre, Almada, Leiria, Coimbra) to the capital, Lisbon or to the second-largest Portuguese city, Porto. The authors' 2006 study had revealed the opposite tendency, in the sense that Chinese business was moving out of the big centres. The crisis seems to have thereby triggered some reversal of this trend. Supplementary interview evidence suggests that the main explanation rests on the decline of business opportunities in smaller cities, with lower income levels and fewer consumers, giving rise to a move to larger centres with a higher *per capita* income and larger numbers of consumers in order to gain a sufficiently large market (niche). The decrease in the cost of rents in the big centres brought about by the aggravation of the crisis might have facilitated this process. Chinese businessmen are hence prepared to take on some risk to meet the challenge of already-established and rather concentrated competitors.

There was also a combination of the strategy of geographical change with downsizing of business/exploration of market niches as to reduce costs and risks. In one case, a businessman, operating in the restaurant sector in Torres Vedras, responded to the decline in demand by changing his business to one of the main avenues of Lisbon (characterised by high immigration and becoming recently fashionable with young people), where he set up a small snack bar to sell doner kebab.

In the change-of-location category, the study evidenced a predominance of businessmen with shorter stays (less than 10 years) in Portugal. This may be explained by the fact that those businessmen opened their establishments in smaller cities upon their arrival in Portugal, given already saturated markets in larger centres. When this proved no longer commercially viable due to changed market conditions, businessmen decided to move their businesses to larger centres.

The strategy of change of sector implies abandoning one sector and entering another, as opposed to diversification, which implies that businessmen remain in the same sector and expand into another one. In our sample, 6.3 per cent of respondents adopted this strategy. There were changes out of the restaurant sector into bazaar-type retailing and a switch from garments and bazaar-type shops into fruit and vegetable shops. The first group reflects a move out of restaurants already identified in the 2006 study, which is linked to saturation of the sector, the second group an adaptation to the change in the pattern of demand in the context of crisis and declining income. As might be expected, changes of sector are more closely associated with Chinese entrepreneurs with longer stays in Portugal (more than 10 years). This finding stands in contrast with what emerged with regard to the change of geographical area. Interview evidence suggests that the concern to preserve the investment made into building up economic ties and a client network over time and the risk of losing it explains the preference for this strategy rather than the change-of-location option.

In the sample, change occurred always as a one-off change from one sector to another, with the exception of one case of a twofold change. In that latter case, a businessman from Lisbon changed from a restaurant to a garment shop around 2008/09 and then to a fruit and vegetables shop in 2012. The last switch of sector occurred in the same premises so as to maintain clients. For the same reasons, Chinese businessmen were careful to remain in the same area of the city to preserve their client network even in the event of a change of shop location (lowering rent).

The strategy of opening a new business for the first time was of marginal importance, accounting only for 3.1 per cent. The two cases in point were Chinese businesspersons who were in Portugal for less than five years. One case regarded a small, more up-market garment shop – the owner had been an employee before and set up her own business in 2012;[27] the other one involved the setting up of a larger-scale and also more up-market shop in Algés. Both adopted a different business model from the traditional Chinese bazaar-type shop, a fact that suggests some concern with innovation of the traditional business model and with attracting more and/or different clients.

Crossing the available data showed that the choice of strategy was related to an entrepreneur's length of stay in Portugal. It is Chinese businessmen with very short stays who tend to start a new business. Those with shorter stays (less than 10 years) tend to prefer a strategy of change of geographical location, while those with longer periods of stay in Portugal (more than 10 years) tend to prefer a strategy of change of sector.

4.2.3.3. *Economic ties with China*

As far as economic ties with China are concerned, the fieldwork indicated that the economic crisis led to a significant decline in economic ties as compared to the pre-crisis period (from 50 per cent in the authors' 2006 study to 16.4 per cent). While this is true for both commercial and investment ties, it is more pronounced in the trade area. One can only hypothesize as to the reasons. They may reflect, on the one hand, the impact of a decline in Portuguese domestic demand, reducing demand for imports from China. However, this phenomenon could also be due to increased sourcing from Chinese producers established within the European Union (such as *pronto moda* from Prato) or from Chinese large-scale traders/importers located in given EU countries (where imports are accounted for) who import from China for Chinese businessmen operating in various EU countries. Those traders can, thereby, explore economies of scale and obtain lower prices than by conducting separate small-scale import operations, a trend already noted in 2006.[28]

On the other hand, demand reduction in the crisis can be expected to have depressed profits and thereby resources that can be invested in China. Several of the interviews conducted with Chinese businessmen confirmed the decline in profits and the entrepreneurs' chief concern to get through the crisis covering their cost so as to ensure the survival of the family. In spite of the general decline in economic ties, evidence however suggests that in the cases where economic ties with China were sustained, they became more relevant as a strategic variable, with a new role and working in an outward direction. Those businessmen who cultivated economic ties with China and used them strategically were involved in business expansion and were found to have coped better with the crisis in Portugal. The main explanation would be that profits generated by their successful operations in China have been used to support operations in Portugal, in clear contrast and reversing the traditional trend of profits obtained in Portugal being used to finance investment in China. For Chinese businessmen, their ties with China have thereby gained a new dimension related to the reinvestment of profits obtained in their business in China in the expansion of their business in Portugal.

4.2.3.4.   Adaptation patterns to the crisis and impacts on the small business community

In conclusion, the impact of the crisis on the Chinese small business community can be analysed at two different levels: the more short-term strategic response to the crisis and the longer-term positioning in the domestic and global economies and the changing internal structure of the community. As for the former, the majority of Chinese businessmen in our sample were found to act pro-actively rather than passively in the face of the crises. They adopted a range of strategies to adapt their businesses, some of which were rather sophisticated. The choice of a specific strategy seems to be influenced by two variables in particular: the entrepreneur's length of stay in Portugal and the existence of economic ties and business deals with China. As a consequence of their more pro-active stance and of a more flexible structure of costs, those businessmen seem to have coped relatively well with the crisis and to have resisted better than similar host economy SMEs.

As far as the longer-term impact is concerned, two trends could be identified: on the one hand is a new emerging pattern of integration in the host economy, associated with some exit from the ethnic economy; on the other hand is a pattern of internationalisation that is changing as a result of both qualitatively different (denser and bi-directional) ties with China and of greater diversification of ties with other Portuguese-speaking countries, which take advantage of Chinese business networks from the same Zhejiang region.[29] The findings confirm the networks' role as key factors of internationalisation[30] despite the fact that the part of the business community involved in internationalisation activities has been shrinking over time. For those who preserved international ties, these became a more strategic variable and a factor of differentiation from other entrepreneurs.

The majority of the community seems to have reacted relatively well to the crisis. Still, the community already displayed some degree of heterogeneity before the crisis (three successive waves of immigration with different characteristics), and a number of factors have exacerbated its level of heterogeneity. On the one hand, the variety of coping strategies in the context of the crisis came to highlight different capacities of taking advantage of economic opportunities and is likely to generate a divide in performance. The same applies to increasing asymmetries in internationalisation. On the other hand, the profile of the more recent flows of

Chinese immigrants from the Mainland depicts greater mobility, higher propensity for entrepreneurship and higher qualifications than previous inflows. In fact, it is the recent immigrants that account for the cases of new business creation in the crisis in the sample.

The existing small business community became more heterogeneous and less cohesive due to differentiated coping strategies, different levels of integration with the host economy and asymmetries in the degree of internationalisation and ties with China. In the crisis, the structure of the community has changed as a result of the recent addition of a new large-scale segment and changes in Portuguese immigration policy, both of which will be analysed in what follows.

4.3. The emergence of a Chinese large-scale business segment in the crisis

4.3.1. *Patterns of large-scale Chinese investment in Portugal in light of European trends*

The crises in Portugal also saw and partly facilitated the emergence of a new kind of Chinese investment in the country, namely large-scale investment by big Chinese firms in the Portuguese economy. This new phenomenon is in line with a similar development going on in the EU as a whole.

In the last few years, the EU has become the leading destination of China's direct investment abroad, which in 2012 reached a total of US$12.6 billion and accounted for 33 per cent of all Chinese outbound investment (A Capital 2013b; *Economist* 2013).[31] This seems to be the result of the interaction among different factors, in particular the opportunity for good deals in troubled European economies, strategic access to brands and technology or China's new strategy to counteract protectionism and improve its image by changing perceptions in Europe. Since 2011, and to a large extent triggered by the privatization process in the context of the Portuguese adjustment programme, this investment has occurred in different sectors in Portugal, with a special emphasis on the energy and public utilities sectors.

In 2012, Portugal was involved in the two largest investments (Petrogal Brasil and EDP) of the top 10 deals in the world concluded by big Chinese investors. Chinese companies have taken advantage of the particular Portuguese situation, i.e. privatisation and capital needs in the context of economic crisis, which enabled them to buy assets (at a discount) and to gain access to infrastructure in the country and to know-how in services sectors. In addition, the targeted sectors are characterised by high rates of return. This trend intensified during 2013 and 2014 and turned Portugal into one of the main recipients of Chinese large-scale investment in the EU (ranking sixth place, behind UK, France, Italy, Germany and Greece).

Different aspects stand out as far as the investment pattern is concerned. To start with, most of the large investment deals that are referred to in Table 4.3 were carried out by large state-owned enterprises (SOEs); the only large deal by a private Chinese conglomerate was the acquisition in 2014 by Fosun of an insurance business (the investment by also private Huawei was small). This finding is in line with the results of a study by A Capital (2013a), which shows that SOEs

Table 4.3 Large-scale Chinese investment in Portugal (per year and sector)

YEAR	INVESTOR	TARGET	SECTOR	AMOUNT (in euros)	FORM OF INVESTMENT
2012	SINOPEC	PETROGAL Brasil	Oil	3.9 billion	M&A; Minority share (30%)
2012	China Three Gorges	EDP	Electricity	2.69 billion	M&A; Privatisation; Minority share (21,35%)
2012	China Three Gorges	EDP Renováveis	Renewables (wind)	359 million	M&A; Minority share (40%)
2012	China State Grid	REN	Energy Grid	287.15 million	M&A; Privatisation; Minority share (25%)
2013	Beijing Enterprises Water Group (BEWG)	VEOLIA Portugal Concession 4 municipalities	Water and sewage	95 million	Takeover
2012	Huawei	Set-up of technical support centre	IT	10 million	Wholly owned
2013	Bank of China	Set-up of office and one branch	Banking	N/A	Wholly owned
2012	Industrial and Commercial Bank of China (ICBC)	Office	Banking	N/A	Wholly owned
2014	China's Fosun International Ltd	Caixa Seguros Saúde (CSS), Insurance arm of Caixa Geral de Depósitos Group	Insurance	1 billion	M&A; Privatisation; majority share (80%)

Source: Newspaper clippings and company reports

tend to account for a large share of investment in Europe, as opposed to the US.[32] However, Hanemann and Rosen (2012: 45) had pointed out that global Chinese investment between 2000 and 2011 has been dominated by SOEs but that this was not true for Europe. In that period, the majority of investment deals in Europe (63 per cent) were carried out by privately owned companies. The apparent contradiction is explained by the fact that the new trend (investment flows into the EU since 2012) differs from the past (stocks). In 2012 and 2013 (first nine months), the share of SOEs (both in terms of value and number of deals) has increased and surpassed private investment, accounting for the large majority of investments (A Capital 2013a, 2013b; *Economist* 2013).

The investment pattern of Chinese large firms in Portugal shows a large focus on energy – oil and electricity production and distribution, renewable energy (wind) and the financial sector (insurance and increasingly banking), complemented by (comparatively smaller) investments in telecommunications, water and sewage. The total investment in the Portuguese economy in 2012–14 amounts to €5.37 billion (of which a third regards the financial sector and two thirds the energy sector), while Portuguese-related assets total €9.27 billion. Studies on Chinese investment in Europe have identified four top industries (Hanemann & Rosen 2012): utilities, chemicals, automotive and coal and oil and gas. In Portugal investment by Chinese large firms is concentrated in the utilities (electricity, telecommunications and water and sewage) and oil sectors; there is no incidence of industrial investment. Although the Portuguese market has a small dimension in many of those sectors, they are often associated with market power positions that generate monopoly rents and hence make them attractive for investment. Its participation in EDP Renováveis allows the Chinese firm to enter the U.S. (American) market in an indirect way (direct access being restricted) and gives access to technology. Huawei's experience in Portugal follows what the Chinese firm has been doing in other European countries, operating several research and development (R&D) centres across Europe. This fact suggests that tapping human talent and research infrastructure in Europe is an important motive for investment.

As for the form that Chinese investment takes in Portugal, the pattern shows a preference for mergers and acquisitions (M&A), with no incidence of greenfield investments. This finding is in line with the observation of Zhang (2013) of M&As being the preferred form of entry in the EU. It is noteworthy that while Chinese investors are increasingly entering the European market through greenfield investments (Hanemann & Rosen 2012), this has not happened in Portugal to date.

Chinese large-scale direct investment in Portugal seems to be motivated by three different factors in different combinations: (1) rent seeking; (2) becoming a global player; and (3) to move upmarket. The first case, rent seeking, refers to taking advantage of market power positions in order to reap and ensure a high rate of return, for instance through firms with monopoly rents. The second case means that Chinese investors take advantage of acquired firms' links and presence in different regional markets to consolidate their global standing (for instance, a Chinese conglomerate position in Brazil and Angola). The cases of EDP and Petrogal Brasil would fit these two first categories. In the third case, a Chinese firm seeks access to technology, brands, skilled labour, distribution channels and so forth in order to move into higher-value-added activities. This move is driven by a concern to compete with foreign conglomerates for the Chinese market to meet (rising) middle-class demand as well as to learn from more sophisticated markets and firms and thereby improve competitiveness in the international arena. Fosun would fit this latter category, having invested in insurance not only to enter the European financial market but also to sell more sophisticated products back in the Chinese home market (healthcare insurance, pension funds). Similarly, Beijing Water's takeover of Veolia Portugal also allows it to gain experience in the sector (constituting the first Chinese investment in the water sector in Europe) and to acquire technology and management know-how with regard to water and sewage systems. Huawei's investment targets R&D skills and market entry. The participation in foreign private firms also opens up the possibility of a Chinese strategy to manage the liberalisation of strategic sectors of its domestic economy in compliance with WTO commitments through a 'round-trip investment' mechanism, which would ensure China's (indirect) influence over foreign formally private candidates to market entry.

The Chinese large-scale investments in Portugal (with the exception of the case of China's Fosun) also confirm another feature identified in the studies on Chinese investment in Europe, namely the option to take minority stakes in large symbolic companies as a strategy to prevent local hostility to outright takeovers and therefore avoid tensions (*Economist* 2013).[33] By the same token, the rising importance of Chinese private investment – motivated by increasing competition in China and promoted by Chinese authorities – can be perceived as a strategy aimed at attenuating concerns about excessive Chinese State influence in host economies.

While the observed motivations for Chinese large-scale investment in Portugal confirm the general pattern observed in Europe, the Portuguese experience is restricted to services investment and hence does not capture other possible motivations important for industrial investment (such as countering trade barriers or protectionism). In addition, the adjustment programme context strongly conditioned investment opportunities in Portugal through the privatisation programme. Significant investment opportunities arose in those sectors where the state had been an important player (infrastructures, utilities) and where revenue maximisation was an important factor. Controlling shares, combined with financing packages and reinforced by multiple investments in the same sectors, may lead to increased market concentration or dominant positions, which highlights the need for effective competition policy and regulation at the national and European levels.

Finally, the new inflows of Chinese large-scale investment had another important impact, not yet analysed in the studies on Chinese investment in Europe, which are related to the pattern of immigration flows insofar as they have generated a new kind of temporary immigration flows into Portugal of highly skilled immigrants. They regard Chinese managers who became members of boards of directors, intermediate staff and trainees (technical staff) of some of the firms that were acquired by Chinese large firms. Although there is no official data on that very recent phenomenon, based on publicly available information on firm sites, it is possible to estimate that since 2012, inflows have involved a minimum of 15 high-level management staff.[34] In addition, there is another more informal inflow of qualified operational staff, who have been coming in for more short-term train-ing, which for instance in the case of EDP involves an estimated 50 to 70 trainees. Considering the various recent large-scale Chinese investments, an estimate of a total of at least 100 Chinese qualified immigrants, who have arrived in the wake of the large-scale Chinese investments during 2013, seems reasonable.[35] This trend in immigration inflows is likely to intensify in the future as a result of the Chinese large firms' twin objectives of actively participating in the management of firms in which they took a share and their intention to take advantage of this opportunity to train Chinese human resources for their global operations. These facts add to the already increasing diversification of Chinese migration inflows.

4.3.2. *Dualism and (potential) inter-linkages*

Chinese large-scale investment in Portugal, concentrated in high-technology sec-tors and in knowledge-intensive services (energy, information technology and financial sectors), stands in stark contrast with the hitherto typical Chinese small family-run firms that focus on low technology and non-knowledge-intensive sectors (retail and wholesale trade, restaurants). The pattern is in line with the one observed in Europe (Zhang et al. 2013: vi). This study revealed a dualistic structure of Chinese businesses in Portugal, characterised by a strong correlation between the size of the firm and the nature and sector of activities. This dualism raises the question whether and to what extent these two segments may (come to) interact and develop synergies or complementarities.

The survey addressed the question whether there are any linkages between the large Chinese firms and the Chinese business fabric in Portugal and the poten-tial impact of those large investments on the businesses of the existing Chinese small business community in Portugal, namely in terms of supply chain relations or attraction of other smaller Chinese investments with a complementary logic. Analysis of sample data demonstrated that the typical Chinese businessman in Portugal, having a small and retail-type establishment, has no links with large Chinese firms investing in Portugal.

Still, there was one exception, a travel agency, which has been working as a service supplier for three large Chinese enterprises (China Three Gorges in the context of EDP, China State Grid in the context of REN and Sinopec in the context of GALP). The travel agency was chosen on the basis of its specialisa-tion and experience in organising travel to various parts of China for Chinese businessmen in Portugal. Chinese ethnicity also played a role. The interesting feature is that the travel agency, which expanded in 2013, was asked to step up the scale of its operations, handling all the travel of the staff of those large Chi-nese firms in Portugal. However, the businessman was reluctant to accept due to the risk and costs involved (having to pay up front for a large number of tickets while waiting for reimbursement). The case of the travel agency is also relevant, as it provides evidence for the fact that large-scale investments are inducing some new inflows of highly skilled Chinese human resources (namely manag-ers), either on a temporary or on a more permanent basis, as mentioned earlier.

Whereas the case of the travel agency indicates Chinese investors' willingness to source locally to Chinese businessmen, it also shows the kind of practical difficulties which still have to be overcome (dimension, type of business). Being but one single case, it is nevertheless meaningful with regard to the potential for cooperation that might emerge over time, for two main reasons. On the one hand, it is because the absence of links in the other cases reflects, above all, an objective misfit between the types of business and sectors rather than a lack of interest in establishing links; as it stands, the nature of the typical Chinese business – retail of food and garments – renders links very unlikely for the time being because they do not fit in with the type of activity that Chinese large firms are involved in. On the other hand, it is because the investments of Chinese large-scale firms are so recent, in some cases dating back less than one year, but nevertheless ties developed very rapidly when the opportunity arose.

There also seems to be some untapped potential that might be developed in the future to the extent that Chinese businessmen manage to exploit complementarities with Chinese SMEs from China. The evolution of China's growth model and the tensions that developed, leading to rising labour costs, over-capacities in production and declining profits, have built up pressure on Chinese SMEs to invest abroad. It gave rise to a twofold strategy, one being lowering costs and the other countering trade protectionism through direct investment (see *China Daily* 2013). Another hypothesis is that Chinese large firms will bring along their suppliers back in China (i.e. SMEs) at a later stage when they take over the firms in the host economy, in which they presently have minority stakes – as they did in the context of investments in Africa, namely in Angola – to operate with them in Portugal, thus partly overcoming some of the cultural distance problems.

Besides firm-to-firm ties, Chinese business associations in Portugal are the other potential catalyst of linkages between the small and large segments in the Chinese business community. They have proliferated in the last decade to more than 15 associations at present. The three main influential associations, each with a different geographical focus, are *Associação Luso-Chinesa em Portugal* (Southern Portugal); *Associação dos Comerciantes e Industriais Luso-Chinesa* (Greater Lisbon); and *Liga dos Chineses em Portugal* (Northern Portugal).

Most strikingly, the associations' main objectives are external rather than domestic, geared to the facilitation of relations with China, in particular with provinces and cities (ibid. 2006). The presidents and vice-presidents of those associations enjoy a special status in China with access to political circles and preferential treatment in business matters in terms of investment in the PRC, which includes better access conditions to credit and land. In several cases, they have been players in the paradiplomacy process of Chinese provinces and cities; they have institutional ties with provincial and county governments and assume the role of "informal economic ambassadors", promoting exports of Chinese regions, attracting direct investment to China and, more recently, facilitating Chinese direct investments in Portugal.[36] In this light and although the associations provide economic intelligence and information about the local business culture to all large-scale Chinese investors, they are likely to be more active in linking with provincial large firms rather than with the global SOEs conglomerates controlled by the central government.

In the past, the Chinese business associations have played an active role as facilitators of small and medium-scale Chinese investments in Portugal, identifying opportunities for Chinese investors and providing economic intelligence on market conditions and the business culture. Even before the outbreak of the crisis, members of the *Liga dos Chineses em Portugal* and of the *Associação de Comerciantes e Industriais Luso-Chinesa* were actively trying to attract Chinese investments.[37] This role has grown in the crisis context, associated with the "golden visa" process, to the extent that the associations' leaders are perceived by potential Chinese applicants/investors as middlemen who may provide information and help in the negotiations (thus contributing to reducing risks and transactions costs).

So far, the Chinese business associations and their leaders have not played any similar role in relation to recent Chinese large-scale investments. By and large, Chinese SOEs have used direct channels. However, the associations constitute a potential platform for interaction and articulation between big firms and small-scale businessmen, provided the new Chinese large firms are interested in joining in. Past experience shows that associations have played such a role: the largest Chinese group in Portugal before the crisis, the Estoril-Sol group owned by Hong Kong–based tycoon Stanley Ho, which operates in the tourism and gambling sectors, has been an active member of *Associação de Comerciantes e Industriais Luso-Chinesa* for a long time, interacting closely with medium- and small-scale entrepreneurs.

4.4. The golden visa regime and the possible emergence of a new segment of the Chinese community

As far as economic factors are concerned, that is, taking into account the effects of the economic and financial *cum* sovereign debt crisis in Portugal from 2008/09 onwards (preceded by scant growth over the first decade of 2000), which triggered a decline in demand and squeezed profits, the aforementioned arrival of new Chinese immigrants/entrepreneurs in recent years looks like a paradox. It raises the question why Portugal still attracts Chinese businesspersons despite appearing less attractive for investment than other (notably EU) countries, in particular for small investments.

One hypothesis is that Chinese entrepreneurs regard the crisis as an opportunity for starting a business and gaining a foothold in the market, in the hope that recovery will bring about better opportunities. In this light, family ties in Portugal would serve as a stepping-stone. Such a strategy implies a long-term view, which downplays shorter-term difficulties. Another hypothesis regards the relevance of non-economic reasons for choosing Portugal. One of those possible factors is the relative ease of obtaining a residence permit in Portugal, which in turn grants access to the European Union and a range of associated market and non-market benefits.

In Portugal, there seems to be a discrepancy between the law and administrative practice as far as the granting of permits is concerned. The law states that, exceptionally, a residence permit can be granted to someone who has entered the country legally, is integrated in the labour market and has no debt towards the tax and social security systems. However, in practice, this seems to have become the rule rather than the exception, making entry and residence easier to obtain in Portugal than in other countries.[38] In 2013, this factor became even more relevant and explicit.

Interestingly, in one of the interviews conducted as part of this research project, a Chinese businesswoman referred to another kind of non-economic factor which had not been mentioned before: educational factors. This was presented as being important for explaining her decision to remain in Portugal in spite of adverse economic conditions and a decline in business. In her view, returning to China, she would have better economic prospects. However, she perceived that for her children, the quality of education and educational opportunities were higher in Portugal, so that the family decided to stay in Portugal and make use of savings.[39]

A new Portuguese government policy openly targets medium-sized foreign investors through the creation of the golden residence permit for investment activity ("golden visa" regime) of August 2012. It constitutes a new mechanism under the "authorisation of residence for investment activities" system, aimed at attracting foreign investors from outside the EU. According to this regime,[40] a foreign investor can obtain a two-year visa that can be transformed into a permanent residence permit if he/she keeps the capital in the country for a minimum period of five years. There are three alternative pre-requisites: (1) invest a minimum amount of one million euros; or (2) create at least 10 new jobs; or (3) buy an asset, a house, with a minimum amount of 500,000 euros.

The most important group of beneficiaries of the golden visa regime were Chinese individuals. The number of granted golden visas increased from 250 in September 2013 to 535 by 23 January 2014, 80 per cent of which (416 visas) were for Chinese (see *Jornal de Negócios* 2014).[41] The rise in the number of visas to Chinese in January 2013 demonstrates increasing interest in the regime. The visas in question allow for free movement in the Schengen space. It stands out that most Chinese investment under the golden visa regime falls into the third category, that is, purchase of real estate rather than productive investment or job creation. Chinese investors might therefore seize opportunities in the housing market, where prices in Portugal have been depressed in the crisis years. Therefore, one can hardly refer so far to any emergence of a new segment of the Chinese business community in Portugal; of course, this is still a potential effect should the number of visas associated with productive investment increase in the future. However, there has been an effect on the existing business community, some of whose members have grasped opportunities as facilitators for investment, organizing visits and meetings for potential Mainland Chinese investors.[42]

The conspicuous absence so far of productive investment under the golden visa regime might be explained either by the crisis impact, with productive investments in Portugal not being perceived as attractive as a business opportunity or could have been delayed by the longer time frame involved in reaching a decision on investment (need for information, business plan, financing, locational issues, etc.) and setting up operations. The Chinese economy is facing increased pressures (slowing down and quality of growth, decline in exports, rising distribution costs, access to credit; see *Financial Times* 2014) and needs to promote the internationalisation of Chinese SMEs. The Portuguese golden visa regime, together with the Portuguese authorities' positive attitude towards Chinese investments, provides conditions that would facilitate this process of internationalisation, potentially leading to an increase of productive investment inflows, which could in turn trigger the emergence of a new middle segment in the Chinese business community.

One may argue that two factors may motivate Chinese golden visa–related investment in Portugal. One is to gain access to the single market and the advantages enjoyed by insiders (such as freedom of movement and non-discrimination but also the right to family regrouping and the possible avenue to Portuguese citizenship). The second aspect, possibly as or even more important, is the legal security issue. The members of the rising Chinese middle class wish to secure their assets abroad given high political risks and a weak legal system in China, which does not guarantee the legal enforcement of their rights and the protection of their newly acquired wealth.[43] The latter political factor would appear to remain relevant in the foreseeable future, thereby reinforcing the more economic factors that will account for increasing inflows of Chinese direct investment. Of course, investment in real estate property in Europe also carries a status symbol effect and contributes to prestige back in China. Investment in luxury real estate (like investing in the wine industry) is a symbol of prestige.[44]

Small-scale entrepreneurs from the existing Chinese business community have been acting as catalysts, performing a relevant role in facilitating the attraction of Chinese investment related to the golden visa system. The interviews conducted with leaders of the Chinese community revealed that at least between 40 and 50 entrepreneurs in Portugal are acting as consultants to potential visa applicants, that is, middle-class investors looking for acquiring real estate in Portugal.[45] These Chinese entrepreneurs in Portugal, who possess the market know-how, Portuguese language skills and knowledge of the local culture that applicants require, perform different roles: (i) organising trips for potential investors using their networks in China; (ii) helping in the negotiation, thereby keeping in check the risk of speculative prices; (iii) monitoring the legal aspects by hiring a Portuguese lawyer to advise the client; and (iv) monitoring the administrative process to obtain the visa, overcoming bureaucratic hurdles. They are naturally perceived as trustworthy interlocutors by other Chinese investors and have therefore developed a new business, which takes advantage of crisis-induced opportunities.

One may expect more future medium-sized investments from China to take place by means of two different processes, driven by different rationales. First, Chinese SOEs and large firms might bring along their SME suppliers. Given the recent nature of those large-scale investments, it is still uncertain whether and when this might happen. In any case, it is not likely to happen before a consolidation of the firms' market positions. However, one may argue that the recent inflow of investments by Chinese large firms produced a "demonstration effect" and might thereby have already played a role in inducing golden visa–related investments in Portugal. Those investments have contributed not only to enhance Portugal's visibility in China but also to sending the message that the country is a good and safe investment destination.

Second, the rising Chinese middle class is starting to invest abroad for the reasons outlined earlier. The choice of location (country and region) seems to be influenced by the existence of institutional links between European local governments and Chinese cities and local governments. The recent report by Zhang et al. (2013: ix) found a strong correlation between the Sino-European sister-city agreements and China's overseas foreign direct investment stock in Europe. Bongardt and Neves (2006) concluded that Chinese provinces' and cities' paradiplomacy was crucial for the expansion of exports and attraction of foreign direct investment to China. The study by Zhang et al. (2013) confirms that the same factors also play an important role in the locational choice of Chinese outward investment. The paradiplomacy ties contribute to lowering transaction costs as well as investment risks and to bridging the cultural gap. At the same time, they provide a more reassuring environment for firms that start to operate in an unfamiliar market.

In the case of Portugal, paradiplomacy ties with Chinese provincial and local governments are little developed, as efforts have been chiefly directed at building ties with the central government in Beijing. As a result, while the golden visa regime intends to attract productive investment, the low density of institutional ties might constitute an impediment, particularly in a context where the perceived risk of investment is high. In this context, the development by Portuguese cities of "sister-city" relations with Chinese regions/cities emerges as a key instrument for attracting new Chinese investment flows on a sustainable basis.

4.5.   Main findings and conclusions

This chapter set out to analyse the joint impact of the (global economic and financial *cum* sovereign debt) crises and of China's intensification of its "go global" strategy on the dynamics and structure of the Chinese business community in Portugal, looking at both economic and non-economic factors and at short- and long-term processes. The crisis had a complex impact on the Chinese business community, and it did so through different channels. Declining consumption and market conditions created constraints and risks that the existing business community had to cope with, a dimension that the survey tries to capture by looking at the different kinds of coping strategies.

Moreover, the crisis facilitated the intensification of China's globalisation through the Portuguese privatisation programme, which opened the door to a novel inflow of large-scale Chinese investments, but also through changes in Portuguese immigration policy aimed at attracting foreign investment, generating inflows of medium-scale Chinese investment. These processes have jointly contributed to changing the structure and the options of the Chinese business community in

Portugal, leading to a more heterogeneous and complex community, both within the traditional small-scale segment and by adding a new segment of large-scale firms and to new types of Chinese immigration flows.

The analysis points to four main conclusions.

First, the crises had a significant impact on the existing Chinese small business community, not only by stimulating the adoption of a variety of coping strategies, which generated disparities in performance, but also by triggering some changes and new trends that touch on the very insertion of the community in the domestic and global economy. The latter are related to increasing signs of exit from the ethnic economy and to a more diversified pattern of internationalisation to countries other than China. In light of the crisis impact, the small business community became more heterogeneous and less cohesive.

The fieldwork showed a diversity of coping strategies in response to the negative impact of the crises. It stood out that the majority of businessmen in the sample reacted by adopting what can be qualified as a pro-active rather than a passive stance, implementing a strategy to restructure their business in Portugal (through change of location, change of sector, expansion of the business or opening a new business) or restructure their business abroad, either by returning to China or re-emigrating to another country. As a result, the majority of businessmen seem to have coped relatively well with the crisis. Among the variables that influenced the choice of a specific strategy, two stand out as possibly having a greater influence on the type of strategy adopted. One is the entrepreneur's length of stay in Portugal. Here a strong correlation emerged between the strategy of change of sector and longer stays (more than 10 years), between the strategy of change of geographical location and shorter stays (less than 10 years) and between starting a new business and very short stays. The other variable is the existence of economic links and business deals with China or in China. It was more associated with the strategy of expansion of the business, most likely financed by profits from operations in China.

At first glance, the crisis appears to have had a somewhat contradictory impact, with economic ties with China shrinking in quantity but being qualitatively transformed in terms of their functions. On the one hand, the crisis is found to have triggered a reduction of economic ties between the Chinese business community in Portugal and the country of origin. On the other hand, for those entrepreneurs who did maintain ties with China, those became more important insofar as profits obtained in China are used as a source of finance for business expansion in Portugal, and some businessmen use the knowledge they have acquired in their host economy for internationalisation beyond the internal market.

The fieldwork also showed that while Chinese businessmen maintained their business model, focused on market needs and counter-cyclical products (already identified in Bongardt & Neves 2006), the crises triggered new trends regarding the insertion of the community in the domestic and the global economy. In the domestic context, there is a re-location trend to larger cities in search of the viability of market niches and an (albeit still timid) exit from the ethnic economy, which results from a re-direction of segments to new products (primary sector) and implies a greater integration in the Portuguese economy. With regard to the global economy, the most pro-active businessmen enhanced the internationalisation of their business, not limited to China as in the past but more widely to Portuguese-speaking countries like Brazil and Angola, hereby making use of products and knowledge from the host economy. With respect to Chinese investment under the Portuguese golden visa regime, some members have seized a new business opportunity by assuming the role of facilitators, bridging the cultural gap and employing their *guanxi* and knowledge of the host economy (real estate, tourism).

Second, the new wave of large-scale Chinese investments has brought about greater complexity. This applies to the Chinese business community in Portugal due to the addition of a new segment, i.e., large-scale global businesses. It also holds true for Chinese immigration flows, where a new type of temporary inflows of highly skilled immigrants has been observed.

This new inward investment has been dominated by large Chinese SOEs that have entered the Portuguese market through mergers and acquisitions, mostly concentrated in the energy sector and in other utilities and taking minority stakes. The investments have driven by three main motivations related to rent seeking; to enhancing the global profile of Chinese multinationals; and to moving up-market by acceding to technology, brands and human talent. The concern was to learn from more sophisticated markets and firms and thereby improve competitiveness in the international arena but furthermore to thereby be able to compete with foreign conglomerates for the Chinese market by satisfying (rising) middle-class demand. Generally speaking, the observed patterns are in line with the trends identified by recent studies on Chinese investment in Europe. However, the Portuguese case also presents specific aspects, namely the strong association with the privatisation programme, the strong concentration in knowledge-intensive services and the building up of strong market positions in what is often considered strategic sectors (i.e. electricity grids and electricity production and distribution).

As for links between the large Chinese private firms and SOEs on the one hand and the local Chinese business fabric on the other, they are not (yet) visible, mainly due to a misfit of activities and lack of complementarity. Judging from a single but paradigmatic case, there is some potential for links to be developed in the future because of a clear willingness of large Chinese firms to cultivate such ties. Therefore, the development of these links would mean that the decline of economic ties with China on the part of the small business community, as noted, could be reversed or rather revitalised through a new type of ties, namely with global Chinese players from the large-scale segment. In addition, the Chinese business associations can play a potentially positive role in functioning as a linking platform between the two segments, not only to explore business opportunities but also to pursue common institutional interests.

These large-scale investments have also led to a new pattern of Chinese immigration. It is associated with a new kind of temporary immigration flows into Portugal of highly skilled Chinese immigrants, i.e. Chinese managers who became members of boards of directors, intermediate staff and trainees (technical staff).

The most striking aspect is the use of the structures, staff and know-how of the large firms where investment was made to train young Chinese skilled workers on the job. Since 2012, these inflows directly associated with large-scale investments can be estimated to involve at least 100 Chinese qualified immigrants. Of course the phenomenon is recent and further research will be needed. However, these inflows are likely to intensify in the future as a result of the Chinese large firms' twin objectives of actively participating in the management of firms in which they took a share and their intention to take advantage of this opportunity to train Chinese human resources for their global operations.

Third, the existing small business community has played a significant role with respect to attracting new small to medium-sized Chinese investment flows, working as facilitators and middlemen and bringing together their *guanxi* networks in China and in Portugal. This has not been the case for large-scale investments so far.

The community's role has been visible in the context of the recent "golden visa" process, that is, changes in Portuguese immigration policy aimed at attracting immigrants with a capacity to invest or create employment. The golden visa process has thus far benefitted, above all, Chinese nationals. The operations have been dominated by real estate operations, with marginal incidence of the productive-investment clause and no use of the employment-creation clause. The regime has come to provide business opportunities for established Chinese businessmen in the real estate sector (for instance as facilitators) but so far had no impact on the business community's structure. Should the category of productive investment increase, this could lead to the emergence of a third, intermediate segment in the Chinese business community, comprising middle-class entrepreneurs and Chinese SMEs suppliers of Chinese big conglomerates. Those tend to be motivated by economic factors but also by political factors, such as the concern to secure abroad their recently acquired wealth to reduce the risk associated with China's limited legal security. The reality of the golden visa process confirms the relevance of non-economic factors and long-term perspectives related to the access to residence status and free movement inside the EU, thus explaining the apparent paradox of continued inflows of Chinese immigrants/entrepreneurs in an *a priori* economically adverse context.

A significant number of small businessmen from the existing Chinese business community have been acting as catalysts of Chinese investment inflows over the last two years, attracting Chinese investment related to the golden visa system. They act as consultants to potential visa applicants insofar as they possess market know-how, Portuguese language skills and knowledge of the local culture that applicants require, thereby filling the business–culture gap. To that end, they organise trips for potential investors, help in the negotiation and monitor both the legal process of acquisition (in coordination with a Portuguese lawyer) and the administrative process to obtain the visa. In that way, being perceived as trustworthy interlocutors by other Chinese investors, they created a new business opportunity, diversifying their activity and attempting to respond to crisis-induced difficulties.

Last but not least, the Chinese business community in Portugal has undergone change in result of the interaction among China's global policy, the crisis impact and Portuguese policy (adjustment programme, immigration laws). First of all, the existing small business community has not only often adopted more sophisticated coping strategies but also reassessed its patterns of insertion in the local and global economy. In addition, the business community's structure has already changed with the addition of a new large-scale segment, while linkages between these two segments are as yet uncertain. Thus far, it has given rise to a dualistic structure of the business community with stark contrasts between the two segments in terms of sheer size and fields of activities. Furthermore, with Portuguese immigration policy encouraging economic immigration, a third intermediate segment might emerge in the future. As a result of these developments, the business community has already become more heterogeneous and complex, less cohesive and eventually more internationalised beyond the single market.

The new reality poses challenges for the EU in various domains, notably in terms of competition policy and sectoral regulation, immigration policy and the coherence of a common policy approach towards China. Chinese investment in Europe has increased in the crisis context, taking advantage of a diversity of bargains and opportunities in the absence of an EU–level common approach. This fact risks fuelling further divisions between EU members and renders a common EU position not only on Chinese investment but also on global relations with China more difficult. For instance, the joint impact in Portugal of Chinese SOE investment in the energy sector at various levels in the supply chain might have an adverse impact on competition (subject to member-state level competition policy and regulation). Beyond that, it could also raise issues about the functioning of the internal market and condition the capacity to create an EU energy policy in the future. To meet these challenges, the EU would need to have an EU–level approach, more holistic, long-term and coordinated among member states.

Notes

1 The authors presented a previous version of this paper at the joint conference "6th Chinese in Prato and 4th Wenzhouese diaspora symposia", organised by Monash University, RSCAS of the EUI and University of Florence held in Prato on 29–30 October 2013. Annette Bongardt should like to acknowledge support by the Robert Schuman Centre for Advanced Studies (RSCAS) of the European University Institute (EUI) in Florence, as this chapter was written while she was a visiting fellow at the RSCAS.
2 That is the issue of competitiveness and of possible distortions, rooted in a variety of factors, among which are trade reciprocity, intellectual property right protection and exchange rate policy.
3 Some representatives have argued that the real numbers are between 40 and 50 per cent higher, thereby accounting for irregular immigrants and for Chinese nationals registered not in Portugal but in another EU country (on this issue, see Rocha-Trindade et al. 2006: 77–8). More recently, Mr Y Ping Chow, president of *Liga dos Chineses em Portugal*, estimated that the size of the Chinese community in Portugal amounted to 22,000 people (cited in Sol, 25 May 2013).

4 Our analysis, based on official data, differs from Latham and Wu's (2013: 28) insofar as they estimate a slowing-down trend and stabilisation of stocks during the crisis for Portugal.

5 Data on the geographical distribution of immigrants by nationality was discontinued after 2009.

6 Based on data from SEF (2005) (the last available year concerning the pre-crisis period). There are no available data for the crisis period, as since 2006, official statistics no longer present disaggregated data on age structure by nationality.

7 Interview with Mr Y Ping Chow (Agência Lusa 2009).

8 Interview with Mr Y Ping Chow, president of *Liga de Chineses em Portugal, Ponto Final* (2012) (newspaper from Macau).

9 For the English version of the questionnaire to Chinese businessmen in Portugal 2013 ("inquérito aos empresários chineses em Portugal 2013" in Portuguese), see Bongardt and Neves (2014).

10 We are grateful to Ngai In Kuan, a Macanese citizen and a lawyer who joined the Portuguese Bar Association and who is currently practising in Portugal, for her help in translating the questionnaire into Chinese and for her valuable cooperation in the interviews with Chinese businessmen.

11 The sections were organised as follows: (i) profile of the entrepreneur (place of origin in China; length of stay in Portugal; motives for choice of Portugal); (ii) firm (location of headquarters; sector of activity; size); (iii) firm's strategy against the background of the economic crisis to understand how Chinese businessmen coped with the crisis impact; (iv) sources of financing during the (previous three) crisis years; (v) Chinese small businesses' links with large Chinese enterprises that have recently started to invest in Portugal; (vi) existence and characteristics of links that Chinese businessmen maintain with China.

12 The only exception was the Algarve region, where the questionnaire could not be applied.

13 According to official SEF statistics in 2009, Lisbon was the first location for Chinese immigrants, with 37.2 per cent, followed by Porto with 13.6 per cent (thus accounting together for more than half of the total), Setúbal 7.9 per cent, Braga 3.4 per cent and Coimbra 2.9 per cent. The districts covered in the sample together represent 65 per cent of all Chinese immigrants (see SEF 2009, Annex "População Estrangeira residente em território nacional – 2009"). These are the last official data on geographical distribution of Chinese immigrants, as from 2009 onwards, official statistics ceased to present the distribution of immigrants per region disaggregated by nationality.

14 As for the identity of sampled firms, the application of the questionnaire did not take into account the identity of sampled firms in the previous study. The firms sampled in the two studies – pre-crisis as compared to the crisis context – are hence different, with a possible marginal overlap. There is some overlap in the group of interviewees, particularly as far as associations are concerned.

15 Data from Bank of Portugal (2013), table 5.1, and Bank of Portugal (2012), table 1. In 2011, Portugal registered negative growth of –1.3 per cent, which worsened in 2012 to –3.2 per cent, while the forecast for 2013 was of a decline of –1.6 per cent.

16 In order to identify Chinese entrepreneurs' coping strategies in the face of the effects of the 2008/9 global economic and financial and the subsequent Portuguese sovereign debt crisis, the questionnaire presented the following nine options: closure of the business (if yes, in which year); change of sector (if yes, indication of initial and present sectors); change of geographical area of the business within Portugal (if yes, from where to where); expansion of the business; starting a new business; return to China; re-emigration to another country; no action; other (if yes, which).
Chinese businessmen were asked to only indicate one – the dominant – strategic option. The interviews revealed that those dominant options were sometimes combined with

other strategic options to tailor them to specific needs and circumstances. Also, there were three cases of "other" strategies, which respondents however did not specify. They counted as pro-active because the option "no action" was not chosen.

17   Note: two non-responses in the sample.
18   Interview evidence (Lisbon, 18 July 2013).
19   The phenomenon of returning Chinese immigrants has been also identified in other EU countries such as Italy and Spain. On Italy, see Pedone (2013) (see also *Financial Times* 2013); on Spain, see, for instance, *El Confidencial* (2013).
20   Interview with director general of Ruoao Wines in Lisbon on 26 July 2013.
21   According to interview evidence, these family sources were not restricted to Portugal but extended to China.
22   Interview evidence (Lisbon, 5 August 2013).
23   The concept of "ethnic economy consists of co-ethnic self-employed and employers and their co-ethnic employees" (Light & Gold 2000: 4). The authors distinguish this concept from an ethnic-controlled economy based on *de-facto* control on the basis of clustering and organization and not on property rights and ownership. One of the key assumptions is that ethnicity is economically advantageous and not neutral. On ethnic entrepreneurship, see Volery (2007).
24   Interview evidence (Lisbon, 5 August 2013).
25   Evidence from interviews (Lisbon, 31 July 2013).
26   Evidence from interviews (Cascais, 2 August 2013).
27   Interview evidence (Cascais, 2 August 2013)
28   Based on an interview with the main Chinese travel agency in Lisbon, specialised in business travels for the Chinese community, it was possible to map the main business destinations, which included Paris (for food for supermarkets and restaurants), Madrid (also for food imports), Florence/Prato (for textiles and garments) and Bologna (for leather goods; see Rocha-Trindade et al. 2006: 141–2).
29   For instance, in March 2014, the largest Chinese wholesale supermarket in Brazil was inaugurated in Rio de Janeiro (China Town Atacado), owned by immigrants from Zhejiang (a business family from Qingtian county; see Conselho Empresarial Brasil-China and Xinhua, http://cebc.org.br/pt-br/dados-e-estatisticas/clipping/chinese-wholesale-supermarket-debuts-rio-de-janeiro).
30   Various authors have underlined the key role, which access to networks plays as a factor in Chinese entrepreneurs' internationalisation. See Guercini et al. (2013) on the case of Italy, while a similar phenomenon has been identified for France, namely a "French connection" of Chinese migrants from Wenzhou who first lived in France and then re-emigrated to French-speaking African countries (Mung 2008: 99). On Chinese migration to Africa, see Park (2009).
31   See also Zhang et al. (2013).
32   SOE investment in Europe accounted for 87.4 per cent of total Chinese merger and acquisition (M&A) investment in industry and services in the first nine months of 2012, compared with 95.6 per cent private investment in North America in the same period.
33   The *Economist* (2013) reports that A Capital estimates that 58 per cent of Chinese deals in the EU now involve minority stakes.
34   For instance four Chinese administrators who sit on the *Conselho Geral e de Supervisão* (Supervisory Board) of EDP, two managers who sit on the board of directors of Be Water and three managers who sit on the Board of Directors of REN (www.edp.pt/pt/aedp/governosocietario/orgaosgovernosocietario/Pages/default_new.aspx; www.bewater.com.pt/pt/gestao; www.ren.pt/investidores/estrutura_societaria).
35   In relative terms, the inflows of 100 or more highly skilled immigrants are significant within the context of total inflows of 1,362 Chinese immigrants in 2012 in official statistics.

36 For instance, Mr Y Ping Chow, president of *Liga dos Chineses em Portugal*, is an "ambassador" of the city of Qingdao from Zhejiang province.
37 That was the case of Mr Y Ping Chow, president of *Liga dos Chineses em Portugal*, who visits China three to four times per year, and Mr Zhou Long, Director of *Associação dos Comerciantes e Industriais Luso-Chinesa*, who since 2005 has promoted a project to create a special industrial zone in which Chinese industrial SMEs could invest and operate alongside Portuguese firms.
38 *Jornal de Leiria* (2013), quoting an anonymous source from SEF (Serviço de Estrangeiros e Fronteiras – Portuguese Borders Police).
39 Interview evidence (Lisbon, 26 July 2013). Interestingly, there seems to be an opposite trend in Prato, Italy, where parents send their children back to China to be educated in Chinese culture and maintain ties with their economically growing homeland (Krause et al., 2013); see also the documentary "L'Occupazione Cinese: Made in Prato" by Massimo Lucconi, DFOR with RAI Cinema.
40 Portuguese law (Law 27/2007, of 4 July) already foresaw a system of authorisation of residence for activities of investment, but it was recently modified and simplified (Law 29/2012, of 9 August). The pre-requisites and procedures of the "regime de autorização de residência para investimento (ARI)" were spelled out in despacho n° 11820-A/2012 of 4 September, recently modified by despacho 1661-A/2013, which simplified conditions and procedures. An English version of the most recent legal requirements is available at www.sef.pt/documentos/35/11820-A-2012.pdf.
41 Until January 2014, these visas led to total capital inflows of 334.26 million euros. Most of these (90 per cent) correspond to the purchase of real estate (Agência Lusa, cited in Sol (http://sol.sapo.pt/inicio/Economia/Interior.aspx?content_id=95745).
42 To give but two examples, the leader of the Chinese business association in Northern Portugal, Y Ping Chow, has been active in matching potential Chinese investors and investment opportunities in Portugal, putting his *guanxi* at their service. Another case in point is the director of the Chinese-language newspaper *Sino*, who has developed the same kind of activities in the region of Lisbon.
43 There has been reference to other factors, namely the desire of wealthy Chinese to escape environmental degradation (air and water pollution) and food safety problems in China, as well as concerns over the impact of anti-corruption policies. The moving-out process is said to be accelerating and increasingly organized by specialised agencies such as the Shenzhen-based China Business Immigration (CBIEC), which is operating in Portugal (*The Straits Times* 2014).
44 Zhang et al. (2013: iv–v).
45 Interview with the director of the *Sino* newspaper, Mr Liang Zhan, on 20 April 2014. He has specific knowledge on this segment, as he has set up his own firm to organize visits for potential Chinese investors.

References

A Capital. (2013a) Dragon Index (9 M 2013), Hong Kong, www.acapital.hk/dragonindex/A%20 CAPITAL%20DRAGON%20INDEX%209M%202013%20ENG.pdf
A Capital. (2013b) Dragon Index (2012 full year), Hong Kong. www.acapital.hk/ dragonindex/A_CAPITAL_DRAGON_INDEX_FY_2012_ENG.pdf
Agência Lusa. (2009, 9 February). A comunidade chinesa em Portugal. www.acidi.gov.pt/ noticias/visualizar-noticia/4cdbf6a13f4af/a-comunidade-chinesa-em-portugal
Bank of Portugal. (2012) *A Economia Portuguesa em 2012, Relatório do Conselho de Administração*. Lisbon: Banco de Portugal.
Bank of Portugal. (2013) *Boletim Económico*, 19 (3). Lisbon: Banco de Portugal.

Beltrán Antolín, J. (2000, October) Expansión Geográfica y Diversificación Económica. Pautas y Estrategias del Asentamiento Chino en España. II Congreso sobre la Inmigración en España. Madrid. http://sirio.ua.es/documentos/pdf/flujos_migratorios/expansion%20geaogrfaica%20y%20diversificacion.pdf

Bongardt, A., & Santos Neves, M. (2006) *The Role of Overseas Chinese in Making China Global: The Case of Portugal.* INA paper 29. Oeiras: INA.

China Daily. (2013, 16 July) Chinese SMEs eye overseas markets for investments. www.chinadaily.com.cn/business/2013–07/16/content_16783354.htm

Economist. (2013, 20 April) Nice to see you, EU. www.economist.com/news/china/21576440-chinese-investors-love-europes-companies-hate-its-bureaucracy-nice-see-you-eu

El Confidencial. (2013, 22 July) Crisis e Inseguridad: los chinos se van de España.

Financial Times. (2013, 6 January) Immigrants abandoning recession-hit Italy.

Financial Times. (2014, 22 January) China abandons its pursuit of growth at all costs.

Guercini, S., Milanesi, M., & Dei Ottati, G. (2013, 29–30 October) *Global and Local Business Networks in the Growth of the Chinese Firm in Prato.* Paper presented at 6th Chinese in Prato & 4th Wenzhouese Diaspora Symposia on "Chinese migration, entrepreneurship and development in the new global economy", organized by the European University Institute/Monash University/University of Florence, Prato, Italy. www.monash.it/files/20131029%20-%20CIP%202013%20-%20Guercini%20et%20al%20-%20For%20web.pdf

Hanemann, T., & Rosen, D.H. (2012) *China Invests in Europe: Patterns, Impacts and Policy Implications.* New York: Rhodium Group.

Jornal de Leiria. (2013, 21 March) Invasão Chinesa, 28 (1497). https://jornaldeleiria.pt/files/_Edicao_1497_514acf9578f5f.pdf

Jornal de Negócios. (2014, 27 January) Governo já entregou 416 vistos de "ouro" a chineses. www.jornaldenegocios.pt/empresas/detalhe/2014_01_27_governo_ja_entregou_416_vistos_de_ouro_a_chineses.html

Krause, E., Bressan, M., & Xu, F. (2013, 29–30 October) *Crooked Capitalism and the Circulation of Children: Considerations and Consequences.* Paper presented at 6th Chinese in Prato & 4th Wenzhouese Diaspora Symposia on "Chinese migration, entrepreneurship and development in the new global economy", organized by the European University Institute/ Monash University/ University of Florence, Prato, Italy. www.monash.it/files/20131016%20-%20CIP%202013%20-%20Program%20with%20abstracts%20and%20author%20notes%20-%201.2.pdf

Latham, K., & Wu, B. (2013) *Chinese Immigration into the EU: New Trends, Dynamics, and Implications.* London: Europe China Research and Advice Network (ECRAN).

Light, I., & Gold, S. (2000) *Ethnic Economies.* San Diego, CA: Academic Press.

Mung, M. (2008, May) Chinese Migration and China's Foreign Policy, *Journal of Chinese Overseas,* 4 (1).

Park, Y.J. (2009) *Chinese Migration in Africa.* South Africa Institute of International Studies SAIIS, Occasional Paper number 24.

Pedone, V. (2013, 29–30 October) *Social Mobility of Chinese Population in Prato.* Paper presented at 6th Chinese in Prato & 4th Wenzhouese Diaspora Symposia on "Chinese migration, entrepreneurship and development in the new global economy", organized by the European University Institute/ Monash University/ University of Florence, Prato, Italy. www.monash.it/files/20131029%20-%20CIP%202013%20-%20Pedone.pdf

Ponto Final. (2012, 24 August) Crise muda face dos negócios luso-chineses. http://pontofinalmacau.wordpress.com/2012/08/24/crise-muda-face-dos-negocios-luso-chineses/

Rocha-Trindade, M. B., Santos Neves, M., & Bongardt, A. (2006) *A Comunidade de Negócios Chinesa em Portugal. Catalizadores da Integração da China na Economia Global.* Oeiras: INA.

Serviço de Estrangeiros e Fronteiras SEF. (2005) *Relatório Estatístico.* Oeiras: SEF.

Serviço de Estrangeiros e Fronteiras SEF. (2009) *Relatório Actividades 2009. Imigração, Fronteiras e Asilo.* Oeiras: SEF. Available at http://sefstat.sef.pt/Docs/Rifa_2009.pdf

Serviço de Estrangeiros e Fronteiras SEF. (2013, May) *Relatório de Imigração, Fronteiras e Asilo 2012.* Oeiras: SEF. Available at http://sefstat.sef.pt/Docs/Rifa%202012.pdf

Straits Times. (2014, 16 February) China's rich migrating in droves. www.straitstimes.com/the-big-story/asia-report/china/story/chinas-rich-migrating-droves-20140216

Volery, T. (2007) Ethnic Entrepreneurship: A Theoretical Framework. In Dana, L.-P. (Ed.), *Handbook of Research on Ethnic Minority Entrepreneurship: A Co-Evolutionary View on Resource Management.* Cheltenham: Edward Elgar, pp. 30–41.

Zhang, H. (2013) The Role of Migration in Shaping China's Economic Relations with Its Main Partners. Florence: Migration Policy Centre, European University Institute.

Zhang, H., Yang, Z., & Van Den Bulcke, D. (2013) *Chinese-Owned Enterprises in Europe: A Study of Corporate and Entrepreneurial Firms and the Role of Sister City Relationships.* Euro-China Investment Report 2013–2014. Antwerp: Antwerp Management School, Euro-China Centre.

5 Chinese investment strategies and migration – does diaspora matter?

A case study on Germany

Margot Schüller and Yun Schüler-Zhou

Abstract

This study analyses the role that Chinese migrants and diaspora networks play in the development of foreign direct investment (FDI) from China in Germany. Based on semi-structured interviews and a questionnaire survey directed at the managing personnel and owners of Chinese-invested companies in the city of Hamburg, we find out that (1) skilled Chinese migrants are important sources and facilitators of FDI from China in Germany; (2) Chinese migrants working in Chinese-invested companies have a crucial bridging role; and (3) private diaspora networks are important platforms for the exchange of business information and knowledge.

Introduction

Chinese migrants have traditionally played an important role in the economic development of neighbouring countries in Asia, especially in Southeast Asia. With China's growing integration into the global economy, not only the mobility of Chinese capital has increased but also that of the country's citizens. Besides the United States and Canada, European countries have become important target locations for Chinese students and businesspeople who function as bridges between their host and home country. Due to its strong economy and well-developed industries, Germany has also seen a growing influx of Chinese citizens over the last decades. Starting with this observation, we ask what role Chinese migrants play in the development of economic relations between China and Germany, especially in terms of foreign direct investment (FDI). Our research design includes both qualitative and quantitative methods. Alongside the outlining of the patterns of Chinese investments and migration to Germany, we also present findings from semi-structured interviews and a questionnaire survey directed specifically at the managing personnel and owners of Chinese-invested companies in the city of Hamburg. Based on our results from the questionnaire survey, we found that diaspora networks do still matter in the FDI context and that Chinese employees working in Chinese-invested companies or German institutions do play an important bridging role.

Previous research argues that immigration can be beneficial for host countries, especially when skilled migrants use their entrepreneurial talents for innovation and the creation of jobs (Briggs and Moore 1994). Genc et al. (2010) find evidence in their meta-analysis that immigration is a complement to rather than a substitute for trade flows between host and home countries. The research by Ivlevs and Melo (2008) on the influence of skill composition of exports on FDI supports this finding. They conclude that the emigration of skilled labour is positively related to FDI, if exports are low-skill intensive. That education matters is also demonstrated in the study on migration and FDI conducted by Gheasi et al. (2011). Using the United Kingdom as an example, they study the relationship between the size of foreign population (by nationality) and the bilateral volume of both inward and outward FDI. The authors find a positive and significant relationship between migration and outward FDI. The more educated migrants were, the stronger the impact on both inward and outward FDI was. In their research on the role that human mobility plays in promoting Chinese outward FDI, Gao et al. (2013) show that the two-way mobility of highly skilled Chinese students and scholars has a significant impact on Chinese outward FDI.

Taking Germany as a case study, Buch et al. (2006) analyse the relationship between migration and FDI. They find a higher volume of inward FDI in those German federal states hosting a larger foreign population from the same country of origin. In their investigation of the migration, FDI and trade nexus, Kugler and Rapoport (2011) argue that migrants are able to reduce transaction costs associated with selling and producing overseas through the formation of business networks and as a consequence of information diffusion. Their study indicated that the ratio of FDI to exports is higher the larger the number of migrants from the buying country living in the seller country is. They also conclude that migration has a stronger impact on FDI than it has on export. Focusing on transnational diaspora entrepreneurship in emerging markets, Riddle et al. (2010) stress that migrants and their descendants can bridge the institutional divides that exist between countries having strongly different institutional and business environments.

Although the statistical data on the number and geographical patterns of distribution of the skilled migrants' countries of origin is still fragmentary, those from Asian countries, and especially China and India, count among the larger groups of expatriates currently present in the OECD countries (Wogart & Schüller 2011). These groups are characterized by a comparably high level of education and training and strong diasporic networks. In the United States, a large number of highly skilled immigrants from China and India are employed as scientists and engineers in Silicon Valley. At the beginning of the last decade, they accounted for one quarter of all engineers working in the region (20,000 Indian and 20,000 Chinese, of whom 5,000 came from Taiwan). Their numbers have risen even further more recently (Kuznetsov 2008: 269; Saxenian 2005: 2).

Chinese migrants have traditionally preferred Southeast Asian countries as their destination, where about 80 per cent of the estimated 25 million "overseas Chinese" (*huaqiao*, 华侨) are currently living. People of Chinese descent living in Hong Kong, Macao and Taiwan are not included in this figure by the Chinese government as they are not counted as being *huaqiao*. Population statistics of Chinese living in the European Union, however, often mix up these different groups (Latham & Wu 2013: 15). The US and certain European countries are the other most popular destinations for migrants from China (Song 2003: 37–40). Although the first wave of Chinese migrants had already arrived in Germany at the end of the nineteenth century, their number then remained relatively small. It is only since the inception of China's economic reform policy in the 1980s – and especially during the last decade – that a substantial influx of Chinese migrants to Germany can be observed.[1]

The literature is not only discussing the motives of individual migrants and patterns of migration but also looks at Chinese diaspora networks as a means to reduce transaction costs in cross-border economic relations. Originally, the term "diaspora" was used only for specific historical groups such as the Jews. However, in more recent studies, it has been applied rather loosely and has been used to denote any group residing outside its place of origin (Gamlen 2008).[2] In this study, we use the term "Chinese diaspora" to refer specifically to those Mainland Chinese citizens and naturalized Chinese living outside of China who still maintain economic and psychological ties with their native country and especially their home regions in it. We focus on members of the Chinese diaspora who are living in Germany with or without Chinese citizenship – and not including those from Hong Kong, Macao or Taiwan.

The important networking function of migrant associations for trade and FDI has been discussed by different authors. Rauch (2001), for instance, stresses the supply of better information on potential business partners by organized migrant associations than is otherwise available on the market or is available only at a higher cost. According to Casella and Rauch (2002), organized migrant networks also rein in any opportunistic behaviour of their members. While Saxenian (2000) points to the importance of Indian professional associations for establishing international contacts, Mitchell and Hammer (1997) study the evolvement and type of Chinese overseas networks. Referring to the differentiation between organized and non-organized migrant associations made by Rauch (2001), Baghdadi and Cheptea (2010) analyse the impact of migrant associations on trade and FDI in France and find a positive role of migrants in both fields as well. They conclude that non-organized networks affect trade via preference and information channels, whereas organized ones have an important informational role. Both types of networks, however, affect FDI via the provision of information to French companies investing abroad.

The term "foreign direct investment" is based on the internationally accepted definition of FDI, which does not include portfolio investment but, rather, the goal of long-term engagement overseas and having an influence on the management of a company (OECD, n.d.).[3] Chinese outward foreign direct investment (OFDI) has increased rapidly in the last few years, making the country the third-largest investor worldwide in terms of OFDI flows in 2013. Germany has become one of the main target locations of strategic asset-seeking companies from China that strive to acquire ownership of high-tech firms, famous brand names and distribution networks in developed countries. Alongside this development, there has been a significant growth in the Chinese population living in Germany, particularly students from China, and in Chinese diaspora networks.

The rest of our contribution is organized as follows. Section 2 provides an overview of the pattern of Chinese investments in Germany in terms of size and sector as well as geographical distribution, the ownership structure of Chinese investors (state-owned companies vs. privately owned ones) and the impact that Chinese investments in Germany have had (in particular, their contribution to employment creation). Next, Section 3 investigates how Chinese migration to Germany has unfolded. It presents statistics on the types of migrants, their skill set and professional focus, as well as on the fields of study of Chinese students. Section 4 then presents the different Chinese diaspora networks in Germany. Finally, Section 5 offers some findings concerning the role that Chinese migrants play as facilitators for FDI from China and the implications therein for the business climate and development of the labour market in Germany. The paper concludes with a short discussion of the findings and implications in section 6.

5.1. Chinese FDI in Germany

Bilateral economic relations are characterized by strong growth in trade and investment in both directions. China is Germany's third-largest trading partner and its most important market in Asia, with exports focusing on high- and medium-tech products. Most of the direct investment made by German companies in China takes place in the same industries in order to overcome export barriers and better adapt to local markets. Bilateral trade almost tripled between 2004 and 2013, with the value increasing from 53.6 billion euros to 140.6 billion euros (Federal Statistical Office Germany [FSOG] 2014). Many German companies have taken advantage of the opportunities for the further global division of labour and have thus relocated parts of their value chains to China (Erber 2012: 28). However, bilateral investment is much lower than bilateral trade. In 2012, the FDI from Germany to China came up to 4.4 billion euros, while Chinese FDI flow to Germany amounted to only 185 million euros. The total FDI stock from Germany in China represented a share of around 3.75 per cent of Germany's total FDI outflow at the end of 2012. In contrast, the cumulative value of Chinese FDI in Germany accounted for only 0.2 per cent of Germany's total FDI inflow (German Central Bank [GCB] 2014). Although Chinese direct investment in Germany is still well below the volume of FDI made by German companies in China, Chinese companies have rapidly expanded their overseas investment operations in Germany in recent years. Especially the German machinery industry has become a focus of Chinese investors in Europe.

5.1.1. *Flows and stocks of Chinese FDI in Germany*

After China's accession to the WTO at the end of 2001, the Chinese government recognized the need to support the internationalization of its domestic companies and thus introduced its "going global" policy. Due to its strong focus on high- and medium-tech industries, Germany has become a recommended target location for Chinese investors. The trend of Chinese companies investing in technologically advanced sectors has sharpened since the global financial crisis of 2008 and the subsequent economic slump. Chinese investors have been able to take advantage of companies struggling against insolvency as a result of a drop in sales within the European market. Many of the smaller companies that found themselves in financial distress were technological leaders in their fields. This was especially true for those working in the machinery- and equipment-related industries (Schüller & Schüler-Zhou 2012).

According to the latest statistics of the German Central Bank,[4] the stock of Chinese FDI in Germany increased from 148 million euros in 1998 to a total volume of 1.4 billion euros in 2012 (GCB 2014). Most of these investments were made between 2007 and 2012 (see Figure 5.1). In addition to the Chinese Ministry of Commerce's (MOFCOM's) annual *Statistical Bulletin of China's Outward Foreign Direct Investment*, the ministry offers a database on its Chinese-language website that includes those FDI projects that had to be registered with state agencies.[5] In this database, 306 investment projects had been registered for Germany as of January 2011. This number had increased to 610 projects by March 2013 (MOFCOM database). Based on the MOFCOM's *Statistical Bulletin*, the stock of Chinese investments in Germany amounted to 3.1 billion USD in 2012 (MOFCOM 2013: 120).

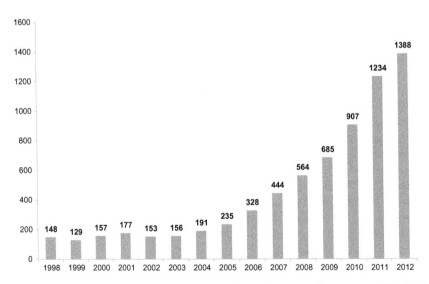

Figure 5.1 German statistics on China's outward direct investment in Germany 1998–2012 (in millions of euros, stock values)

Source: German Central Bank (1998–2014)

According to the German trade and investment promotion agency GTAI (Germany Trade and Invest), China ranked first among the country's foreign investors in terms of the number of investment projects listed by local investment promotion agencies in 2011. While 158 investment projects originated from China, 110 projects were conducted by companies from the United States and 91 by companies from Switzerland (GTAI 2012). The distribution of these Chinese investment projects (greenfield and expansion investment projects) by sector shows a strong focus on automotive, industrial machinery and equipment (28 per cent), followed by electronics and semiconductors (22 per cent), consumer goods (including foods and beverage; 12 per cent) and ICT and software (8 per cent) in the period 2007 to 2011. The analysis of the Chinese investment projects according to business activities reveals that the majority of these projects were related to sales, marketing and support (62 per cent), followed by headquarter activities (13 per cent), manufacturing (6 per cent) and logistics, distribution and transportation (5 per cent; GTAI 2012).

With regard to the geographical distribution of China's investments among the federal states in Germany, GTAI reports that the city of Hamburg ranked first in terms of FDI (greenfield) stock (215 million euros) in 2010, followed by Hessen (186 million euros), North Rhine-Westphalia (110 million euros) and Bavaria (70 million euros). In terms of the number of Chinese investment projects (not including M&As) undertaken between 2007 and 2011, North Rhine-Westphalia was able to attract the largest share (137), followed by Hessen (63), Baden-Württemberg (15) and Bavaria (11) (GTAI 2012). These data only allow, however, a first glimpse at the geographical distribution of Chinese investments and are challenged to some extent by the views of representatives from local GTAI agencies (Interview with Bavaria Invest 2013).

5.1.2. The patterns of Chinese FDI in Germany

In addition to macro-level data, firm-level statistics complement the depiction of patterns of Chinese investment activities in Germany. Based on data collected by the authors and retrieved from the Zephyr M&A database, a total number of 74 Chinese M&A transactions took place in Germany between 1996 and 2012. The geographical distribution of M&A transactions within Germany reveals that most transactions took place in North Rhine-Westphalia, followed by Baden-Württemberg and Bavaria. The machinery and equipment industry attracted most investment (25 M&A cases), followed by the automobile sector (9 cases) and the electronic and IT industry (8 cases). The data also reveal that the number of M&A transactions, especially in machinery and equipment, grew rapidly after 2004 (see Figure 5.2).

Most of the Chinese acquirers from the machinery and equipment sector in our sample of M&A transactions were state-owned companies (16 out of 25 companies). They belonged to the group of those state-owned companies that have undergone restructuring and modernization in China in the last few years, increased their international competitiveness and are now looking for high-end

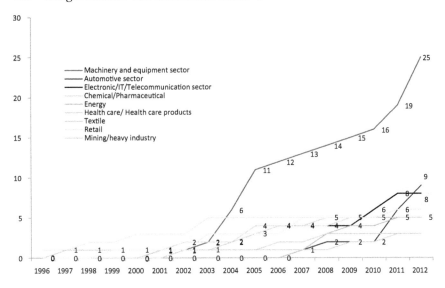

Figure 5.2 Chinese M&A in Germany by sector 1996–2012 (accumulated number of cases)

Source: authors' compilation of M&A transactions and Zephyr M&A database

and technology-intensive companies to acquire or to cooperate with. In another study, we found that the acquisition of these companies is often driven by the need to increase their own reputation in the domestic market in China, which is extremely competitive. With the latest technology and the "made or designed in Germany" label, Chinese companies expect to enjoy a better domestic product image and higher sales volumes (Schüller, Meuer, & Schüler-Zhou 2012).

With the acquisition of German companies that in many cases faced financial difficulties and were threatened by bankruptcy, Chinese investors contributed to the stabilization of local employment. Looking at the employment record of the German companies acquired, we found that – with the exception of the seven companies which had to shut down after takeover – employment was mostly stabilized at a slightly lower level than before or otherwise increased. Among the companies acquired between 2003 and 2006, for example, a small decrease or increase in employment was recorded for: Dürrkopp Adler, Wohlenberg, Waldrich Coburg, Zimmermann, Wirth, HPTec and Bullmer and TopCut (Hoppenstedt Company Profiles).

In contrast to the acquisition strategies of many Chinese investors, the so-called "Chinese Champions" – in other words, technology-intensive companies such as Huawei and ZTE – prefer greenfield investment as the predominant entry mode. To them, greenfield investment represents the most effective means for transferring their competitive advantages to Germany. The telecommunications company Huawei has, for example, established 18 subsidiaries in Germany and employs 1,600 persons, most of them Germans. In addition to these greenfield investments, the company is cooperating in R&D with telecommunications providers such as Deutsche Telekom and certain German universities (Huawei company website).

The creation of new employment through greenfield investment is one of the major policy goals of local German investment promotion agencies. However, there is no systematic reporting of employment figures for Chinese-invested companies by the local or national branches of GTAI. In addition to large M&A transactions and greenfield investment, there are thousands of small-scale Chinese-invested companies and self-employed Chinese persons in Germany who might not appear in any of the official statistics. Therefore, only broad estimates of the total employment created by Chinese FDI in Germany are possible. For the year 2010, for example, GTAI estimated that the approximately 700 Chinese-invested companies employed about 6,600 people (GTAI, cited in Xu, Petersen, & Wang 2012: 31).

In sum, the analysis of Chinese FDI in Germany demonstrates that there has been a significant increase in OFDI from China. Most of the large- and medium-scale investments have been concentrated in Germany's machinery and equipment, automobile and electronic/IT industries. Although the majority of investment activities are still related to market-seeking pursuits, we can observe a growing interest in manufacturing and R&D endeavours on the part of Chinese companies.

In order to analyse the linkages between foreign investment and migration, the following section studies the historical development of Chinese migration to Germany. First, we look at the overall size of the Chinese population in Germany and its geographical spread across the country. Second, we scrutinize the influx of Chinese students to Germany, focusing specifically on their geographical distribution and chosen fields of study.

5.2. Chinese migration to Germany

In 1967, the first statistical record of ethnic groups conducted in Germany identified around 2,400 persons as having an ethnic Chinese background, with four fifths of them noted as coming from Taiwan. Another key group of ethnic Chinese are the so-called boat people, who came from Vietnam. In the 1960s and 1970s, most of these migrants worked in Chinese restaurants or as nurses. They lived in close communities with strong family ties, and interactions took place mostly within their territorial associations (*Landsmannschaften*). Some of the successful businessmen among them established internal saving associations that provided loans to fellow ethnic Chinese on the basis of trust (Yü-Dembski 2005: 40–8). Traditionally, many Chinese migrants in Germany came from Zhejiang Province in China, especially from the cities of Wenzhou, Qingtian and Lishui. Most of the Zhejiang Chinese diaspora worked in the catering industry and used their strong family networks to help other Chinese family and non-family members to migrate to Germany (Giese 2005: 105–12).

In contrast to this group of migrants, who fit into the traditional concept of the diaspora, those (mainland) Chinese people coming to Germany in the 1990s were characterized by their belonging to transnational communities. The reform and opening-up policy of the Chinese government since the 1980s triggered a new wave of migration by students, both with the assistance of government scholarships and through self-funding. After the Tiananmen Square incident of 1989, a larger number of them decided to seek permanent residence in Germany. The new generation of migrants (called *Xinyimin*) commute between China and Europe, are spread across different cities and regions in Germany and pursue attractive work or housing conditions instead of looking for the solace of close ethnic communities (Yü-Dembski 2005: 48–51).

5.2.1.   Trends in Chinese migration to Germany

Data on the Chinese population and Chinese students in Germany are based on the statistics released by the Federal Statistical Office Germany (FSOG) and the German Academic Exchange Programme (DAAD). These statistics are complemented by the estimations about the extent of the Chinese population in Germany that have been made by various scholars. German statistics differentiate between those members of the population with a so-called "migration background" and the statistics on the overall foreign population. In 2012, the number of people with a migration background totalled 16.3 million. This statistic divides between migrants and persons born in Germany with at least one parent who is a migrant. According to the Micro Census of 2011 (FSOG 2011a), the total number of the population with a Chinese migration background amounted to 102,000 people. Out of this total, 45,000 persons were registered as being part of the labour force, 7,000 as being self-employed and 32,000 as employees. The distribution of the labour force by sector revealed that the majority of the labour force is engaged in trade, catering and transportation (21,000 persons, 47 per cent), followed by other services (17,000 persons, 38 per cent) and manufacturing (6,000 persons, 13 per cent).

According to FSOG statistics (FSOG 2011b), the number of Chinese citizens (those registered as foreigners) in Germany increased from 18,376 in 1990 to 86,436 in 2011 (see Figure 5.3). In the following, we focus specifically on the population statistics for the years from 2004 to 2011. Although Chinese citizens represent only a small proportion of all foreigners living in Germany, their number increased by 20.7 per cent between 2004 and 2011. The gender ratio also changed during this period, with the share of women increasing from 46.3 per cent in 2004 to 51.3 per cent by 2011 (see Table 5.1).

The age range of this Chinese population in Germany is characterized by a predominance of people of working age – in other words, those between 15 and 65 years of age. Within this group, the number of people aged between 15 and 35 years is twice as large as that of people aged between 35 and 65 years (see Table 5.2). Compared to the German population at large, Chinese citizens living in Germany are on average much younger.

Most Chinese people only stay in Germany for a relatively short period of time, typically between one and four years. In 2011, the share of these short-term

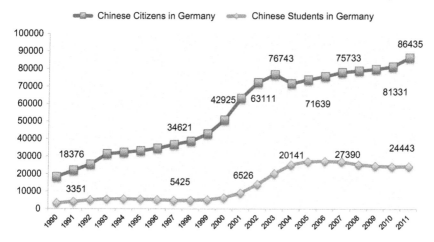

Figure 5.3 Chinese citizens and students in Germany 1990–2011

Source: FSOG (2011b, 2012)

Table 5.1 Number of Chinese citizens living in Germany, 2004–2011

Year	2004	2006	2008	2011
Total	71,639	75,733	78,960	86,435
Male	38,444	39,710	40,067	42,052
Female	33,195	36,023	38,893	44,383
Proportion of women as a %	46.3	47.6	49.3	51.3

Source: FSOG (2011b)

Table 5.2 Age range of Chinese citizens living in Germany in 2011

	< 5–15	15–35	35–65	65–95+	Average
Total	5,357	55,642	24,621	815	31.1
Male	2,746	27,302	11,576	428	31.0
Female	2,611	28,340	13,045	387	31.2

Source: FSOG (2011b)

residencies in the total Chinese population amounted to 43.8 per cent. The second-largest group of Chinese persons living in Germany stay for a period of up to eight years (20 per cent), while 26.4 per cent were registered as having stayed in Germany for up to 15 years or more (see Table 5.3).

The geographical distribution of Chinese citizens in Germany shows that there is a strong concentration in those federal states with a vibrant economy and a

Table 5.3 Duration of the stay of Chinese citizens living in Germany as of 2011

< 1–4 years	4–8 years	8–15 years	15–25 years	25–35 years	35–40+ years	Average
37,859	17,249	22,808	7,430	940	149	6.7
43.8 %	20%	26.4%	8.6%	1.1%	0.2%	

Source: FSOG (2011b)

Table 5.4 Geographical spread of Chinese citizens among German federal states in 2011

Baden Württemberg	Bavaria	Berlin	Branden-burg	Bremen	Ham-burg	Hesse	Mecklenburg–West Pomerania
12,360	12,385	6,701	969	1,085	4,671	8,172	460
(14.3%)	(14.3%)	(7.7%)	(1.1%)	(1.3%)	(5.4%)	(9.7%)	(0.1%)
Lower Saxony	North Rhine–Westphalia	Rhineland-Palatinate	Saarland	Saxony	Saxony-Anhalt	Schleswig-Holstein	Thuringia
5,581	21,813	2,550	800	3,571	2,416	1,540	1,361
(6.6%)	(25.2%)	(3.0%)	(0.9%)	(4.2%)	(2.9%)	(1.8%)	(1.6%)

Source: FSOG (2011b)

well-developed higher education system. This distribution is essentially consistent with the demographic spread of the German population across all of the federal states. In 2011, the most populous federal state, North Rhine-Westphalia, attracted 21,813 Chinese, or 25 per cent of all Chinese citizens living in Germany, while Baden-Württemberg and Bavaria each absorbed a share of 14 per cent. Generally speaking, the newer federal states (those which were previously part of the German Democratic Republic) have been less popular destinations for Chinese citizens. Within this group of federal states, Saxony absorbed the highest share of Chinese immigrants (around 3 per cent or 3,571 persons). Among the city-states, Berlin and Hamburg were the most attractive locations for Chinese migrants, absorbing a share of 7.7 and 5.4 per cent, respectively (see Table 5.4).

5.2.2   Chinese students in Germany

Since the 1980s, students have come to represent an important and growing proportion of Chinese citizens living in Germany. The number of Chinese students rose from 3,351 in 1990 to 24,443 persons in 2011, after a peak in 2006 (see Figure 5.4). They represented the largest group of foreign students studying in Germany.

Three federal states absorbed the largest number of Chinese students – namely, North Rhine-Westphalia (22 per cent or 4,697 persons), Baden-Württemberg (15 per cent or 3,259 persons) and Bavaria (11 per cent or 2,350 persons). Within

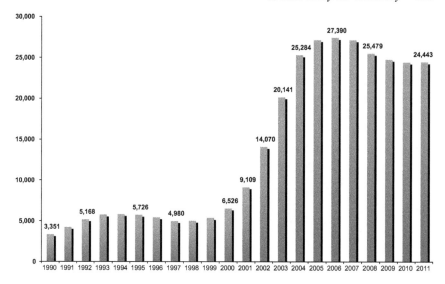

Figure 5.4 Number of Chinese students in Germany 1990–2011

Source: FSOG (2012)

Note: 2011 represent the Winter Term 2010–2011; this applies also to the other years.

the so-called New Federal States, the number of Chinese students is still small, but they nevertheless also constitute the largest group of foreign students there as well.

Chinese students have a strong study focus on engineering. Figure 5.5 indicates that since 1997, the number of students in this field has significantly increased, rising from 1,368 to 9,126 persons. The next most important fields chosen by Chinese students were law, economic business administration and the social sciences. By 2011, there was a total number of 5,041 Chinese students active in these fields in Germany. Mathematics and the natural sciences ranked third among the most attractive fields of study, with 4,310 such Chinese students in 2011. Analysing the motives of Chinese students coming to Germany, Chen Hongjie from the Beijing University, German Studies Centre, points out that these individuals are in most cases not laying the foundations for a future academic career at home but aiming to enhance their CV with a Master's or doctoral degree from a foreign university in order to increase their competitiveness on the Chinese labour market. Another motive for studying in Germany is the country's strong reputation in China, as well as Germany's comparatively favourable costs for study and living. The country's strong economic presence in China and the perception of good career prospects after the completion of their studies in China or Germany are other motives cited. Chen also explains the increase in the number of Chinese students coming to Germany as the result of the closer cooperation that has taken place between German and Chinese universities in recent years (DAAD 2012).

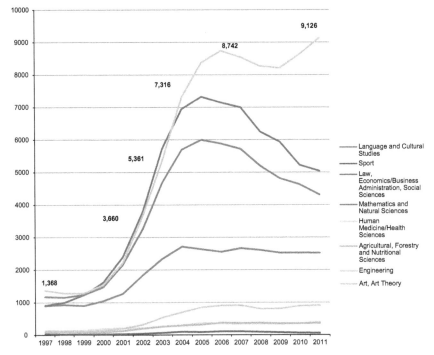

Figure 5.5 Chinese students' fields of study in Germany 1997–2011

Source: FSOG (2012)

In sum, we can observe an increase in the number of Chinese citizens and students coming to live and work in Germany since the end of the 1990s. There is a strong concentration of this population in economically developed federal states and in those fields of study which directly relate to Germany's industrial strength, namely, engineering and the natural sciences. Following the assumption that migrants can reduce transaction costs by establishing business networks and by facilitating the diffusion of information (Kugler & Rapoport 2011), we can expect well-educated Chinese with a strong knowledge of German economic and social institutions to assume a bridging role for Chinese investors coming to Germany as well as for the trade and investment activities of German companies or institutions. After they return to China, there is a strong possibility that they will work in companies that then invest in Germany. During their study time in Germany, they might also use their knowledge and understanding of both the Chinese and German business cultures to link companies from the two countries.

That cultural factors are significant for the investment decisions of Chinese companies is also one of the findings of a recent KPMG study undertaken on behalf of the EU. The presence of Chinese diaspora in an EU country as well as the number of Chinese students and the level of Chinese tourism were regarded as key factors that determine the perceived business environment for Chinese investors (KPMG 2013). Furthermore, Chinese graduates in Germany are also

Box 5.1. Mang Chen: the founder of Caissa Touristic, Hamburg

Mr Chen came to Germany to study business administration in 1988 and founded the Caissa Touristic (Group) AG in Hamburg in 1993. It is one of "China's Top 10 Outbound Travel Wholesalers" and is the market leader in terms of inbound tourism from China, with 28,000 bookings for travellers from China in 2012. Today, Caissa encompasses more than 10 branches in major European and Chinese cities like London, Paris, Hamburg, Munich, Beijing, Guangzhou and Shanghai. In China, Caissa has nearly 3,000 employees. In Germany, the total number of employees is 70, with 60 per cent of the staff belonging to the Chinese diaspora. Half of the staff consists of Chinese graduates. In addition to the travel agency Caissa Touristic (Group) AG, Mr Chen stressed his involvement in business collaboration and information exchange between both countries.

As a member of the Chinese diaspora and as someone who has lived in Germany for more than 20 years, Mr Chen is well connected with other members of this diaspora. He is CEO of the German Association of Chinese Entrepreneurs, founded in 1999. This network of Chinese entrepreneurs currently has more than 100 members. Almost all of them are small and medium-sized companies privately owned by members of the Chinese diaspora. These owners are almost all naturalized German citizens, and all do business related with and to China. Only a few of the network's members are state-owned Chinese companies. The main tasks of the association are the promotion of economic and trade cooperation between China and Germany, the engagement in scientific and technical exchange, the improvement of the understanding between the peoples of China and Germany and the organization of economic and trade fairs, exhibitions and professional seminars.

(*Source:* Interview conducted by the authors in December 2012)

entitled to establish their own company. An example of this is Mang Chen, who founded the largest Chinese travel agency in Germany during his time as a student in Germany (see Box 5.1).

5.3.   Chinese diaspora networks in Germany

Traditionally, Chinese migrants used to set up ethnic networks abroad based on mutual assistance so as to better cope with an unfamiliar and often unfriendly environment. Given both the relaxation of immigration policies in the EU and the more international orientation of the new Chinese migrants, the role of diaspora networks might in recent years have changed as well. Our main research questions with regard to this potential development are as follows:

*   What kind of Chinese diaspora networks can be found in Germany?
*   To what extent are these networks important for Chinese companies investing in Germany?
*   What role do Chinese diaspora have in the FDI decision-making process of Chinese companies?

The term "Chinese diaspora" has been used by Cheung (2004: 664–5) to describe the nature of specific economic and networking relations, especially those sustained through cross-border activities. He attributes the "social capital" generated among the Chinese diaspora to ethnicity, languages/dialects, social or business associations and Confucian beliefs. Defined as "a set of informal values or norms shared among members of a group that permits cooperation among them" (Fukuyama 1999: 16), social capital can be successfully used within both business and personal networks. Given the challenges posed by certain informational barriers in international transactions – such as a lack of information on trade opportunities, restrictive government regulations or uncertainty about the trustworthiness of potential business partners – networking activities can play an important role in allowing business to take place (Rauch & Trindade 2002).

While the importance of Chinese diaspora networks in Southeast Asia has long been the subject of many different academic studies, to date not much research exists regarding the impact that these networks have in developed countries characterized by a high level of institutional development. Applying a gravity model to the analysis of this question, Tong (2003) concludes that ethnic Chinese networks facilitate FDI not only between China and Southeast Asian economies but also between China and economies in other parts of the world. While these networks offer the better enforcement of sanctions in countries with weak institutions, the core purpose of Chinese networks in countries with strong institutions is to supply information – and thus reduce transaction costs.

Although the Chinese migrants' identities and diaspora networks are gradually undergoing change, there are nevertheless still quite a significant number of both official and private Chinese overseas organizations that work as a bridge between mainland China and those living abroad. The Chinese government discovered already in the 1960s the important role that the *huaqiao* could play and thus tried to organize them under the joint leadership of the Communist Party and the government. Up until today, the government pays close attention to the development of overseas Chinese cultural and business associations and supports their development. In April 2012, about 570 representatives from 110 countries and regions attended a global conference of overseas Chinese co-sponsored by the State Council's Overseas Chinese Affairs Office and the China Overseas Exchange Association. That overseas Chinese organizations continue to enjoy a great deal of attention was reflected in the fact that not only Jia Qinglin, Chairman of the Chinese People's Political Consultative Conference National Committee, but also Hu Jintao, Xi Jinping and Li Keqiang met with their delegates (*China Daily* 2012).

According to recent estimates, there are around 10,000 Chinese overseas organizations currently active worldwide – with nearly 1,000 of them focusing on commercial issues (Baike, website). Among the most important of all of them is the China Chamber of Commerce in the United States. It is the biggest overseas chamber, representing more than 100 large Chinese companies and more than 1,200 members. After the visit of Chinese Prime Minister Li Keqiang to Germany in May 2013, the first Chinese Chamber of Commerce in Germany was established in Berlin. The main goal of this business association is the promotion of Chinese investment in Germany. According to the president of the chamber, Chen Fei, member companies will be carefully selected, with a focus on ensuring healthy and trustworthy Chinese companies becoming members.

Established in 1992, the European Association of Chinese Organizations unites more than 100 Chinese associations across 20 different European countries. One of its core goals is to strengthen the dialogue between European countries and China (Barabantseva 2005: 20). The ethnic Chinese networks currently active in Germany include various voluntary associations of overseas Chinese business-people and academics (see Table 5.5).

Chinese diaspora networks are often based on a person's native region in China, place of residence in Germany or alumni networks. These associations offer the opportunity to exchange information and also help to establish connections with home regions in China. Some of them enjoy financial support from the Chinese Embassy or the consulates, from the local governments of their hometowns in China and from overseas Chinese business leaders. One of the most important networks in this regard is the Federation of Chinese Scholars and Students Associations in Germany, founded in 2002 and located in Frankfurt/Main. Its primary mission is to promote communication and interaction among Chinese students, scholars and local Chinese communities and German society at large. It consists of 68 student unions from different cities around the country as well as 11 professional associations (interview with Zhao Dan, president of the Federation of Chinese Scholars and Students Association in Germany, on 9 December 2012).

Gao (2003: 614) underlines that "many overseas Chinese associations consider establishing connections between members and their ancestral hometowns in China as one of their major goals". These associations invite delegates from native regions in China to Germany so as to promote trade and investment

Table 5.5 Selection of Chinese associations in Germany

Gesellschaft Chinesischer Physiker in Deutschland e.V. (Association of Chinese Physicists in Germany)
Gesellschaft Chinesischer Informatiker in Deutschland e.V. (Association of Chinese Computer Scientists in Germany)
Association of Tongji Graduates and Members in Germany
Chinesischer Verein in Hamburg e.V. (Chinese Association in Hamburg)
Bund der Chinesen in Deutschland e.V. (Chinese Union in Germany)
Federation of Chinese Associations in Germany
Association of Overseas Chinese from Qingtian in Germany
Ningbo Vereinigung (Ningbo Association)
Federation of Chinese Scholars and Students Association in Germany
German Association of Chinese Entrepreneurs
Chinese School Association Germany
Laiyin Chinesisches Kulturzentrum e.V. (Laiyin Chinese Cultural Centre)
Chinesisches Kulturzentrum München (Chinese Cultural Centre, Munich)

Source: World Chinese Public Welfare Organization

opportunities and in order to offer further employment opportunities to Chinese immigrants. Based on the information published by the World Chinese Public Welfare Organization, nearly 60 overseas Chinese associations are currently in existence in Germany.

In sum, we have pointed out in this section that Chinese diaspora networks exist in Germany as well but have undergone significant changes in the last decades. These changes can be related to the new type of migrants who have recently come to Germany and who seem to be less interested in forming or joining traditional diaspora networks. The newcomers represent a well-educated group of people who belong to transnational communities. They are more mobile and thus less dependent on diaspora networks. Whether this new type of migrants facilitates the inflow of FDI from China to Germany will be discussed in the next sections.

5.4.   Chinese migrants' role as facilitators of OFDI from China

The existence of the Chinese diaspora can facilitate Chinese OFDI in Germany in two ways. First, members of the diaspora set up business in Germany and undertake investment themselves. Second, they build bridges between the Chinese and German business community by working for Chinese or German companies, service organizations or non-profit associations. In order to discover what specific role the Chinese diaspora plays for the facilitation of Chinese direct investment in Germany, we have taken a two-tiered approach. First, we conducted semi-structured interviews; second, we carried out a questionnaire survey. In the following part of this section, we present the preliminary results from the interviews and the questionnaire survey.

5.4.1.   *Interviews: the voices of the Chinese diaspora*

During the five-month period of December 2012 to April 2013, we conducted semi-structured interviews with representatives from various Chinese diasporic networks, Chinese governmental agencies, German investment promotion agencies and other Chinese and German business and cultural associations (see Table 5.6). These interviews focused on the role that the Chinese diaspora networks play with regard to the attracting of Chinese direct investments to the host country, thus acting as a bridge between Chinese companies and the German institutional environment.

The 11 respondents, 9 of them ethnic Chinese, represent different aspects of the Chinese diaspora in Germany. Two of them work for German investment promotion agencies with a focus on German–Chinese investment relations, one based in Bavaria and the other in Berlin. One of the respondents is employed by a German company and responsible for the liaison with and support of Chinese clients. Five Chinese respondents are the owners or CEOs of companies based in Hamburg. They have either set up the company in question or acquired it from another ethnic Chinese person. One of the respondents works for a Chinese government agency based in Germany. The Chinese respondents' educational background is also quite diverse – with five out of nine of the respondents having studied in Germany, while three of the other four obtained their university degrees in China. They represent the group of high-skilled Chinese professionals who have good German language skills and multi-cultural experiences, which enables them to take on a bridging role between companies from China and Germany. Due to their strong educational background and their experience of having lived in Germany, they are suited for establishing their own businesses here. They are particularly able to facilitate the flow of knowledge and information between companies from both countries and to set up networks that provide useful platforms for Chinese companies' going global. By diffusing knowledge and information, they help Chinese investors to reduce the risks and uncertainty that are part of the liability of foreignness.

Our interviews confirmed that Chinese diaspora networks are regarded as being highly important. However, they often operate as open platforms for bringing

Table 5.6 List of semi-structured interviews

Name	Network Type/Position Therein	Date of the Interview
	Scholarly Network	
Mr Zhao	President of Federation of Chinese Scholars and Students Association in Germany; entrepreneur	December 2012
	Business Networks	
Mr Chen	Founder of Caissa Touristic (Group) AG in Hamburg; CEO of the German Association of Chinese Entrepreneurs	December 2012
Mr W.	Representative of a traditional network of Chinese restaurant owners, Hamburg	April 2013
Mr L.	Representative of a traditional business network; owner of a Chinese–invested hotel, Hamburg	April 2013
	Cultural Network	
Mr C. Q.	Vice President of a German-Chinese cultural association in Hamburg, Managing director of a company in Hamburg	March 2013
	Investment Promotion Agency Representatives	
Mr N.	Bavaria Invest	February 2013
Mr H.	Hamburg Invest	February 2013
Ms Cao	Germany Trade and Invest, Berlin	March 2013
Mr Li	Bavaria Invest, Munich	February 2013
	Chinese Government Agency Representative	
Mr Jiang	Head of the educational department at the Chinese embassy in Berlin	March 2013
	Chinese Consultant to German Companies	
Ms L. P.	Senior consultant at a German company	April 2013

Source: Interviews conducted by the authors and their China team

Chinese migrants and companies together. An example of this activity is the organization of job fairs by various networks. According to the president of the Federation of Chinese Scholars and Students Associations in Germany, one of the major functions of his association is to connect Chinese graduates in Germany with prospective employers in both China and Germany. The organization of the "Chinese Talent Days" in Cologne in April 2011 in collaboration with the Campus China organization and the German Overseas Chamber of Commerce is an example of this kind of activity. In 2012, more than 300 German companies participated in this event, demonstrating the keen interest here in the employment of highly skilled migrants from China. The Beijing Automotive Group has also previously organized a job fair in Germany in tandem with the Federation of Chinese Scholars and Students Associations (interview with Mr Zhao, Dan).

The Chinese Embassy in Germany also sponsors the organization of such events by Chinese students. According to the head of the educational department at the embassy, students play a bridging role by recruiting personnel for Chinese companies based in China and by becoming managing personnel for Chinese-invested companies in Germany. Due to their high-level qualifications obtained in Germany, Chinese companies openly and enthusiastically welcome these graduates (interview with Mr Jiang, Chinese Embassy). According to Mr C. Q., representing a German-Chinese cultural association, the Chinese Embassy and the consulates play an important role in bringing overseas Chinese together and in supporting small and medium-sized Chinese companies as they seek to invest abroad. In his own case, for example, the Chinese Consulate in Hamburg played an intermediary role and introduced his current business partner to him. Together, they established an import and export company here in 2010 (interview with Mr C. Q.).

That diaspora networks are still important for the diffusion of information about the German investment environment and for other support services was pointed out by Cao, the Chinese representative at GTAI in Berlin (interview in March 2013). She is in close contact with those Chinese companies looking for an appropriate investment location or industry in Germany. In the interview, Cao pointed to the various Chinese associations in Düsseldorf as an example of a well-functioning network that has attracted a large number of Chinese investment projects to the region. The interview conducted with Chen, president of the German Association of Chinese Entrepreneurs and founder and president of Caissa Touristic (Group), also revealed the important role that Chinese diaspora networks play.

Two Chinese diaspora networks in Hamburg – the Association of Chinese Overseas Merchants in Hamburg and the Association of Overseas Chinese in the Catering Industry in Hamburg – are directly concerned with the representation of their members' interests. One of our respondents, who owns a Chinese restaurant, noted that the latter association represents half of the about 130 Chinese restaurants currently existing in Hamburg. On average, they meet once every month and are an important source of information on business regulations and helpful for the purchase of materials. Communication takes place mostly in Chinese because many members' German language skills are limited (interview with Mr W.). The Association of Chinese Overseas Merchants in Hamburg fulfils an important consultative function for their members, especially in legal affairs and regarding the diffusion of information (interview with Mr L.).

Interviews with the Chinese representative from the national GTAI in Berlin and the representative from the local GTAI in Munich illustrate that these two members of the Chinese diaspora have the ideal attributes to be able to bridge the cultural and information gaps that first-time Chinese investors face in entering the German market. They not only disseminate information to Chinese delegations coming to Germany on investment opportunities and challenges but also coach companies in China and influence these companies' investment decisions.

Our interview results confirm previous studies conducted by the authors on the role of Chinese expatriates. In the case of the machine tool company Schiess/ Aschersleben, the Chinese manager from company headquarters played a crucial role as an intermediary between the two different business cultures in the initial takeover period (Schüller & Schüler-Zhou 2008). Another typical example is the role of the Chinese CEO of the machine-building company Wohlenberg in Hannover. After he studied machine building in China, he came to Germany in the middle of the 1980s and did his PhD at a German university. He worked in various German companies before he was asked by Shanghai Electric Group to assume the role of CEO at Wohlenberg. His technical knowledge combined with the understanding of both the Chinese and German business cultures helped him to successfully rebuild Wohlenberg following the company going bankrupt in 2005 (Schüler-Zhou & Schüller 2013).

5.4.2. Results from the questionnaire survey

We carried out our questionnaire survey in March and April 2013. The questionnaire was formulated in German and Chinese and directed specifically at the management personnel and owners of Chinese companies in the city of Hamburg. Based on the information from the Investment Promotion Agency Hamburg (HWF) and the Chamber of Commerce Hamburg, there are 564 Chinese companies located in Hamburg. The survey was conducted with the help of three Chinese students, who were required to contact each Chinese-invested company at least three times by phone. Some of the questionnaires were filled in directly during a telephone interview. In total, we collected 81 questionnaires from Chinese managerial personnel or owners of Chinese-invested companies in Hamburg. The respondents worked in 70 companies registered in Hamburg, representing a share of around 13 per cent of all Chinese-invested companies in Hamburg (see Appendix). The questionnaire explored:

1. The individual characteristics of the respondents – including gender, age, family status, nationality and residence permit status. The latter reflects the migration background of the respondents.
2. The educational background of the respondents. Questions were related to the educational achievements and the respondents' fields of study in both Germany and China, whether the study was supported through a grant or was

self-financed and how important the field of study was for the respondents' later employment or founding of a business. The respondents were also invited to self-appraise their German language skills.

3.   The respondents' employment situation and their assessment of the extent of the role that the Chinese diaspora plays in the investment activities of Chinese companies in Germany or of the company he or she works for. The questionnaire also asked questions related to the time period of foundation of the company, its size (number of employees), legal form and the percentage of company profits reinvested in the company.

4.   The importance of diaspora networks. The questionnaire asked participants to evaluate various networks by their contributions to their own professional success. If the respondent was a member of a particular diaspora network, the questionnaire asked how often he or she would meet with network members and what he or she expected from other members of the network. Further, the respondent was required to appraise the importance of his or her individual network for the OFDI decision-making process and whether he or she thought that networks are more important in China than in Germany or, alternatively, equally important in both countries. Complementary to formal networks, informal ones may play a role in the OFDI decision-making process as well. Therefore, the questionnaire asked whether formal or informal networks were more important to the interviewee or if both kinds of networks were equally important and overlapped.

The breakdown of the 81 respondents' individual characteristics reveals that 51 participants were male and 30 were female. The majority of the respondents were less than 50 years old and were mostly married, with their wives or husbands and children living in Germany. Almost all of the respondents were born in China, with 56 of them having Chinese citizenship (see Table 5.7).

Fifty-four of the 56 respondents with Chinese citizenship answered the question about whether they hold a limited or unlimited residence permit. The majority (41 of 54 Chinese citizens) possess an unlimited residence permit. It was revealed that most of the respondents had no particular problems in obtaining a residence

Table 5.7 Breakdown of respondents' individual characteristics

Gender		Age Range		Family Status		Nationality and Place of Birth	
Category	*Total*	*Category*	*Total*	*Category*	*Total*	*Category*	*Total*
Male	51	Under 30	5	Single	10	Chinese	56
Female	30	31–40	26	Married	71	German	21
		41–50	25			Other Nationality	1
		51–60	22			n/a	3
		over 60	3				

permit. Out of the 75 respondents that answered this question, only 11 of them were very unsatisfied or unsatisfied with the application procedure for the residence permit.

The educational background of the respondents (see Figure 5.6) demonstrates that most of them are highly skilled. About 79 per cent of the respondents (64 respondents) had a tertiary education, while nearly 20 per cent (16 respondents) had a primary or secondary education. Among the 64 respondents who held a university or college degree, 27 had graduated from an institution of higher education both in China and in Germany. Thirty-five respondents had only graduated from a university or college in China. The majority of the respondents who had studied in Germany said that they self-financed their study abroad.

Thirty-eight respondents received their education in Germany. Among them, 26 established their own company in Germany, while the other 12 respondents worked for a Chinese company (Table 5.8). Twenty-two of the 35 respondents who graduated only from a university or college in China came to Germany to set

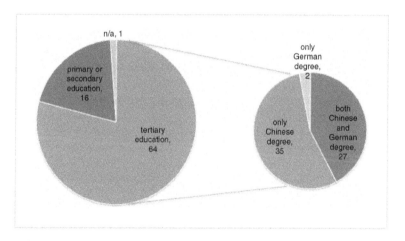

Figure 5.6 Respondents' educational background (*N* = 81)

Table 5.8 Breakdown of respondents' German educational background in relation to employment

	Employee	Entrepreneur	Total
German university degree	11	18	29
German primary or secondary education	0	3	3
Without German university degree	1	5	6
	12	26	38

up a business. Eleven of them were sent to Germany by the Chinese headquarters of their employer.

In total, the survey included 58 entrepreneurs and 23 employees. Among the 64 respondents with a tertiary education, there were 42 entrepreneurs. In other words, more than 70 per cent of those who were self-employed held a university or college degree. Almost all of the employees in managerial positions graduated from a university or college (see Table 5.9).

Regarding the self-appraisal of German language capabilities by employees and the entrepreneurs, it is important to note that half of all respondents assessed their German language skills as being good or very good. Only 21 per cent considered their German language skills to be bad or very bad (Table 5.10).

Most of those interviewed said that their field of study had been important for their current employment. Among the group of self-employed respondents who answered the question, 43 out of 54 said that their study had been either very important, important or somewhat important. For the group of employees, there was a similar result, with 78 per cent of them rating their study as having been important to varying degrees for their current employment (see Figure 5.7).

Assuming that not only the entrepreneurs but also the employees themselves are involved in the process of OFDI decision making, the questionnaire asked which specific function(s) Chinese migrants had with regard to Chinese investment in Germany.

More than half of the entrepreneurs stated that overseas Chinese have an important or very important influence on Chinese investment in Germany. They are crucial for Chinese companies' market entry and operations in Germany, as well as for accessing information on the German domestic market. Consequently, overseas Chinese are seen as being an important bridge between the home country and

Table 5.9 Breakdown of respondents' educational background in relation to employment

	Employee	Entrepreneur	Total
Tertiary education	22	42	64
Primary or secondary education	0	16	16
n/a	1		1
	23	58	81

Table 5.10 Breakdown of respondents' German language skills in relation to employment

	Employee	Entrepreneur	Total
Good	12	28	40
Middle	5	19	24
Bad	6	11	17
	23	58	81

the host country. In contrast, only 15 entrepreneurs stated that overseas Chinese could be helpful for the process of integration into Germany (Figure 5.8). With regard to the employees, similar results were obtained. They consider themselves to be taking the role of intermediary within Chinese companies (Figure 5.9).

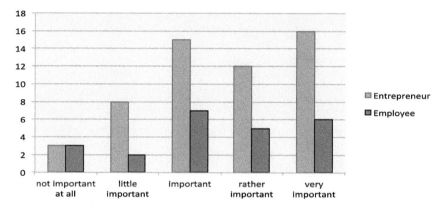

Figure 5.7 Respondents' assessment of the role of study for their current employment/ self-employment (entrepreneur = 54, employee = 23)

Note: Not all of the interviewees answered the question.

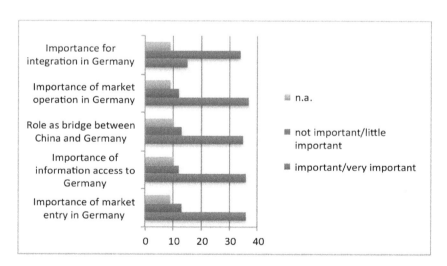

Figure 5.8 Entrepreneurs' assessment of the influence of overseas Chinese on Chinese investments in Germany (*N* = 58)

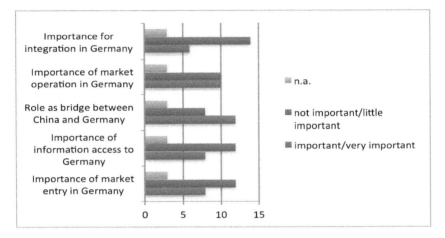

Figure 5.9 Employees' assessment of the influence of overseas Chinese on Chinese investments in Germany (*N* = 23)

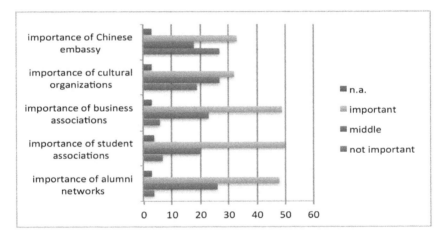

Figure 5.10 The role of Chinese diaspora networks (*N* = 81)

In their assessment of the importance of various diaspora networks, the majority of respondents stressed the crucial role that business and student networks, as
well as the alumni ones, play. Cultural associations were regarded by both entrepreneurs and employees as not important (Figure 5.10). The role of the Chinese
Embassy or consulates was assessed very differently. Nearly half of the entrepreneurs viewed the Chinese Embassy and consulates as important or very important
for the conducting of business in Germany, while nearly half of the employees
assigned Chinese Embassy and consulates less importance.

To our surprise, only 10 out of 77 respondents stated that they were a member of a formal overseas Chinese network. On the other hand, 63 out of 78

respondents declared that their own personal network was important with regard to business contacts leading to Chinese investments in Germany. Another interesting finding was that 50 respondents (out of the 74 who responded to this question) thought that networks were equally important in both China and Germany. An even larger number of respondents (64 out of 76 respondents) stated that formal and informal networks were difficult to distinguish from one another and often overlap.

5.5. Conclusion

In sum, the preliminary findings of our questionnaire survey suggest, on the one hand, that diaspora still matters. The success of Chinese migrant entrepreneurs in Germany is an important source of motivation for companies in Mainland China. Their business experience helps to reduce the transaction costs – associated with locational choice and information diffusion – that Chinese companies incur. Overseas Chinese working in Chinese-invested companies or German institutions have an important bridging role as well and therefore represent a positive diaspora externality. On the other hand, we can observe that many overseas Chinese do not establish or enter into traditional Chinese diaspora networks. This can be explained to some extent by the changes in the type of Chinese immigrants arriving since the late 1980s. The new generation of Chinese migrants are highly qualified, flexible and mobile – and thus less dependent on formal networks. We agree with the findings of Latham and Wu (2013: 12–13), that "the Chinese 'ethnoscape' has become more complex and diversified in recent years and Chinese communities have become more diverse not only in origin, education, skills and migration experience, but also in economic activity".

The Chinese migrants participating in our survey reflected the age demographic of Chinese citizens in Germany. They were mostly less than 50 years old and had a stable family background. They were almost all born in China but had lived in Germany for a long period of time before deciding to stay. Most of them possessed an unlimited residence permit or held a German passport. Our survey group's educational background is also in line with the strong number of highly skilled Chinese people living in Germany. Chinese migrants in our survey mostly had a tertiary education. This emphasizes the need to obtain a university or college degree as a precondition for later reaching a managerial position in a Chinese or German institution or company. The field of study played at least an important role for most of the Chinese migrants in our survey. In contrast, having advanced German language skills seems not be as important for those who are employed or entrepreneurs.

Overseas Chinese people living in Germany and the Chinese diaspora networks are important platforms for the exchange of business information and knowledge. Although formal networks such as business associations can reduce transaction costs for Chinese companies or individuals, most highly skilled Chinese migrants do not enter into traditional overseas Chinese associations – with the exception of into student associations. To some extent, they rely on the networking function of the Chinese Embassy or consulates – but generally prefer informal, private networks instead of formal networks.

In sum, our contribution has shown that Chinese migrants living in Germany help to overcome the psychic distance that exists between the two countries. This distance results in high information costs for Chinese companies with regard to investment opportunities, government regulations and/or the trustworthiness of potential business partners in Germany. Our paper pointed out that the number of Chinese students in Germany increased rapidly after 2001, with a strong focus on engineering, machinery, business and natural sciences. Although most of these students return to China after graduation, they possess specific knowledge about the German business culture and institutions that enables them to fulfil a bridging role between companies from both countries. Those Chinese students who decide to stay in Germany tend to set up their own companies, relying on their acquired expert knowledge and cultural understanding. They help Chinese investors who are unfamiliar with Germany and the German business landscape to reduce transaction costs.

Notes

1 Following UNESCO's definition of a "migrant", we use the term to denote a person living temporarily or permanently in a country where he or she was either born or not born and who has acquired some significant social ties to this country. This group does not include refugees but only those persons who made voluntary choices about when to leave and where to go.
2 The International Organization for Migration (IOM) provides a broad definition for those considered part of a diaspora as being "members of ethnic and national communities who have left, but maintain links with their homelands. The term 'diaspora' conveys the idea of a transnational population, living in one place, while still maintaining relations with their homeland, being both 'here' and 'there'". The European Commission (EC) shares the same understanding of the term and stresses the diaspora's "commitment to and/or interest in the country of origin" (Wickramasekara 2009: 3).
3 In the analysis of the patterns of Chinese outward foreign direct investment (OFDI), we differentiate between "greenfield investment", relating to the setup of companies, and "mergers and acquisitions" (M&A), which include the takeover of companies. Greenfield investment is regarded as the most effective means for transferring a company's competitive advantages to foreign countries. In contrast, acquisition is seen as being more effective when the absorption of knowledge from the acquired foreign company is intended (Sarala & Sumelius 2005). Following this line of argument, companies which are more technologically developed, such as the telecommunications giants Huawei or ZTE, will have a preference for greenfield investment. In contrast, M&A investment will be chosen by Chinese companies when they invest in a country with mature industries in order to gain access to strategic assets. Acquisitions in developed countries provide Chinese firms with the opportunity to access higher-value-added markets and to catch up with global market leaders. This also bolsters their ability to compete with multinationals in their home market (Child & Rodrigues 2005: 389).
4 Data collected by the GCB on FDI flows to Germany includes foreign companies with a balance sheet total of more than 3 billion euros and who possess an equity stake of more than 10 per cent.
5 The MOFCOM database includes the registration number of the investment project (证书号), the target country of the investment (国家/地区), the Chinese name of the investor (境内投资主体), the name of the overseas company or institution (境外投资企业（机构）), the subordination of the investor to the central government or local

government/province (省市), the business activities (经营范围), the date of approval (核准日期) and the registration date overseas (境外注册日期).

References

Baghdadi, L., & Cheptea, A. (2010) Migrant Associations, Trade and FDI, *Annals of Economics and Statistics*, No. 97/98, January–June, 71–101.

Barabantseva, E. (2005) *The Party-State's Transnational Outreach: Overseas Chinese Policies of the PRC's Central Government*. Greater China Occasional Papers No. 2. www.uni-tuebingen.de/uploads/media/2.pdf

Briggs, V. M., & Moore, S. (1994) *Still an Open Door? U.S. Immigration Policy and the American Economy*. Washington, DC: American University Press Public Policy Series.

Buch, C. M., Kleinert, J., & Toubal, F. (2006) Where Enterprises Lead, People Follow? Links between Migration and FDI in Germany, *European Economic Review*, 50, 2017–2036.

Casella, A., & Rauch, J. E. (2002) Anonymous Market and Group Ties in International Trade, *Journal of International Economics*, 58 (1), 19–47.

Cheung, Gordon C. K. (2004) Chinese Diaspora as a Virtual Nation: Interactive Roles Between Economic and Social Capital, *Political Studies*, 52 (4), 664–84.

Child, J., & S. B. Rodrigues (2005) The Internationalization of Chinese Firms: A Case for Theoretical Extension, *Management and Organization Review*, 1, 381–410.

Deutscher Akademischer Austausch Dienst (DAAD)/German Academic Exchange Service. (2012) *Wissenschaft weltoffen, Facts and Figures on the International Nature of Studies and Research in Germany, Focus Chinese Students at German Universities*. Bertelsmann Stiftung: Bielefeld. www.research-in-germany.de/dachportal/en/downloads/download-files/104658/daad-his-wissenschaft-weltoffen.pdf

Erber, Georg. (2012) German-Chinese Economic Relations – Opportunities and Risks, *DIW Economic Bulletin*, 3/2012, Berlin.

Federal Statistical Office Germany (FSOG). (2011a) *Micro Census 2011*. Berlin: Author.

Federal Statistical Office Germany (FSOG). (2011b) Ausländische Bevölkerung – Fachserie 1 Reihe 2–2011. Berlin: Author.

Federal Statistical Office Germany (FSOG). (2012) Hochschulstatistik (Statistics for Institutions of Higher Education). Wiesbaden: Author.

Federal Statistical Office Germany (FSOG). (2014) Trading Partner. www.destatis.de/DE/ZahlenFakten/GesamtwirtschaftUmwelt/Aussenhandel/Handelspartner/Handelspartner.html#Tabellen

Fukuyama, F. (1999, 1 October) Social Capital and Civil Sociology. International Monetary Fund. www.imf.org/external/pubs/ft/seminar/1999/reforms/fukuyama.htm

Gamlen, A. (2008) *Why Engage Diasporas?* Working Paper No. 63. Oxford: University of Oxford, ESRC Centre on Migration, Policy and Society. www.compas.ox.ac.uk/fileadmin/files/Publications/working_papers/WP_2008/WP0863%20A%20Gamlen.pdf

Gao, L., Liu, X. H., & Zou, H. (2013) The Role of Human Mobility in Promoting Chinese Outward FDI: A Neglected Factor? *International Business Review*, 22, 437–49.

Gao, T. (2003) Ethnic Chinese Networks and International Investment: Evidence from Inward FDI in China, *Journal of Asian Economics*, 14, 611–629.

Genc, M., Gheasi, M., Nijkamp, P., & Poot, J. (2011) *The Impact of Immigration on International Trade: A Meta-Analysis*. Norface Migration Discussion Paper No. 2011-20, www.norface-migration.org/publ_uploads/NDP_20_11.pdf

German Central Bank (GCB). (1998–2014) FDI Stock Statistics. Special Statistical Publication April 2014, 32–5 and 64–7, www.bundesbank.de/Navigation/DE/

Veroeffentlichungen/Statistische_Sonderveroeffentlichungen/Statso_10/statistische_
sonderveroeffentlichungen_10.html

Germany Trade and Invest (GTAI). (2012, 2 October) Germany Major Investment Partners. China. www.gtai.com

Gheasi, M., Nijkamp, P., & Rietveld, P. (2011) *Migration and Foreign Direct Investment: Education Matters*. Discussion Paper 136/3. Amsterdam: Tinbergen Institute.

Giese, K. (2005) Die Zhejiang Connection: Irreguläre Migration in der ersten Hälfte der neunziger Jahre. In Goeling-Che, H. W., & Dagmar, Y. D. (Eds.) *Migration und Integration der Auslandschinesischen in Deutschland*. Wiesbaden: Deutsche Morgenlandische Gesellschaft, 105–32.

Huawei Website. (n.d.) www.huawei.com/ilink/de/about-huawei/Huawei-in-Deutschland/index.htm

Ivlevs, A., & Melo, de M. (2008) *FDI, the Brain Drain and Trade: Channels and Evidence*. Working Paper, EUDN 2008–06, European Development Research Network, Namur. www.eudnet.net/download/wp/EUDN2008_06.pdf

Kugler, M., & Rapoport H. (2011) *Migration, FDI, and the Margins of Trade*. CID Working Paper No. 222. Cambridge, MA: Center for International Development at Harvard University.

Kuznetsow, Y. (2008) Mobilizing Intellectual Capital of Diasporas: From First Movers to a Virtuous Cycle, *Journal of Intellectual Capital*, 9 (2), 264–82.

Latham, K., & Wu, B. (2013) *Chinese Immigration into the EU: New Trends, Dynamics and Implications*. London: Europe China Research and Advice Network.

Ministry of Commerce of China (MOFCOM). (2013) *2012 Statistical Bulletin of China's Outward Foreign Direct Investment*. Beijing: China Statistics Press.

Ministry of Commerce of China (MOFCOM) Database. (n.d.) http://wszw.hzs.mofcom.gov.cn/fecp/fem/corp/fem_cert_stat_view_list.jsp

Mitchell, K., & Hammer, B. (1997) Ethnic Chinese Networks: A New Model? In Safarian, A. E., & Dobson, W. (Eds.) *The People Link: Human Resources Linkages Across the Pacific*. Toronto: University of Toronto Press, 73–97.

OECD. (n.d.) *Glossary of Foreign Direct Investment Terms and Definitions*. Paris: Author. www.oecd.org/daf/inv/investmentfordevelopment/2487495.pdf

Rauch, J. E. (2001) Business and Social Networks in International Trade, *Journal of Economic Literature, 39* (4), 1177–1203.

Rauch, J. E., & Trindade, V. (2002) Ethnic Chinese Networks In International Trade, *Review of Economics and Statistics*, 84 (1), 116–30.

Riddle, L., Hrvnak, G. A., & Nielsen, T. M. (2010) Transnational Diaspora Entrepreneurship in Emerging Markets: Bridging Institutional Divides, *Journal of International Management*, 16, 398–411.

Sarala, R., & Sumelius, J. (2005) The Impact of Entry Mode on Outward Knowledge Transfer in MNCs: International Greenfield Investments and Acquisitions, *Finnish Journal of Business Economics*, 4, 510–30.

Saxenian, A. (2000) *Silicon Valley's New Immigrant Entrepreneurs*. San Francisco: Public Policy Institute of California, Center for Comparative Immigration Studies.

Saxenian, A. (2005) From Brain Drain to Brain Circulation: Transnational Communities and Regional Upgrading in India and China, *Studies in Comparative International Development*, 40 (2), 35–61.

Schüler-Zhou, Y., & Schüller, M. (2013) Empirical Study of Chinese Subsidiaries' Decision-Making Autonomy in Germany, *Asian Business and Management*, 12 (3), 321–50.

Schüller, M., & Schüler-Zhou, Y. (2008) Chinesische Unternehmen kaufen in Deutschland. In Lucks, K. (Ed.), *Mergers & Acquisitions Jahrbuch*. Frankfurt: Bundesverband Mergers & Acquisitions, 18–20

Schüller, M., & Schüler-Zhou, Y. (2012) Markteintritt chinesischer Unternehmen: Direktinvestitionen und staatliche Flankierung. In VDMA (Verband Deutscher Maschinen- und Anlagenbau) (Eds.) Wettbewerber China. Herausforderungen und Trends. Frankfurt: VDMA Außenwirtschaft, 39–45.

Schüller, M., Meuer, J., & Schüler-Zhou, Y. (2012) *China's OFDI Footprint in Europe: Investment Patterns, Drivers and Implications*. Research Report for DG Enterprise and Industry, Manuscript, Hamburg and Zurich.

Song, X. M. (2003) Auslandschinesen. In Staiger, B., Schütte, H. W., & Friedrich, S. (Eds.) *Das große China-Lexikon*. Hamburg: Institut für Asienkunde, 37–44.

Tong, B. (2003) *The Chinese Americans*. Boulder: University Press of Colorado.

Wickramasekara, P. (2009) Diasporas and Development, Perspectives on Labour Migration No. 9. www.globalmigrationpolicy.org/articles/development/Diasporas%20&%20Development%20Conceptual%20&%20Measurement%20Issues,%20WICKRAMASEKARA%20%20ILO%202009.pdf

Wogart, J. P., & Schüller, M. (2011) The EU's Blue Card: Will It Attract Asia's Highly Skilled? *GIGA Focus International*, 3, 1–8.

Xu, T., Petersen, R., & Wang, T. L. (2012) *Cash in Hand. Chinese Foreign Direct Investment in the U.S. and Germany*. Report for the Bertelsmann Foundation, Berlin.

Yü-Dembski, D. (2005) Huaqiao – Geschichte der Auslandschinesischen in Deutschland. In von Groeling-Che, H. W., & Yü-Dembski, D. (Eds.) *Migration and Integration der Auslandschinesen in Deutschland*. Wiesbaden: Deutsche Morgenländische Gesellschaft, 27–56.

Appendix

Chinese Investment in the City of Hamburg based on the company registration

Year of establishment	Total number of companies registered	Number of active companies
–1989	49	21
1990–1994	102	32
1995–1999	144	71
2000–2004	351	167
2005–2009	242	165
2010–2012	118	108
2000–2007	496	256
2008–2012	214	184
k.A.	84	
Total	**1090**	**564**

Size of Chinese-invested Companies in Hamburg Based on Registered Capital (in euros)

Year	Total investment	Number of companies	Active companies' investment	Number of companies	Not active companies' investment	Number of companies
–1989	8,325,000	47	4,425,000	20	3,900,000	27
1990–1994	10,491,300	102	6,015,000	32	4,476,300	70
1995–1999	16,217,000	143	11,927,500	71	4,289,500	72
2000–2004	25,977,300	348	20,202,300	167	5,775,000	181
2005–2009	47,000,112	242	20,387,112	165	26,613,000	77
2010–2012	10,713,146	117	9,351,146	107	1,362,000	10
2000–2007	**58,994,550**	**495**	**37,731,550**	**254**	**21,263,000**	**241**
2008–2012	**24,846,008**	**213**	**12,209,008**	**185**	**12,637,000**	**28**
Total	118,723,858	999	72,308,058	562	46,415,800	437
Total	**118,873,858**	**1000**	**72,308,058**	**562**	**46,565,800**	**438**

6 Chinese investment strategies and migration – does diaspora matter?

Chinese migrants in Poland

Paweł Kaczmarczyk, Monika Szulecka and Joanna Tyrowicz

Abstract

For centuries, Poland has been – and still remains – a net emigration country, sending thousands of migrants to the United States and Western European countries. Notwithstanding, since the early 1990s, along with the socio-economic changes related to the transition from a socialist towards a market economy and liberalization in admission policies, Poland started to play a role in the European migration system. China was never an important sending country in the case of Poland. Contrary to some other countries of the region – particularly Hungary – inflows of immigrants from this country were of marginal importance. This situation started to change only recently. The scale of this phenomenon remains relatively low, but it presents some interesting features. Thus, the aim of this chapter is twofold. The first goal is to assess in quantitative terms the scale of flows and stocks of Chinese migration to Poland. The second is to ask the question whether it is possible to relate recent migration flows to investment activities of Chinese companies.

1. Introduction

For centuries, Poland has been – and still remains – a net emigration country, sending thousands of migrants to the United States and Western European countries. Notwithstanding, since the early 1990s, along with the socio-economic changes related to the transition from a socialist towards a market economy and liberalization in admission policies, Poland started to play a role in the European migration system. Already in the 1990s, Poland hosted various categories of migrants – transit migrants, asylum seekers and refugees, petty traders, highly skilled professionals and labour migrants. The most important countries of origin were post-Soviet countries (predominantly Ukraine) and Vietnam (as a side effect of close cooperation between these two countries in the communist era). The immigration grew in importance after Poland's accession into the European Union (1 May 2004). However, due to massive outflow of Polish citizens in the post-enlargement period, inflows of foreigners do not counterbalance emigration, and net migration remains clearly negative.

China was never an important sending country in the case of Poland. Contrary to some other countries of the region – particularly Hungary – inflows of immigrants from this country were of marginal importance. This situation started to change only recently. The scale of this phenomenon remains relatively low, but it presents some interesting features.

Against this background, the aim of this chapter is twofold: First, to assess in quantitative terms the scale of flows and stocks of Chinese migration to Poland. Second, to discuss the question whether it is possible to relate recent migration flows to investment activities of Chinese companies.

Due to the almost non-existent Chinese diaspora in Poland, we propose three possible ways of explaining links between migratory flows and FDI:

1. Chinese multinationals in Poland recruiting foreign line workers;
2. Chinese multinationals in Poland employing managerial staff (conditional on local/regional labour market conditions);
3. Endogenous investment process stipulated by Chinese migrants present in the country (explicit impact of the diaspora).

The structure of this chapter clearly refers to those three possible strategies. Section 2 looks at the recent Chinese migration to Poland but presents it in a broader context – of both Chinese migration worldwide and flows/stocks of immigrants in Poland. Section 3 provides an analysis of foreign direct investment (FDI) in Poland, with particular emphasis on Chinese capital. The next section is based on available quantitative and qualitative data and assesses links between Chinese FDI in Poland and migration flows. In this section, we refer to three potential explanatory avenues as suggested. Finally, section 5 concludes.

2.   Chinese migration to Poland

In general, in terms of Chinese migration, Poland is a negligible destination country, both when compared to the OECD and with reference to the EU as a whole. In fact, Poland attracts roughly as many Chinese as does the Czech Republic, with the latter being about four times smaller in terms of population; see Figure 6.1. As opposed to, for instance, Vietnam, the tradition of Chinese migration to Poland has never been prominent, which explains relatively lower inflows of Chinese to Poland following the economic transformation as of 1989. A second explanation consists of the observation that Poland is traditionally rather a sending country than a receiving one and, despite positive economic developments, is not perceived as an immigration magnet. Consequently, Chinese migration to Poland is economically and politically minor. Because of this, recent phenomena are even more intriguing.

The objective of this section is to present the scale and characteristics of Chinese migration to Poland. We first describe Chinese migration in general. We then move to describing the migration situation of Poland, which is a typical sending country. Finally, we discuss in detail Chinese migration to Poland. The analysis

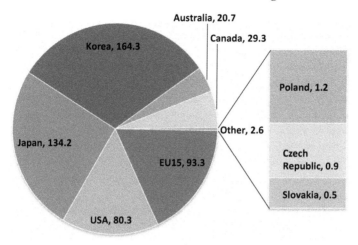

Figure 6.1 Major Chinese destination countries (thousands), data for 2008
Source: OECD

of the Chinese migration to Poland comprises the analysis of general inflows and inflows of workers (as two separate categories). We also present some evidence relating to industry and sector location of Chinese immigrants in Poland.

2.1.   Chinese migration – general overview

As clearly pointed out by Pieke and Speelman (2013), there is a clear structural break in China's migration history. Transcontinental Chinese migration on a massive scale started in the late nineteenth century and was related mainly to the so-called coolie trade (recruitment of indentured workers) and employment of coolie workers in labour-intensive sectors of American or Asian economies (e.g. sugar cane and cotton plantations).[1] The process of mass emigration from China was interrupted when the most important receiving countries, including the USA and Australia, introduced anti-immigration laws.[2]

The new wave of Chinese migration started only in the second half of the twentieth century along with political (and economic) changes in the People's Republic of China. The initial driver of the new wave of Chinese migration was a fundamental relaxation of the emigration policy, particularly, imposing – in 1985 – the new immigration law which allowed to travel abroad (relatively) freely and to make business with partners abroad (Pieke & Speelman 2013; Piłat & Wysieńska 2012). Chinese migration of that time (1970s to 1980s) has been relatively ordered both in terms of destinations (United States, well-established destinations in Europe) as well as regions of origin (Guangdong province, Zhejiang province; Pieke & Speelman 2013).

Importantly, these patterns of migration from China changed drastically in the 1990s and 2000s. According to many authors, the changes were driven mainly by changes in the Chinese society (economic reforms producing both winners and losers).[3] As a consequence, previous patterns of massive internal migration ("floating population") could be easily translated into a high propensity to migrate in international terms. This process was supported by rapid expansion of supporting services (migration as a business), growing scale of professional and scientific mobility and expanding role of China as source of capital (FDI)[4] (Pieke & Speelman 2013; Piłat & Wysieńska 2012). These changes were accompanied by a gradual change in immigration policies of the most important receiving countries – there is a clear tendency visible to move from strictly exclusivist policies introduced in the late nineteenth and early twentieth centuries towards far more friendly post-war policies (particularly in the USA and Canada). Consequently, migration has become a social mobility avenue for people of all social backgrounds (Pieke & Speelman 2013; Zhang 2013).

Today's China is one of the most migrant-sending countries worldwide. According to the estimates available, the size of the Chinese diaspora is as large as 35 million (80 per cent living in other Asian countries, 13 per cent in North America; Zhou 2009, quoted by Piłat & Wysieńska 2012). The number of Chinese migrants staying abroad (first generation only) is estimated at 8.3 million (2010), or 0.6 per cent of the total population (OECD 2012). The most important destination countries include Hong Kong, the United States, Japan, Canada, Singapore, Thailand, Australia, the Republic of Korea and EU countries (UK, France, Germany, Italy and Spain). Figure 6.2 presents the dynamics of recent Chinese migration to main destinations.

Interestingly, the scale of outflow from China remained high despite the economic crisis and was as high as 440,000 to 540,000 annually over the period 2005 to 2010 (OECD 2012). As the proxy of the importance of recent migration from China, the scale of remittances may serve – according to the MPI data, China is

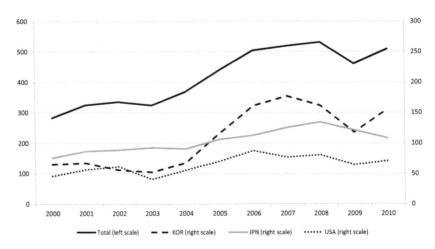

Figure 6.2 Legal migrant flows from China to the OECD (total and selected destinations), 2000–2010 (thousands)

Source: OECD

the second-largest recipient of migrants' remittances; in 2010, the scale of the transfer equalled more than 53 billion USD (MPI Data Hub).

Against this background, Chinese migration to Europeans destination is highly specific. First, its scale is far smaller than in the case of other continents. Estimates of the number of Chinese in Europe vary significantly. In 2008, it was assessed by Eurostat at 670,000 (2.1 per cent of total foreign population). Chinese sources provide far higher figures: 2.6 to 3.2 million in 2010 (Pieke & Speelman 2013). Figure 6.3 presents the main destinations of Chinese migrants and points to relatively small importance of European destination countries as compared to traditional migration magnets such as the United States, Canada, Australia or Asian countries.

Second, according to Laczko (2003), the structural features of this migration stream are also specific, being marked by relatively high shares of students, highly educated persons and, at the same time, irregular workers. The structure of receiving countries is also interesting. According to the recent data, since the 1990s the most dynamic inflow in Europe was noted in Southern European countries (particularly Italy and Spain) but also in Central and Eastern European countries (particularly Hungary[5]). The structural features and activities performed by Chinese migrants in European destinations differ significantly. In the case of Southern Europe, Chinese are very active in the business field (services, gourmet industry, gastronomy). In Central and Eastern Europe, trade and wholesale trade dominate. In Western European countries (particularly the United Kingdom), student migration plays the most important role.[6]

The presence of Chinese in Central and Eastern Europe was related both to political factors (as shown clearly by the Hungarian case) as well as to economic conditions. Chinese migrants were eager to set up informal "shuttle trade" and tool advantages

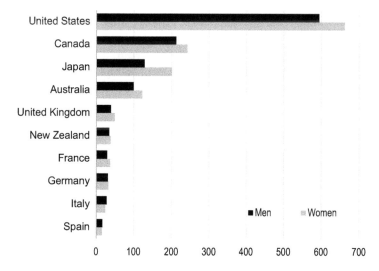

Figure 6.3 Ten main destination countries of Chinese emigrants in 2005/06 (thousands)
Source: OECD

of malfunctioning socialist economies. Nyiri (2003) pictures a new flow of Chinese entrepreneurial migrants who, having no prior connections in this part of Europe, managed to utilize even brief periods of liberal migration controls. According to Nyiri, there were two main factors responsible for increasing the scale of Chinese migration to Central and Eastern Europe: the political and social situation, particularly the Tiananmen Square movement that created anxiety among Chinese entrepreneurs regarding the private sector, and the recession that China experienced between 1989 and 1991 acting as the main push factor. As a consequence, Hungary became one of the main distribution centres of Chinese wholesale trade in Central Europe, supplying most of the neighbouring countries (see also Zhang 2013).

The scale of irregular migration of Chinese to Europe remains largely unknown. In the early 2000s, the stock of illegal Chinese migrants staying in Europe was estimated as high as 200,000. Notwithstanding, some institutions (e.g. European Federation of Chinese Organizations) provide far higher figures (roughly 1 million). Experts suggest taking a rather conservative stance on this point (Laczko 2003).

2.2.   Migration to Poland – general overview[7]

For centuries, Poland has been a traditional country of emigration. This situation started to change only in the early 1990s when, along with socio-economic changes, the first mass inflows of foreigners appeared. Notwithstanding, Poland remains a net emigration country; the scale of outflow significantly outnumbers the scale of immigration.

This statement can be supported by all kinds of available statistical data. The basis source of information on immigration to Poland is the Central Population Register, which provides information on persons who came from abroad and register for a permanent stay in Poland. The problem is, however, that these data comprise both Polish nationals and foreign nationals: they concern not only immigrants but also Polish returnees. The scale of registered immigration to Poland is very low – in the period 2001 to 2012, 142,900 persons registered in Poland for a permanent stay; in 2011, the number of permanent immigrants was around 15,500 persons; in 2012, it decreased to 14,600. However, the vast majority arrived from the countries of the European Union (72 per cent), which leads to an obvious conclusion that these data seem to include information rather about the return migration or migration of persons with Polish descent than inflow of foreigners.

A similar picture refers to the stock of temporary migrants, i.e. persons who arrived from abroad and registered for a temporary stay of more than 3 months in Poland (both foreigners and Polish nationals). According to the Central Population Register, in 2011, around 66,000 persons registered for a temporary stay in Poland, and 69 per cent of them stayed in the country less than 1 year. The main countries of previous stay included Ukraine (18,200, 28 per cent), Germany (8 per cent), Belarus (7 per cent), Vietnam (5 per cent), Russian Federation (4 per cent) and China (2,800, 4 per cent). Thirty-five per cent of them were staying in the Mazowieckie voivodship. In 2011, 42,600 residence permits were issued (a slight decrease as compared with 2010), and the structure of immigrants was similar to that already noted.

According to the 2011 National Census,[8] around 675,000 permanent residents of Poland (1.8 per cent of the total population) were born abroad. The major countries of origin were the territory of Ukraine (227,500), followed by Germany, Belarus and Lithuania. This number – relatively high by Central European standards – says nothing about the actual immigration: a significant portion of "foreign-born population" constitutes persons born outside the Polish territory, i.e. Polish citizens born either in pre-war Poland or abroad but relocated or displaced during the Second World War. In fact, only 7 per cent of foreign-born persons do not hold Polish citizenship. According to the 2011 Census, 55,400 (0.1 per cent) of those staying in Poland permanently were citizens of other countries, including 13,400 citizens of Ukraine (24 per cent), 5,200 citizens of Germany (9 per cent), 4,200 citizens of Russia (8 per cent), 3,800 citizens of Belarus (7 per cent) and 2,600 citizens of Vietnam (4.7 per cent). Most of foreign citizens live in Mazowieckie voivodship (17,200 – 31 per cent of the total). Importantly, the metropolitan region attracted 73 per cent citizens of Vietnam and approximately 30 per cent of citizens of Ukraine and Russia.[9]

A similar scale of the stock of immigrants can be estimated on the basis of the Labour Force Survey (LFS) data. Like other sources quoted, the LFS reveals a very low scale of immigration to Poland: in the years 2011 to 2012, the number of foreign citizens (aged 15 and above) was as high as around 40,00 to 45,000.

All the presented data show that the scale of both short-term and long-term immigration to Poland is very small or even marginal. It comprises mostly persons originating from former Soviet Union countries. The vast majority of all migrants reside in large cities, with around 30 to 40 per cent of them staying in Warsaw or Mazowieckie voivodship. The trends are very stable.

Contrary to this picture, there is a steady increase visible with regard to foreign labour admitted to Poland. The number of work permits granted in Poland has been increasing constantly since 2007 and in 2011 reached around 39,500 (13 per cent more than in the previous year; in 2012, this number decreased to around 38,100). Additionally, around 1,300 work permits granted to foreign sub-contracting companies were issued. The largest groups of foreign workers were citizens of Ukraine (35 per cent of the total), China (5,854, 14 per cent), Vietnam (6 per cent), Belarus (4 per cent) and Nepal (3 per cent). The main economic sectors of foreign employment included construction (22 per cent), retail and wholesale trade (17 per cent), household services (11 per cent), manufacturing (10 per cent), professional, scientific and technical activities (8 per cent) and hotels and gastronomy (7 per cent). A clear division of foreign workers is visible: work permit holders are dominated by qualified workers and workers performing simple jobs, employed mostly in retail and wholesale trade (the case of citizens of China, Ukraine, Vietnam), manufacturing (the domain of citizens of Ukraine), the construction sector (Ukraine and China), transport (Belarus) and households (Ukraine). More than half the work permits granted individually in 2011 were issued in the Mazowieckie region.

Since 2006, there has been a possibility to employ foreigners without the necessity of obtaining the work permit. According to the so-called simplified procedure, the citizens of Belarus, Georgia, Moldova, Ukraine and Russia are allowed to work up to 6 months during 12 consecutive months without work permit on the basis of a Polish employer's declaration of intent to employ a foreigner. The number of employers' declarations has risen steadily since 2006: it increased from almost 22,000 in 2007 to 260,000 in 2011 (235,000 in 2012). Ninety-two per cent of all persons who obtained the declaration were citizens of Ukraine. In 2011, the main economic sectors represented by the employers were agriculture and the construction sector, followed by manufacturing, household services and transport. The scale of the phenomenon shows significant potential for the increase of foreigners' employment in Poland.

2.3.   Chinese migrants in Poland – flows and stocks

The aim of the previous section was to provide a general background for the analysis of the presence of Chinese migrants in Poland. It was necessary to have a clear point of reference when looking at recent flows and stocks of Chinese citizens and analysing its structural features – both in terms of general patterns of Chinese migration as well as recent immigration to Poland.

Contrary to other countries of the region (particularly Hungary), Chinese immigrants were hardly present in Poland till the early 2000s. The scale of the phenomenon started to change only in the late 2000s. According to Piłat and Wysieńska (2012), reasons for such low interest in Poland as destination country were manifold:

- First, the Polish market was not perceived as an attractive one – in terms of the wholesale trade of goods imported from Asia, it was monopolized by a few businessmen from China. Also, there was harsh competition from the side of Armenian and Vietnamese immigrants;
- Second, the relatively strict migration policy of Poland was perceived as a serious barrier;
- Third was the unfriendly attitude of Polish administration towards Chinese immigrants;[10]
- Last but not least – and this is extremely important in the context of this report – as one potential reason, the very low level of Chinese FDI in Poland was treated. In the late 1990s, China was ranked 26th among all foreign investors in Poland (see section 3).

Apart from the low or very low scale of the phenomenon in absolute terms, it is important to analyse its relative importance. The presented data show that in 2000, inflow to Poland constituted 0.14 per cent of the total Chinese migration flows to OECD countries and 0.64 per cent of the inflow to the EU countries. Nine years later, those figures tripled or quadrupled (to 0.45 per cent and 2.47 per cent, respectively) but still remain very low. Poland as a potential destination for Chinese migrants is far less important than Germany, France or Southern Europe as well as – relatively speaking – other Central and Eastern European (CEE) countries.

It is believed that EU Enlargement posed a direct impulse for change in previously observed migration patterns. According to the Ministry of Foreign Affairs (2008), since 2005, a gradual increase with regard to main entry categories was noted. It refers to border crossings, visas and all kind of permits (as well as attempts for illegal border crossing). This tendency is clearly visible while analysing the dynamics of Chinese immigration to Poland – see Figure 6.5.

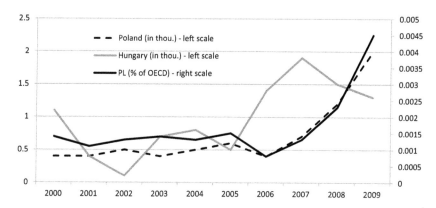

Figure 6.4 Chinese migrants to Poland and Hungary

Source: Own elaborations based on OECD data

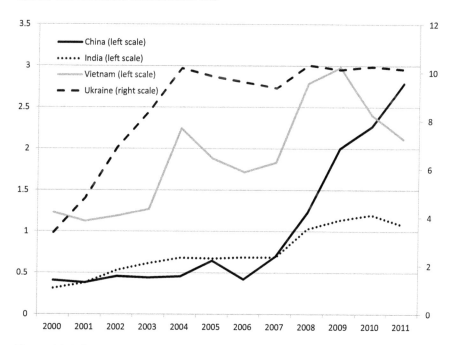

Figure 6.5 Inflows of foreigners to Poland (thousands) – selected immigrant groups

Source: Own elaborations based on OECD data

The data presented above show that there is a steady increase in scale of Chinese immigration visible since 2006. Since China is gradually becoming the most important migrants' sending country in Asia, so this increase is not a strange phenomenon. However, given that Poland is a country with a relatively low influx of foreigners, the growth of the number of Chinese migrants to Poland has shifted China to being currently (in 2011) the second-most-important sending country. In fact, China has outnumbered India and Vietnam, i.e. traditionally the second-most important sending country of immigrants to Poland. Possible reasons for this change will be discussed in section 3.

In 2011, 2,800 Chinese citizens registered for temporary stay in Poland. They constituted 0.42 per cent of all registered immigrants – a similar number to registered Vietnamese (0.49 per cent) and significantly fewer than Ukrainians (27.6 per cent; Kaczmarczyk 2013). Only 26 persons from China registered for permanent stay in Poland (0.17 per cent of all registered migrants), and this number was far lower than that of immigrants from Vietnam (0.35 per cent) and much lower than that of Ukrainians.[11]

As for the end of 2011, 3,821 Chinese immigrants were holding residence permits, and this number was much higher than a few years before (e.g. in 2007, it was only 1,095 persons). At the same time, an increase was noted in the number of work permits (see what follows).

As a consequence, the stock of immigrants from China in Poland remains extremely low. According to the PESEL database, in 2009, the number of registered Chinese immigrants was as high as 400 or 0.79 per cent of the total. The outcomes of the 2011 National Census have not been revealed yet, but according to the 2002 National Census, the number of Chinese immigrants (foreign born) amounted to 740 (0.09 per cent, according to OECD data). All presented data may suggest that inflow from China is of marginal importance for Poland. And it is important to note that this refers to the country with generally low intakes of foreigners. At the same time, however, Chinese immigration is growing in importance and recently outnumbered inflow from Vietnam, one of the most important migrants' sending countries in the Polish case.

2.4.   Chinese workers in Poland

Similar trends refer to mobility of foreign workers. There seems to be a clear division between migrant workers originating from neighbouring countries (not to mention persons relying on the simplified procedure) and those coming from more remote places, Figure 6.6.

Despite the economic slowdown, numbers of migrant workers from nearly all countries increased in Poland, but the growth was most pronounced in the case of Ukraine (as the most important country of destination). Nonetheless, since 2007, a clearly rising trend in inflow of Chinese workers is visible; see Figure 6.7. The scale of this phenomenon is far lower than inflow of immigrant workers from Ukraine, but in the last few years, Chinese overcame not only Indian immigrants but also migrant workers from Vietnam, i.e. one of the most important groups in Poland.

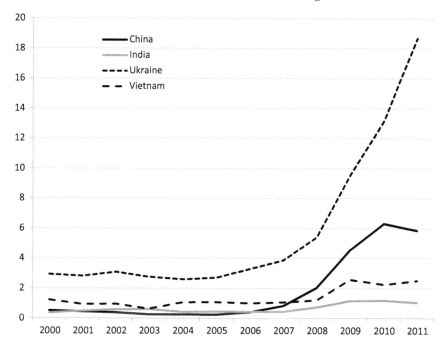

Figure 6.6 Inflows of foreign workers to Poland (thousands) – selected immigrant groups

Source: Own elaborations based on OECD data

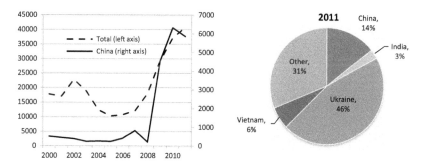

Figure 6.7 Inflows of foreign workers to Poland – selected immigrant groups

Source: Own elaborations based on OECD data

Between 2009 and 2011, Chinese workers constituted around 15 to 17 per cent of the total inflow as compared to 1.5 to 3.0 per cent in the early 2000s. In 2011, the scale of the inflow from China was more than twice as high as the inflow of workers from Vietnam. The data presented above may indicate a serious change in the migration patterns of Chinese in Poland, particularly if this trend continues in 2013 (preliminary data for 2012 show a significantly smaller number of work permits issued to Chinese citizens).

Except for the scale of inflow (in 2005, the number of Chinese immigrants holding work permit was as high as 240; in 2011, this number amounted to almost 6,000), the structure of work permits issued changed as well. Till the mid-2000s, the vast majority of work permits were issued to managers and specialists (more than 70 per cent). It reflected both the marginal scale as well as specific forms of inflow in that period. In contrast, in 2011, the share of these professions was lower than 20 per cent, and the majority of foreign workers constituted unquali-fied workers employed mainly in retail and wholesale trade (2,500) and construc-tion (1,300).[12]

Figure 6.8 reveals the change in the structure of Chinese employment patterns since the early 2000s (as noted). In 2011, except for managers or specialists, the relatively important group constituted manual (unqualified workers) – the share of this category was much higher than in a theoretically similar group, i.e. Vietnam-ese immigrants. The same holds true in the case of sectoral division of immigrant labour, as shown in Figure 6.9.

Chinese workers are employed predominantly in construction (roughly 20 per cent) and trade (around 40 per cent). This structure differs significantly from patterns observed of persons originating from Vietnam: work permits issued to Vietnamese workers were referring mainly to trade (around 60 per cent) and hotels/gastronomy (further 25 per cent). Thus, these data potentially reveal quite diverse migration strategies of migrants originating from these two Asian countries.

At the same time, Chinese citizens dominate among foreigners who obtained work permits for posted workers; see Table 6.1. In 2011, around 900 such permits (C-type permit) were issued for Chinese citizens, who constituted as much as 44 per cent of the total (twice as many as for Ukrainian immigrants!).

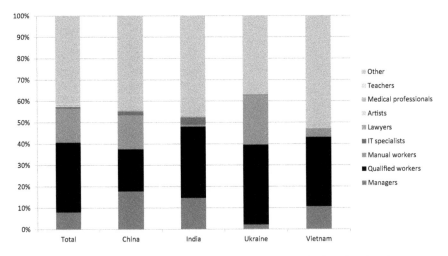

Figure 6.8 Work permits issued (individually) in 2011, by profession (% of total)

Source: Own elaboration based on Ministry of Labour and Social Affairs data

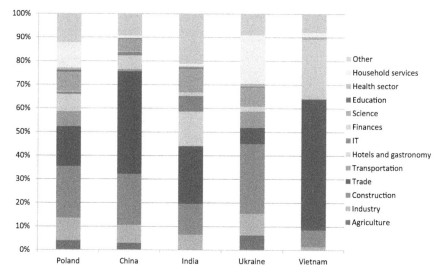

Figure 6.9 Work permits issued (individually) in 2011, by sector of economy (% of total)
Source: Own elaboration based on Ministry of Labour and Social Affairs data

Table 6.1 Work permits issued for posted workers, 2011, by type of profession

Country of origin	Total	Managers, experts	Qualified workers	Unqualified workers	Other
In thousands					
Total	2,136	280	532	687	637
China	**932**	**41**	**51**	**685**	**155**
India	129	19	3	0	107
Ukraine	454	43	316	1	94
Vietnam	17	0	17	0	0
As percentage of the total (for a given country)					
Total	100	13.11	24.91	32.16	29.82
China	**100**	**4.40**	**5.47**	**73.50**	**16.63**
India	100	14.73	2.33	0.00	82.95
Ukraine	100	9.47	69.60	0.22	20.70
Vietnam*	–	–	–	–	–

* not reported due to low number of observations.

Source: own elaboration based on Ministry of Labour and Social Affairs data

The majority of these workers constituted unqualified workers, and this pattern was significantly different in comparison with Ukrainian (mainly qualified workers) or Indian (large share of managers/specialists) posted workers.

Differences between main categories of posted workers are clearly visible while analysing data on sectoral composition; see Figure 6.10. Contrary to Ukrainian workers, who are being posted mainly by firms active in the industrial sector,

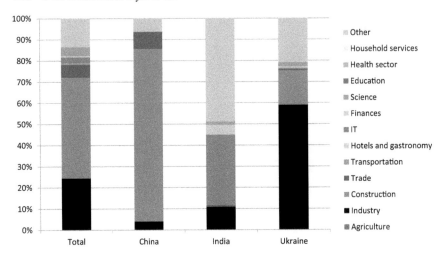

Figure 6.10 Work permits issued for posted workers, 2011, by sector of economy (% of total)

Source: Own elaboration based on Ministry of Labour and Social Affairs data

Chinese posted workers are predominantly employed in construction (around 90 per cent of the total). This tendency is related to changing patterns of Chinese investments in Poland as well as growing interest of Polish employers in foreign labour from China (Piłat & Wysieńska 2012).

3.   Chinese investments in Poland

FDI arriving to Central and Eastern Europe played two major roles. On the one hand, foreign strategic investors have been important for the privatisation of the state-owned enterprises. On the other hand, numerous greenfield investments as well as acquisitions of the incumbent private enterprises have contributed to changing the market structures as well. The inflow of FDI is widely believed to contribute greatly to increasing access to foreign trading networks, facilitate technology transfer and spillovers and enable the passing of the so called X-efficiency, i.e. superior management techniques to the transition countries. As research demonstrates, however, many of the FDIs have in fact been cherry-picking, thus having negligible effect on the firm performance (Hagemejer & Tyrowicz 2011). Notwithstanding, access to the foreign trading networks has been an important channel of raising the sales and export shares.

These arguments seem perfectly reasonable if one comprises FDI as flows from Triad countries[13] to transition economies of the CEE countries. However, flows between CEECs and across transition countries are less likely to be motivated by transfer of technology and more likely to be led by scope and scale economies. From this perspective, China, being the second-largest economy in the world, is not particularly interested or well fit for being active in CEECs. This long-lasting trend is partly changed, however, with the growing interest of the Chinese companies in supplying high-quality products to the markets of the industrialised countries. From this perspective, location in CEECs may be seen as a gateway to the EU15 markets. Observing FDI patterns, it seems that many of the Chinese FDI entries in the region were governed by either specific interest in that market or because CEECs were considered a gateway to EU15 markets.

The objective of this section is to describe the foreign direct investment flows to Poland as a background for the Chinese investments.

3.1. FDI flows to Poland – general overview

Being the largest country in Central and Eastern Europe, Poland has also consistently attracted most of the FDI that came to the region since the onset of transition. While both the flows and the stocks of FDI have been large in total numbers, in per-capita terms, countries like the Czech Republic or Hungary have outpaced Poland over the last two decades. It should also be noted that many FDI projects in the region have benefited from a number of tax-redemption instruments (including special economic zones) in the 1990s. Accession to the EU as of 2004 made it impossible to continue the preferential tax treatment policies, but for a many non–EU firms interested in easy access to EU15 markets, investment in Poland, the Czech Republic or Slovakia was a viable business strategy in the late 1990s and early 2000s.

In terms of origin, despite temporary trends, these were predominantly Triad countries that invested in CEECs, and Poland is no different in this respect. However, tax regulations in Poland until 2009 favoured investors from a few countries, i.e. Sweden, Luxembourg, Cyprus and the Netherlands. Consequently, the majority of non–EU originated FDI coming to Poland has arrived via these three countries, making it quantitatively impossible to infer from the official statistics what is the origin of foreign capital coming to Poland. This limits the scope of bilateral analyses to only EU countries (with the exception of the abovementioned four). The problem of gateway countries has been identified recently in the UNCTAD report on global FDI (UNCTAD 2013).

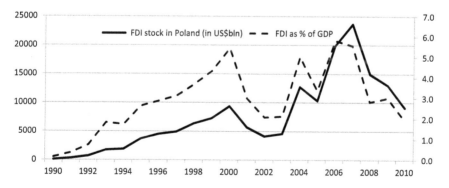

Figure 6.11 FDI stock in Poland

Source: Own elaboration based on OECD data

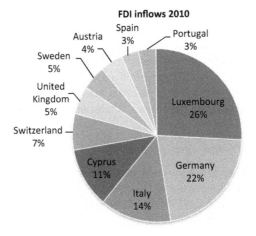

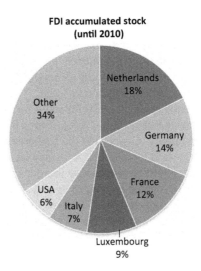

Figure 6.12 Foreign direct investment in Poland – inflow of capital in 2010 (% of total)

Source: Own elaboration based on the National Bank of Poland data

Given this important legal constraint, numbers concerning the origin of FDI coming to Poland should be interpreted with caution. In accumulated terms, major investors are Germany, France and Italy, as well as the United States. Nonetheless, gateway countries such as Luxembourg and the Netherlands play important roles, accounting for 27 per cent of the accumulated FDI stock. According to the official estimates, major investors in Poland consist of Luxembourg, Germany, Italy and Cyprus. Whereas Germany and Italy denote actual country of origin, Luxembourg and Cyprus are gateway countries through which FDI from other non–EU countries came.

3.2.   Chinese investments in Poland

Official numbers concerning Chinese FDI to Poland amount to as little as €2 million – €246 million over the past 10 years. These values are extremely low as compared to the total value of Chinese FDI, which amounted to US$366 billion globally and US$24.5 billion in Europe (in 2011; Zhang 2013). However, they do not reflect accurately the extent of engagement of the Chinese companies in the Polish economy. In fact, just one of the TV factories located in Koszalin (Digital View Inc.) has consisted of investment amounting to nearly €34 million in only the first year. Nuctech, having established one factory worth €25 million, planned to open another one, triple the size. Both these investments took place in a year when aggregate FDI inflow to Poland from China amounted to €19 million. This suggests that the extent of using the gateway countries may be considerable in the case of Chinese FDI to Poland.

With reference to industry composition, the FDI inflows of 2010 identifiable to China consist mostly of computers and electronics (27.5 per cent of total Chinese FDI to Poland) and trade (21.8 per cent of total Chinese FDI to Poland). These two sections dominated also in 2011, amounting to 48.6 per cent and 26.9 per cent of total Chinese FDI to Poland, respectively.[14] It should be noted, however, that these numbers may be misleading, as an unknown part of Chinese FDI to Poland comes *via* gateway countries. This observation is clearly consistent with the analysis of Zhang (2013) who pointed out that Luxembourg is the most important host country for Chinese FDI in Europe (around 37 per cent of the total European FDI) while hosting only 0.01 per cent of Chinese migrants.

4.   Does diaspora matter? Chinese migration and FDI flows

The picture presented in the previous section proves that analysis of links between Chinese diaspora and FDI flows to Poland need to be conditional on the specific position of Chinese migrants in the country, particularly on the fact that Chinese diaspora is hardly existent. Thus, what might make sense in the Polish context is to look rather at the impacts (or potential impacts) of capital flows on migration process rather than vice versa. Following this line of reasoning, next, two short sections discuss potential impacts of Chinese FDI on inflows of both unskilled and highly skilled migrants from China. The last one focuses on a clear case of endogenous investments undertaken by members of the Chinese community in Poland.

4.1.   Chinese FDI as a driver of mass migration

The answer to the question whether Chinese FDI can lead to a massive inflow of Chinese workers is highly conditional on the labour market conditions in Poland. The point is that while the *de nomine* difference in wages in Poland when compared to China is considerable, manual workers' compensations usually do not exceed substantially a minimum wage level. Minimum-wage legislation is relatively strictly enforced in Poland, which implies that any investor willing to lower employment costs by seeking cheaper labour from its country of origin would need to comply with this requirement. Furthermore, legislation requires the employer to prove that adequate Polish workers are not available before work permits for foreigners are granted. While this legislation is not strongly enforced, the majority of larger-scale investment projects involve the engagement of the local authorities, who are interested in creating jobs for their constituency. Consequently, there is a variety of stakeholders able to use formal constraints on employing foreign manual workers accompanying the FDIs.

Moreover, wages are still relatively low in Poland when compared to Western Europe. The majority of FDIs locating in CEECs establish their production sites to lower the transportation costs to the European Union. In the case of Poland, the relatively large size of the internal market is an additional driver. Business-wise, employing local workers offers a sufficient cost advantage. Thus, in most cases, linking FDI activity with importing of foreign labour seems not to be the most efficient strategy.

Finally, depending on sector, local workers may actually be more able than expats. COVEC constitutes one such example. COVEC (China National Overseas Engineering Corporation) is one of the largest Chinese companies operating in the construction sector (and the world's third largest). It is a member enterprise of China Railway Engineering Corporation (CREC), a large-scale construction company operating under the supervision of the Chinese government. Observing large-scale public infrastructure investment projects undertaken by the Polish government, COVEC has participated in a tender for road construction (two sections of the A2 highway for a cost of US$450 million[15]). Having won the contract (in 2009), COVEC has realised that with the intensifying of public investment, the subcontractors and suppliers are not able to satisfy the demand for services and raw materials.[16] These problems were common to all investors at that time, but local engineers and logistic specialists were able to at least partially by-pass the physical constraints. It seems that COVEC's strategy was to employ local subcontractors and offer them far lower rates than the market ones. This strategy turned into complete failure. Under the circumstances, COVEC, which largely relied on Chinese specialists, was unable to fulfil the contract and had to abandon the project without settling with the subcontractors. In early May 2011, most of the Chinese workers did not return to work, and machinery operations were suspended. A few weeks later, COVEC suggested a new price around 70 per cent higher than the original bidding price, but this was rejected by the Polish government (and the whole issue ended in court).

In purely speculative terms, it is possible that the positive example of COVEC might have positively impacted attitudes towards large-scale Chinese investments and also fostered import of Chinese workers. On the contrary, COVEC's failure significantly impacted public perception of Chinese business activities in Poland.

4.2. *Chinese FDI as a driver of highly skilled and managerial mobility*

According to Piłat and Wysieńska (2012), spatial concentration of Chinese migrants in Poland is strictly correlated with Chinese FDI. A report presented by

KPMG in 2011 (KPMG 2011) suggests that Chinese investments are concentrated in several Polish locations, and those locations are becoming migration magnets for Chinese people. Obviously, large a share of them constitute highly skilled migrants – managers and professionals; see section 3.4.

However, due to data limitations – as shown in the previous section – this hypothesis cannot be verified empirically. From the data presented in section 3.4, it follows that the share of managers among Chinese labour migrants is twice as high as compared with Vietnamese (and much higher than in case of Ukrainian workers); see Figure 6.8. At the same time, there is a clear structural pattern visible, with large numbers of Chinese workers employed in construction and industry. Nonetheless, there is no empirical evidence linking these patterns to investment activities of Chinese companies.

Another explanation for this phenomenon is related to the highly skilled migrants from China. Many investors prefer to delegate managerial and specialist positions to expats, and Chinese FDI does not differ in this respect. However, the majority of Chinese FDI occurs in relatively capital intensive industries, where the production workers require only small "human" supervision and management. For example, due to automatisation, a production line staffed mostly with Polish manual workers may require one manager at each shift. Production levels as well as more strategic decisions are taken at the headquarters of the FDI sending company. So are research and design as well as financial management. This lowers substantially the scope for demand for Chinese managers and experts.

On the other hand, the very fact that the Chinese diaspora is present in Poland generates a need for ethnic services, which in the future may reinforce the originally minuscule effect (see next section).

4.3. *Chinese investments as an endogenous process*

The main aim of this section is to assess one particular case of Chinese investment activity in Poland which is strictly related to migration process and, in our opinion, may serve as an example of endogenous investment process conditional on the presence of a Chinese community. In parallel, we will attempt to compare two important Asian communities in Poland: Chinese and Vietnamese immigrants.

As noted, regarding immigration from Asia, Vietnamese constitute the largest and the most visible migrant community in Poland. The history of their presence is longer and far richer than in the case of Chinese immigrants, who are definitely less numerous in Poland. Interestingly, migration researchers tend to compare the Vietnamese community not with other Asian groups[17] but with the Ukrainian one. This kind of comparison is marked by significant differences: different patterns of integration (in every dimension), different opportunity structure stemming from legal rules (privileges for Ukrainian nationals), different language and cultural distance influencing the potential for integration and, last but not least, different patterns of mobility (e.g. Grzymała-Kazłowska 2008). It could be assumed that fewer differences would be observed when comparing Vietnamese with Chinese migrants in Poland. With regard to sectors of activity, Chinese, similarly to Vietnamese, are involved in trade and catering. However, Chinese's involvement in the Polish economy is not limited to these two sectors, as it is (to a large extent) in the case of Vietnamese. Chinese are also significantly present in other sectors of economy (see section 3).

Although Vietnamese in Poland are treated as the best-organized migrant community, which is visible through many formal and informal associations and organizations (Piłat & Wysieńska 2012), Vietnamese seem to be acting more independently than Chinese. However, this is rather the Chinese community, which is more scattered in Poland. Chinese investments in Poland cover not only the trading centres, restaurants or ethnic services, like in case of Vietnamese, but also many other sectors. The advantage of Chinese in Poland, in economic terms, depends mostly on the size of investments and international business contacts. This feature is extremely important due to the fact that far more numerous Vietnamese communities in Poland became dependent on the Chinese, at least in the sector that is occupied by the majority of Vietnamese immigrants in Poland, namely trade in imported goods from Asia.

Migration and adaptation patterns of immigrants from Vietnam and China differ as well. Although both communities are strongly based on the collectivistic attitude, respect for elderly people, specific perception of the family, attachment to home country, mother tongue and culture and readiness to support families and co-ethnics, their functioning in Poland shows that there are many differences in how they find themselves in the receiving societies and how their relationships with others look. Chinese, as those coming from the "Middle State",[18] seem to treat others in a way that emphasizes their superiority. This does not allow them to establish close relationships with the representatives of either the receiving society or, for instance, the Vietnamese community. Next, the majority of Chinese migrants in Poland are temporary migrants, and this differs significantly from migration patterns of Vietnamese who declare to be in Poland only temporarily while establishing more and more ties to Poland and becoming settled migrants.

Both similarities and differences are particularly well identifiable in such places that concentrate migrants from both ethnic groups. One of the most known cases of such concentration is the huge trading centre or, to be more precise, wholesale market, in Wólka Kosowska near Warsaw.[19] It concentrates mostly Chinese and Vietnamese entrepreneurs, but also Polish, Turkish and Indian ones. The fact that large numbers of representatives of several national groups meet there does not mean that there is interethnic communication that would relate to other things than business issues. National groups, including Chinese, limit their social contacts to co-ethnics. Although in Poland there are many other places that concentrate lower numbers of Chinese traders (e.g. in Jaworzno, where only Chinese entrepreneurs act next to less numerous Polish traders), the trading centre in the village being the suburbs of Warsaw, in Wólka Kosowska, constitutes a perfect place to be studied in several contexts regarding Chinese diaspora, including types of economic activity, interethnic relations, relations with local authorities, motivation to learn Polish legal, economic and social norms, culture, language and the role played in the wholesale market offering imported goods from Asia. The situation observed in Wólka Kosowska may reveal many features of Chinese migration to Poland in general and its linkages to investment activities.

Wólka Kosowska is a small village situated about 30 kilometres from the centre of Warsaw. In the 2000s, it became famous not only in Poland but also in the CEE region because of the establishment of the large trading centre. The first market halls were built by the Chinese investors (GD Poland company) in the mid-1990s. Other halls were built a few years later, at the beginning of the 2000s, by other foreign investors, mainly Vietnamese and Turkish immigrants. Although currently, the complex of market halls is owned by several national groups, these are the Chinese who established the trading centre and still have significant shares in it ruling the conditions of trading space for rent or offering goods to be sold in wholesale or retail trade. Interestingly, already in the mid-1990s, Chinese businessmen chose the agricultural area near Warsaw to build there large market halls, supposed to serve mainly wholesale purposes and to become the centre of wholesale trade of goods imported from Asia (mainly from China) in the region. And their vision of the future of this locality in Wòlka Kosowska is claimed to be very accurate, which according to some businessmen from the trading centre in Wólka Kosowska is not surprising, since Chinese are treated as those who carefully study the conditions for possible investments and very rarely make mistakes.[20] In the early 2000s, Vietnamese and Turkish investors, following the Chinese investment, found this locality perfect for further business development. The appearance of other foreign investments in Wólka Kosowska was to some extent linked to the more and more real perspective of closing the main open-air market located in the area of the 10th Anniversary Stadium in the centre of Warsaw ("Jarmark Europa"), which for several years constituted the place of work for many migrant salespeople, starting from small retail traders to very influential businessmen, owning various businesses often linked to both trade and catering.

As already indicated, representatives of other migrant communities (especially the Vietnamese one) perceive the Chinese choices as a guarantee of success and often follow them in business terms. Moreover, these are the Chinese who have the best contacts and opportunity to import directly from China, which facilitates their trading activity and causes other migrant traders to become dependent on them. Thus, in practice, Chinese may dictate terms and conditions of cooperation. And this is mainly due to direct contacts in China and knowledge about the manufacturing process there. Their position in the trading centre in Wólka Kosowska seems to be more advantageous than the position of other migrants. This also causes the Chinese investments in trade to attract other Chinese investors or workers, not only those interested in wholesale but also those who plan to operate in other sectors, e.g. in real estate. However, the admission policy, in particular obtaining visas, sometimes occurs to constitute a significant barrier on the way to Poland, where other Chinese migrants already reside (often temporarily) and do their business or work in Poland. Nevertheless, Chinese migrants still own a large part of the whole market in Wólka Kosowska, which means that hiring trading boxes is also ruled and valued by them. In business relations, they are not focused on cooperation with co-ethnics only. They offer their services and trading space for rental to anyone who can afford to run their own trading company in Wólka Kosowska.

The main Chinese investment in Wólka Kosowska is the "GD Poland Investments Ltd", often called the Chinese Trade Center. It is presented by the company as "the largest distribution location of goods and merchandises from China and entire Asia and it is at the same time the greatest Chinese investment in the region. The investment reached over 50 million USD and is situated on 200 thousands sq. meter yard".[21] The centre consists of six trading buildings, three warehouses and a hotel for people renting trading boxes in the centre or clients coming from distant places. The premises of the centre serve not only trading purposes. There are many additional services available in GD centre, namely bank office, exchange offices, restaurants, grocery shops, legal and tax advisory offices and a post office. In general, the offer of the sellers (mostly wholesale traders) in the GD halls includes clothes, shoes, accessories, small electronics and AGD appliances and fancy goods (also original Asian food is available in the centre). To emphasise the role and significance of this investment, the GD company presents the trading centre as "beyond competition in this craft", stating that the centre "is visited by the customers from all over Poland and neighbouring countries as well. Networks of hypermarkets like Auchan, Geant and Carrefour also do some shopping here".[22] In this way, the Chinese investors try to dispel the myth that hypermarkets are threats for such trading centres, at the same time inviting people to shop in Wólka Kosowska, which will be cheaper than shopping in the hypermarkets. Nevertheless, the character of the GD trading centre in Wólka Kosowska is based on wholesale, which means the centre is not a real alternative for retail buyers. For such people, Chinese have another offer: numerous small Chinese markets in many Polish towns and even villages, especially in the regions considered less wealthy (eastern and southern part of the country).

In the qualitative study (Klorek & Szulecka 2013), it was confirmed that the fact that many Chinese run their businesses or work as hired employees in the trading centre causes that specific services, targeted at the Chinese, became available in the surroundings. For instance, Chinese enjoy gambling: they play cards, use slot machines or visit casinos. One of Warsaw's casinos is located in Janki, on the way from Warsaw to Wólka Kosowska, and part of its personnel constitute Chinese. It is possible to have driving lessons in Chinese in the neighbourhood of Wólka Kosowska. Chinese may be also provided with translation services, although the demand for them seems to be bigger than the current supply. Importantly, many services advertised in the area of the trading centre are presented also in Chinese. This shows that the presence of Chinese contributed to the development of services that are aimed at satisfying not only social needs (restaurants, casinos) but also needs that will improve the conditions of daily routines, such as work, commuting, taking care of children and housekeeping. Thus we have to do with a very interesting case: the first impulse was given by Chinese investment; at the moment, the presence of a growing Chinese community attracts investors from China and from other countries. The impact of diaspora is clear in this case.

In the area of Wólka Kosowska, Chinese invested not only in the trading halls. They also built luxury housing, which now constitutes the place of living for those well-to-do immigrants. To some extent, buying a house in such an area could be seen as a form of another investment, since it happens that part of the houses or other premises (e.g. a garage) are used to accommodate co-ethnics who are newcomers and have to start their living in Poland being dependent on those who are wealthier and more familiar with the economic reality in Poland. Such practices constitute a kind of an incentive for the newcomers, who would not decide to come to a foreign country if they were not convinced that they would get support from co-ethnics.

In terms of adaptation/integration, Chinese are rather distanced towards the receiving society and other immigrant communities. The relations established by Chinese immigrants in Wólka Kosowska are mostly based on economic ties, and these are usually Chinese who rule these contacts due to their better access to goods produced in China. The relations with another Asian community, namely Vietnamese, who are claimed to be still more numerous than the Chinese in Wólka Kosowska, are perceived as strained. Although with regard to business matters, they have to communicate with each other, even if they are not interested in establishing more social contacts. It happens, however, that in order to maintain positive business relations, Chinese and Vietnamese invite each other to social events, such as weddings or special dinners for business partners. It is of note that this is often done in basic Polish, which constitutes the language of their communication. In general, however, Chinese are not eager to learn Polish. They treat this country or even this specific place as only a temporary place of residence, which will change immediately if staying in this concrete location becomes no more profitable. In that sense, Chinese are claimed to be very mobile, not focused on establishing stronger ties with the receiving community. As representatives of the receiving society claim, Chinese are convinced that their tongue should be learnt by others rather than they should learn the language of the receiving society.

Often, Chinese are seen as people who express their superiority in various aspects of life. For instance, this refers to mixed marriages or sending children to schools. Importantly, those Chinese immigrants who can afford this send their children to American or British schools in Poland, which causes that still there are no opportunities for the children to learn the Polish language. However, on the level of relations between those who have a kind of power and influence (e.g. owners of GD company and local government), the situations looks different. Chinese investors show their interest in improving various aspects of the local area and even invest in local infrastructure. According to information acquired in the course of qualitative studies (Klorek & Szulecka 2013), the Chinese community concentrated in the suburbs of Warsaw comprises mostly economic migrants, single persons, without families. However, there are exceptions: mixed marriages and families with small children. Recently, a new multicultural kindergarten (called Panda) was opened in the area, and from the very beginning it was planned for both Chinese and Vietnamese children.[23]

Importantly, Chinese investments in trade in Poland are sometimes associated with an enormous threat to local economy and tax interests. Chinese are blamed for the bankruptcy of small Polish entrepreneurs, "flooding" the market with cheap and low-quality goods produced in Asia. The way they operate in such places as the trading centre in Wólka Kosowska is associated with the informal economy and fraud. The sight of luxury goods (cars, mobile phones) possessed by Chinese migrants, even by "ordinary sellers", provokes negative comments among the members of the receiving society, who consider the way they acquire their capital as not fully honest. Although the significant extent of informal operations may be observed in the economic activity of many Chinese migrants, it should be also emphasised that perceptions of Chinese migrants do not often involve any reflections referring to Asian culture, in which, for instance, economic status is shown through such attributes as luxury goods (vehicles, clothing, communication devices), and business is based on many informal arrangements and negotiations (see, e.g., Klorek & Szulecka 2013; Żabowska 2012).

In terms of migration strategies, Chinese do not treat Poland as an attractive destination country. Rather, they plan to return to China as soon as they accumulate satisfactory capital in Poland (or in any other country of the EU; Klorek & Szulecka 2013). Additionally, opposite to Vietnamese, their declarations about return are more likely to become reality. The fact that Chinese parents send their children to British or American schools in Poland or to study abroad also shows that this is not the return to China, which is the main aim of immigrants who are currently in Poland. The choice is, however, the "luxury" of those who can afford to be independent and have stable sources of income to support themselves and their families, who are often still in the home country. Individual strategies of less wealthy Chinese migrants differ significantly from the strategies of more influential investors. Despite the crisis, businessmen still have plans to occupy next positions in the market of wholesale and retail trade. Some Chinese see that consumers appreciate low prices offered in the Chinese markets, appearing in more and more locations in Poland, and respond to this accordingly. As the observation in Wólka Kosowska showed, Chinese running their own smaller businesses notice and experience the competition and try to create more and more attractive conditions of trading operations. Nonetheless, they will put efforts in improving their economic situation through entrepreneurships or work in Poland as long as they see it profitable. Supposedly, Chinese operating in Wólka Kosowska will increase their dominance over other national groups, even if Chinese stay less numerous. However, their success is also dependent on the presence and entrepreneurial activities of other groups, including mostly Vietnamese.

5.   Conclusions

Growing FDI activity of Chinese companies together with the increase in Chinese international mobility raises important questions about linkages between these two processes. In this chapter, we aimed at referring to this issue, but it was clear that the answer is conditional on data availability (quality) and the very nature of this process itself.

Data suggest that while both FDI and migration from China to Poland is growing, they are still phenomena of relatively limited scale. Some past experiences suggest that there are some industries in which FDI will continue to grow, perhaps fostering the migration processes as well. Such investment projects create jobs locally, partly for the Polish workers, and, from the perspective of a local community, contribute significantly to the local economy. The case of Wolka Kosowska presented in this report (section 4.3) constitutes one such example. The contrasting case of COVEC shows that Chinese business strategies do not necessarily fit European reality, and they can negatively impact both future capital and labour flows.

On the other hand, a large proportion of the Chinese migrants to Poland work as ethnic entrepreneurs, occupied in either trading or gastronomy. While these inflows contribute to expanding ethnic diversity in Poland, they were not large enough to affect aggregate scale processes. Again, the case of Wolka Kosowska shows that the presence of a growing Chinese community can easily induce endogenous investment processes and lead to perpetuation of both Chinese investments and immigration. Due to extraordinary changes in migration dynamics observed in recent years, Poland is thus to be perceived as a very attractive field to trace development of Chinese diaspora (and its impacts on business activities).

Notes

1 Altogether, several millions of Chinese were sent as indentured workers to more than 40 countries between the 1830s and 1940s (Castles & Miller 2009).
2 It is important to note that the first anti-immigration measures such as Chinese Exclusion Act (United States) or Immigration Restriction Act 1901 (Australia) were aimed at this particular immigrant group.
3 In this respect, China may serve as a perfect example of the hypothesis stated by Douglas Massey (1999) that migration is not a product of stagnation, but it rather results from socio-economic change.
4 The best example of this kind of mobility is Chinese migration to Africa. According to the data available, the number of Chinese companies investing in African countries is close to 1,000. These companies are often followed by migration streams – their size was estimated at 200,000 to 300,000 annually in the late 2000s (Kuang 2008; Politzer 2008; Sautman 2006).
5 Chinese migration to Hungary constitutes a very special case. This is mostly due to very close relations between the Hungarian and Chinese governments in the communist era. In 1988, a bilateral agreement on the visa-free regime was signed, which led to a significant increase in the number of Chinese migrants in Hungary. According to Nyiri (2003), the scale of border traffic increased from 11,000 in 1990 to almost 30,000 in 1991. Due to the very large scale of the inflow (45,000 between 1989 and 1991), in 1992, the migration policy concerning Chinese citizens was changed; however, this first impulse gave a chance for gradual development of a Chinese diaspora in Hungary (Nyiri 2003; Piłat & Wysieńska 2012).
6 For example Chinese students are the single most important group among foreign students admitted at British universities.

172 *Paweł Kaczmarczyk et al.*

7 This section is based on Kaczmarczyk (2013). For the sake of comparability with the National Census data, year 2011 is taken as a point of reference (but in some cases, we refer to the most recent data available).

8 Full outcomes of the census are not available yet.

9 Additionally, the 2011 National Census revealed around 56,300 permanent residents of other countries staying temporarily in Poland; therein, 40,100 were staying in Poland for at least 3 months. Thus the total number of foreigners could be estimated around 110,000.

10 In fact, Chinese immigrants are subject to the same set of rules as other third-country nationals. They are obliged to possess a visa to enter Poland. However, the number of entries based on the visa procedure does not cover all Chinese coming to Poland. According to the Polish data, about 50 per cent of all entries by Chinese into Poland are performed within the visa-free regime. This is possible because about 8 million Chinese possess official passports, issued by 56 governmental institutions in China. This category of travellers as well as those possessing diplomatic passports may enter Poland (and other EU countries) without the need to possess a visa, which makes assessment of the whole story really difficult (MSWiA 2008).

11 Available data suggest that the scale of irregular migration from China is relatively low, particularly as compared to Vietnamese migrants (Piłat & Wysieńska 2012).

12 There are methodological problems with the data provided by the Polish Ministry of Labour and Social Policies. Categories presented are not necessarily exclusive; additionally, the scale of not-qualified permits remains extremely high.

13 The so-called Triad is a group of three major trading and investment players in the global scale and includes the United States, the European Union and Japan.

14 Data courtesy of the National Bank of Poland.

15 Importantly, the price proposed was about half the costs estimated by the Polish government.

16 Reports by the government and by industry representatives suggest that the whole sector had problems in accessing concrete, asphalt, drainage channels and so forth. Imports were infeasible because the ability of the transport companies to relocate such heavy and voluminous cargo was already exhausted.

17 Other than Chinese or Vietnamese groups are subject of the study on Turkish, Pakistani, Armenian and Indian migrants in Poland, conducted by the Institute of Public Affairs in 2012–1013; see www.isp.org.pl/ygiel-kulturowy-czy-getta-narodowosciowe-wzory-integracji-i-wzajemne-relacje-imigrantow-z-azji-i-bli,688.html.

18 Although the tradition of treating others as barbarians is much weaker, still treating China as the centre of the world determines the mentality of both non-migrants and emigrants from China, including those who came to Poland. See Tomala (2001).

19 Information regarding Chinese migrants functioning within the trading centres in Wólka Kosowska is based on the results of the study focused on migrants' economic institutions and their influence on the local community as part of a wider project titled "Różni, ale równi – badania nad równym traktowaniem migrantów w Polsce" ("Different, but equal – the study on treatment of migrants in Poland"), conducted by Stowarzyszenie Interwencji Prawnej (Association for Legal Intervention) and Instytut Spraw Publicznych (Institute of Public Affairs) in 2012. For more information about the study and main results, refer to Klorek and Szulecka (2013).

20 Opinion provided by Vietnamese entrepreneur functioning in Wólka Kosowska for more than a dozen years now.

21 The website of the GD company: www.gdpoland.pl/en/onas.php

22 The website of the GD company: www.gdpoland.pl/index.php

23 Although the owners expected that foreigners would be more interested in sending children to this educational unit, the effects were not very satisfactory at the beginning. Nonetheless, the owners still see the Chinese as the main immigrant community

in Wólka Kosowska and even consider learning Chinese themselves, treating this as prospective investment. On the contrary, as was mentioned earlier, Chinese in Poland do not see the need to invest time and money to learn Polish.

References

Castles, S., & Miller, M. J. (2009) Migration in the Asia-Pacific region. *Migration Information Source*. Washington, DC: MPI.

Grzymała-Kazłowska, A. (Ed.) (2008) *Między jednością a wielością. Integracja odmiennych grup i kategorii migrantów w Polsce* [Between unity and multiplicity. Integration of different groups and categories of migrants in Poland]. Warsaw: OBM WNE UW.

Hagemejer, J., & Tyrowicz, J. (2011) Not All That Glitters, *Eastern European Economics*, 49 (3), 89–111.

Kaczmarczyk, P. (Ed.) (2013) *Recent Trends in International Migration in Poland*. The 2012 SOPEMI Report. CMR Working Paper 71 (129).

Klorek N., & Szulecka, M. (2013) *Migranckie instytucje ekonomiczne i ich wpływ na otoczenie. Przykład centrow handlowych w Wolce Kosowskiej. Analizy – Raporty – Ekspertyzy 2/2013*. Warsaw: Stowarzyszenie Interwencji Prawnej. http://interwencjaprawna.pl/docs/ARE-213-Wolka-Kosowska.pdf

KPMG. (2011) *Poland's Position as a Business Partner for China. How Chinese Investors Are Looking at Poland*. Warsaw: KPMG. www.kpmg.com/PL/pl/IssuesAndInsights/ArticlesPublications/Strony/Raport-postrzeganie-Polski-przez-inwestorow-z-Chin.aspx

Kuang, E. (2008) The New Chinese Migration Flows to Africa, *Social Science Information*, 47, 643–60.

Laczko, F. (2003) Understanding Migration Between China and Europe, *International Migration* 41 (3), 5–19.

Massey, D. (1999) Why Does Immigration Occur? A Theoretical Synthesis. In Hirschman, C., Kasnitz, P., & DeWind, J. (Eds.) *The Handbook of International Migration: The American Experience*. New York: Russell Sage Foundation, pp. 34–52.

MSWiA. (2008) *Migracje z Chin*. Departament Polityki Migracyjnej. Warsaw: MSWiA (unpublished).

Niyiri, P. (2003) Chinese Migration to Eastern Europe, *International Migration*, 41 (3), 239–65.

OECD (2012) *International Migration Outlook 2011*. Paris: Author.

Pieke, F., & T. Speelman, T. (2013), *Chinese Investment Strategies and Migration*. Report prepared for MPC EUI. Florence: EUI.

Piłat, A., & Wysieńska, K. (2012) Społeczności wschodnioazjatyckie w Polsce oraz w wybranych krajach regionu i świata. In Wysieńska, K. (Ed.) *Sprzedawać czy budować? Plany i strategie Chińczyków i Wietnamczyków w Polsce*. Warsaw: ISP, pp. 9–76.

Politzer M. (2008) Passage to China. *Foreign Policy* Magazine, January-February.

Sautman, B. (2006) Friends and Interests : China's Distinctive Links with Africa, Center on China's transnational relations, Working Paper No. 12 Hong Kong: Center on China's Transnational Relations.

Tomala, K. (2001) Kilka uwag na temat chińskiej emigracji. In Zamojski, J.E. (Ed.) *Diaspory. Migracje i Społeczeństwo* 6. Warsaw: NERITON, pp. 156–166.

UNCTAD. (2013) *Global Investments Trade Monitor No. 12* (UNCTAD/WEB/DIAE/IA/2013/6). Geneva: UNCTAD.

Wysieńska, K. (Ed.) (2012) *Sprzedawać czy budować? Plany i strategie Chińczyków i Wietnamczyków w Polsce*. Warsaw: ISP.

Żabowska, J. (2012) *State (of Exception). An Ethnography of "Grey Zone" in a Chinese Wholesale Market in Poland*. Copenhagen: University of Copenhagen, Department of Anthropology (mimeo).

Zhang, H. (2013) *The Role of Migration in Shaping China's Economic Relations with Its Main Partners*. Report prepared for MPC EUI. Florence: EUI.

7 The Chinese in Russia – friends or foes?

Investment strategies and migration patterns between neighbours

Ekaterina Selezneva

Abstract

Since the beginning of the 1990s, the Chinese government has promoted the idea of complementarity with neighbouring economies. While Russia has rich natural resources, a big consumption market, unused arable land and highly educated specialists in technical professions, a low- and medium-skilled labour force and large-scale investments are lacking, especially in the Russian Far East. In the framework of its "go global" strategy, China invests mainly in resource and power production industries and in the development of infrastructure in relevant areas. Investments and border-trade flows are often accompanied by labour force flows.

Introduction

From the moment of the re-animation of political and economic relationships between Russia and China at the beginning of the 1990s, the Chinese government has promoted the idea of the complementarity of the two economies. Cooperation has been developing unevenly at two levels, namely at the state level and at the regional level. A combination of push and pull factors drives the flow of migrants and investment from China to Russia. The flows are subject to fluctuations induced by a combination of stimulative and prohibitive legislative measures from both sides.

The purpose of this study is to provide an overview of the existing – quantitative and qualitative – evidence on the character and the extent of Chinese migration to Russia and the characteristics of the migrant community, as well as the development of economic cooperation including (large-scale) direct investment to Russia by Chinese firms and cross-border trade. The main sources of quantitative information include the open-access databases of a number of official Russian and Chinese bodies, namely the Russian Federal Statistical Service (Rosstat), the Russian Federal Migration Service (FMS), the Central Bank of Russia (CBR) and the Ministry of Commerce (MOFCOM) of China. Sources of qualitative information include news sections of the aforementioned institutions' websites, newspaper and academic articles and the results of attitude and opinion polls.

The present analysis has several limitations. Data from official sources are likely to underestimate the real size of the Chinese presence in Russia, especially by region. A large share of Chinese migrants do work in the grey sector of the economy. Moreover, the official data are collected by different services using a variety of definitions and methods, and therefore estimates may vary. In addition, Chinese migration to Russia and especially to the Russian Far East and Siberia is a sensitive issue in the Russian media. This might lead to a biased representation of the phenomenon, especially in non-scientific sources.

The text is organized in the following way: section 2 is dedicated to the theme of migration. I start with a short overview of the migration dynamics and relevant legislative measures. Then facts on Chinese legal and illegal migration are summarised. Then I paint a portrait of Chinese migrants in Russia and list characteristics of the migrant community. Section 3 starts with an overview of the economic relationships between China and the Russian Federation, with particular attention to Chinese (large-scale) direct investment in Russia and border-trade problems. Finally, the chapter concludes with a discussion on the motivations behind migration and investment flows.

7.1.   Migration to Russia

7.1.1.   General facts

Over the more than 20 years that have passed since the breakup of the Soviet Union, Russian migration policy has undergone a shift from repatriating Russian nationals from the former Soviet Republics to attempting to attract labour migrants from Commonwealth of Independent States (CIS) countries and repopulating the Russian Far East (RFE) and Siberia (Concept 2012). Over the 2000s, a course towards the simplification of bureaucratic procedures (issuing working and residence permits, granting citizenship) was taken, with some restrictions introduced in the second half of the decade. Net migration exchange with foreign countries peaked in 1994 with 845,732 people; by 2003, it collapsed to a low of 35,126. Since 2004, however, arriving migrants have outnumbered those leaving the country. In 2011, the number of immigrants (356,535) was already 9.6 times greater than the number of emigrants.

   The recent (since 2010) increase in immigration figures was driven by the simplification of issuing procedures for work permits for highly qualified foreign specialists and by the introduction of job permits for employment in the private sector (so-called patents) for citizens of countries with no-visa requirements. On the contrary, immigration quotas for the medium- and low-qualified labour force from the "far abroad", meaning foreign countries beyond the frontiers of the former Soviet Union, declined from 3.97 million people in 2009 to 1.7 million in 2012 and then even further to approximately 1.6 million in 2014. Officials reported that shrinking quotas reflected a constantly declining demand for foreign workers from the "far abroad". However, one of the reasons was the deliberate cut of quotas by the Russian government, which was aiming to protect national workers during 2008-crisis conditions. While medium- and high-level skill segments were occupied mainly by locals, foreign labourers were engaged in mining, installation and repair and construction works, which remained a highly requested professional category (more than 0.5 million requests in 2012).

According to the Federal Migration Service, "the number of employed foreigners in the country is about 10.6 million – many times more than the 2014 quota". While official statistics only account for legal migrants, the pool of undocumented migrants could be as big as 4 to 5.5 million people (estimate for 2010 by Mukomel 2012). The shrinking number of illegal migrants may be expected as a result of severe penalties for regulatory infractions and the simplification of the procedure which grants Russian citizenship to entrepreneurs and highly qualified specialists, both of which were measures proposed in the framework of the New Concept for State Migration Policy of the Russian Federation up to 2025 (Concept 2012).

7.1.2. Recent history of Chinese migration to Russia

The pool of Chinese nationals in Russia – although small compared to that of CIS–country migrants – is one of the most important groups stemming from the so-called "far abroad". The last USSR Census of 1989 reported 11,355 Chinese residing in the USSR. Approximately one half (5,197) lived in the territory of present-day Russia. The community of Chinese permanent residents expanded by more than six times between the censuses of 1989 and 2002, but then growth slowed down and even reversed by 2010. Between Russia's two censuses, a decline of approximately 5,500 people (or 16 per cent) was registered (from 34,577 to 28,943). The number of Chinese residents, both in terms of absolute numbers and as a share of the total population of Russia, declined in urban areas (from 0.031 to 0.026 per cent of the total population of Russia), although it grew in the rural areas (from 0.003 to 0.006 per cent).

Census data are likely to count a number of Chinese citizens with valid residence permits, but other Chinese may reside in Russia "without a permit, based on multiple-entry, extendible visas, either for work or study" (Chudinovskikh 2012: 22). For example, in Amur Oblast, many Chinese entrepreneurs are not reflected in official statistics. Thus the census data do not provide a complete picture of the extent of the Chinese presence in Russia (e.g. Ryasantsev 2014; Ryzhova & Ioffe 2009). In order to assess the presence more clearly, a short excursus into the history of the relationships between the two countries is needed.

Indeed, Chinese working in Russia is not a new phenomenon. At the end of the nineteenth century, approximately half a million Chinese worked in the Russian Far East alone (Minakir 1996). Over the Soviet era, political and economic relations between the USSR and China were unstable for a number of reasons. About 30,000 Chinese were working in the Russian Far East in the 1930s, but most of them suffered from Stalinist repressions in 1937 (Kim 1994). However, at the beginning of the 1950s, an unbreakable partnership between the countries' two leaders, Mao and Stalin, seemed to be established. Just a decade later, however, an armed conflict over several islands in the Amur River in the 1960s created a hostile climate against Chinese in the USSR (Kurt 2007). It is only at the beginning of the 1990s that a revitalization of the cooperation between the two countries in the sphere of tourism and exchanges of labour/specialists was reinstituted. The opening of the Russian border in 1988 was critical for the inflow of Chinese workers into the country. They predominantly worked in timber cutting, farming, construction and light manufacturing (Kim 1994). Over the last two decades, the number of border crossings as well as the number of permanent and temporary Chinese residents in Russia oscillated significantly in response to a series of both stimulative and prohibitive (e.g. fighting illegal migration) legislative measures. At present, Chinese nationals as a group have constantly growing net migration figures, although the relative share of Chinese nationals in migration exchange with Russia has just exceeded only 2 per cent (Table 7.1).

Among the measures stimulating cooperation, the first agreement on tourist group exchanges with no visa requirements was signed in May 1993. Holders of ordinary passports travelling in tour groups organised by authorised travel agencies of both countries received a right of no-visa entry. The number of border crossings soared. Due to low levels of control, pseudo-tourism began to flourish. Both Chinese and Russian citizens exploited the availability of visa-free tours for cross-border "shuttle/suitcase trade". Some Chinese workers also used it as an instrument to get access to illegal work at construction and agriculture firms in the Russian Far East. However, cases of illegal migration among business/commerce visa holders were even more commonplace. As many as one third of Chinese citizens who entered Primorskiy Kray in 1994 to 1995 didn't leave the country within the validity period of their permit (Kireev 2013). The strengthening of controls and clampdowns on Chinese "shuttle merchants" by Russian authorities over the second half of the 1990s resulted in a 50 per cent decrease in the number of border crossings from 1994 to 1996 (from approximately 751,000 to 349,000, as cited in Kurt 2007 and Kireev 2013). In 1997 already 99 per cent of Chinese tourists had returned home. Amendments to the mutual visa-exemption agreement in December 2000 further reduced possibilities for using the no-visa regime as a channel for the illegal migration of Chinese to Russia.

Activities in the framework of the Year of Russia in China (2006) and the Year of China in Russia (2007) pushed forward cooperation between the two countries (see a special issue of *Rossijskaja Gazeta* for a number of initiatives from 26 March 2007). Border regions – Khabarovsk, Vladivostok and Blagoveshchensk – took the most active participation, promoting and hosting not only economic but also cultural initiatives (Kozlov & Nasakova 2008). Right before the crisis of 2008, bilateral relations between Russia and China were "at the peak of amity and warmth". From 2009 to 2013, a 36 to 48 per cent growth in the number of tourists was observed each year. In 2012, 343,000 Chinese tourists came to Russia, more than half of whom (185,000 people) came using the no-visa channel.

As for legal labour migration, the recruitment of foreign workers was made possible in the beginning of the 1990s through inter-governmental agreements and enterprise-to-enterprise agreements (Kim 1994). Chinese local governments

Table 7.1 Migration exchange with foreign countries

	1997	1998	1999	2000	2001	2002	2005	2010	2011	2012
Arrived to the Russian Federation, total	597,651	513,551	379,726	359,330	193,450	184,612	177,230	191,656	356,535	417,681
From CIS countries	571,903	488,087	362,708	326,561	183,650	175,068	163,101	171,940	310,549	363,955
China	2,861	6,854	3,871	1,121	405	410	432	1,380	7,063	8,547
% arrivals to total										
From CIS countries	95.69%	95.04%	95.52%	90.88%	94.93%	94.83%	92.03%	89.71%	87.10%	87.14%
China	0.48%	1.33%	1.02%	0.31%	0.21%	0.22%	0.24%	0.72%	1.98%	2.05%
Net arrivals										
total saldo	364,664	300,174	164,763	213,610	72,284	77,927	107,432	158,078	319,761	294,930
CIS countries	424,942	357,037	234,901	246,051	122,080	122,969	127,683	150,734	287,981	268,383
China	1,639	2,605	1,074	463	249	259	−24	1,132	6,556	4,189

Source: Own calculations based on the data from Rosstat, www.gks.ru

played a crucial role in sending labourers to the Russian Far East. Upon the request of Russian firms, local Chinese governments mobilised worker groups, controlled the activities of businesspeople organizing labour migration and monitored the return of their citizens (Biao 2003). Due to the outflow of the native (skilled) population, the Russian Far East became dependent on foreign workers, who were mainly employed in construction, agriculture and light manufacturing (Kim 1994). At the beginning of the 2000s, approximately 50 Chinese cities facilitated a procedure of issuing passports for foreign use. About 200 companies appeared specializing in the selection of labourers for work abroad (Gelbras 2004). On the Russian side, the simplification of procedures for issuing some categories of temporary Russian work permits – for a period up to one year and work permits for temporary residents for up to three years – was exploited by a great number of Chinese migrants beginning in 2002. At the same time, some of the Russian initiatives hampered the development of the (cross-border) suitcase trade. Others introduced restrictions regarding the professional occupations of migrants. For example, from 4 January 2007, foreign workers were banned from employment in retail trade in Russian open markets and business booths, namely from selling goods directly to customers. The measure was active for a period of four years.

In general, the number of foreign workers in Russia grew until the crisis of 2008 then diminished rather abruptly in 2010 (Table 7.2). According to the official data, the percentage of Chinese citizens with valid working permits decreased gradually over the period of 2005 to 2012. In 2010, the share of Chinese labour migrants in the pool of total working migrants in Russia stayed above 11 per cent and accounted for about 186,500 people. By the end of 2013, approximately 1.1 million foreign workers had Russian working permits, including 85.3 per cent CIS citizens (approximately 941,700) and 6.4 per cent (approximately 71,000) Chinese. The Federal Migration Service reported a threefold increase (235,500) in Chinese citizens with valid work permits by mid-2014. It is noteworthy that being

Table 7.2 Number of foreign citizens who had valid working permit (at the end of each year)

	2000	2005	2006	2007	2008	2009	2010	2011	2012
Total, ths.	213.3	702.5	1014	1717.1	2425.9	2223.6	1640.8	1027.9	1148.7
In %	100.0	100.0	100.0	100.0	100.0	100.0	100.0	100.0	100.0
CIS	49.9	48.9	53.0	67.1	73.4	74.0	76.0	83.6	84.3
EU	10.5	2.9	2.4	1.8	1.5	1.6	1.8	1.3	0.7
China	12.3	22.9	20.8	13.3	11.6	12.1	11.4	6.8	6.7
Other "far abroad" countries	27.3	25.3	23.7	17.7	13.5	12.3	10.7	6.8	7.3

Source: Rosstat (Российский статистический ежегодник, different years), www.gks.ru/wps/wcm/connect/rosstat_main/rosstat/ru/statistics/publications/catalog/doc_1139916801766

a legal working migrant did not mean having completely legal status. In 2007, about 40 per cent of legal working migrants were hired unofficially, and many of them were even unaware of this fact (Ioffe & Zayonchkovskaya 2010).

The increased migration exchange in 2011 to 2013 was accompanied by the conclusion of international agreements that called for government operations to mitigate illegal migration (for example, "Nelegal – 2012"). Approximately 69,000 violations of the migration legislation were disclosed, including 2,773 cases from the side of Chinese citizens. From 2010 through 2013, according to the vice-chief of the FMS, Anatoly Kuznetsov, 12,500 Chinese had violated migration laws during their previous period of stay.

7.1.3. *Portrait of Chinese (im)migrants in Russia*

Officially, slightly more than 6 million Russian citizens live in the Russian Far East, while the three Chinese provinces bordering Russia have a combined population of approximately 100 million Chinese citizens (in 2009; Ryzhova & Ioffe 2009). "The Chinese represent a small segment of the migrant population in Russia, though they are of enormous psychological importance in the Russian Far East" (Repnikova & Balzer 2009: 8, 10). The latter authors state that Russian fears of a Chinese invasion are rooted in "imperfect information and misperceptions about history, government policy, and the desirability of living in Russia" (11). Russian media persistently present Chinese migrants and workers in a negative way, "influencing public opinion and, in turn, political strategies" (Repnikova & Balzer, 2009: 10).

In the Russian mass media, the word "diaspora" – when applied to workers from China – is often used as synonymously with "migrants" (Kireev 2013). The former term, however, is much more contentious; several preconditions need to be fulfilled for an ethnic group of migrants to constitute a diaspora. As Kireev argues, one cannot yet speak about a Chinese diaspora established in Russia. Therefore, further in this text, I refer to the population of Chinese migrants in Russian territory as a migrant community. The main characteristics of the community are listed in what follows.

As already noted, there are significant differences of opinion on the number of Chinese actually residing in Russian territory. Kireev (2013) quotes an estimate of 200,000 people who were residing temporarily or permanently in the Russian Far East in 1996. However, the number halved to approximately 80,000 by 2000. Since 2010, in the aftermath of the severe shuttle-trade regulation measures and the world economic crisis of 2008, the number of Chinese migrants to Russia started to grow again.

If the demographic composition of the pool of Chinese migrants to Russia is considered, it is clear that families resettled from China to Russia up until 2002, but then after this date, young men started arriving (Gelbras 2004). The censuses of 2002 and 2010 registered twice as many men as women among Chinese residing permanently in Russia. As for the Russian Far East, it is only by 2010 that an equalization in the shares of two sexes was observed; by that time, the migrant community was noted to have become more rooted (Kireev 2013).

Table 7.3 Age distribution of foreign citizens with valid working permits (by end of 2012)

| | Total, thousands | Including, by age | | | | | |
		18–29	30–39	40–49	50–54	55–59	60 years and older
Total	**1148.7**	**501.2**	**306.9**	**236.4**	**68.4**	**27.2**	**8.6**
Including those from CIS countries	968.6	458.6	258	175.2	51.4	19.6	5.9
	100%	47.3%	26.6%	18.1%	5.3%	2.0%	0.6%
Including those from China	76.9	16	19.8	30.2	7	3.1	0.7
	100%	20.8%	25.7%	39.3%	9.1%	4.0%	0.9%

Source: Rosstat

Table 7.4 Demographic characteristics of Chinese migrants (on 01.06.2014)

Chinese	younger than 17	18–29 y.o.	30–39 y.o.	40–49 y.o.	50–59 y.o.	Older than 60	Total
men	5,497	37,872	32,972	45,721	21,070	12,194	155,326
	3.54%	24.38%	21.23%	29.44%	13.57%	7.85%	100.00%
women	3,666	19,217	13,485	19,946	13,875	9,997	80,186
	4.57%	23.97%	16.82%	24.87%	17.30%	12.47%	100.00%

Source: FMS, (accessed on 10.06.2014) www.fms.gov.ru/about/statistics/data/details/54891/

At present, the most numerous age group among Chinese migrants with valid working permits is from 40 to 49 years old among both sexes (whereas this is the third-biggest group among CIS labourers). The second-biggest Chinese group is aged 18 to 29 (the first-biggest group for CIS labourers), among both sexes (Tables 7.3 and 2.4). Over the last two years (2012–2014), the share of this younger group increased approximately 5 percentage points.

Kireev (2013) summarised the results of several surveys conducted among Chinese migrants in different parts of Russia. The following demographic characteristics of migrants can be gleaned from the survey descriptions: from 1995 to 1998, the percentage of males among migrants ranged from 66 to 90 per cent, and only 19.7 per cent of men lived with families, including 4 to 6.1 per cent families with children (Larin in 1995–7 and Gelbras in 1998). By 2005, 78 per cent of respondents were already living with a spouse (see Kireev 2013).

Chinese workers – like other foreign migrant workers – are noted to be distributed unevenly across the regions of Russia. Di Bartolomeo et al. (2014) write about three centers of gravity: the City of Moscow and Moscow region, the Ural Federal District (FD) and the Far Eastern Federal District, which accounted for

36 per cent, 16 per cent and 10 per cent of foreign migrant workers in Russia, respectively. While the Moscow region requests migrant workers from a variety of occupations, the demand for migrant labour in the Ural Federal District is driven by its oil-producing industries and in the Far East by construction, agriculture and forestry. Within the Far Eastern FD, more than 60 per cent of residing migrants are settled near the China–Russia border, where there is the highest demand for the Chinese goods and services (Kireev 2013; Ponkratov 2007). While in 2008, 53.03 per cent of migration flows throughout Russia came from CIS countries, in the Russian Far East, 76.79 per cent of migrants came from the "far abroad" (Motritsch 2010). Foreign workers residing in the Russian Far East come predominantly from China, Democratic People's Republic of Korea and Vietnam (Di Bartolomeo et al. 2014).

At the more disaggregated level, Chinese migrants are noted to reside – often compactly in a house or guest house – near infrastructure (complexes) such as restaurants and markets, where Chinese migrants operate. This may be creating pre-conditions for the development of true Chinatowns in the future (Kireev 2013).

But why do Chinese workers migrate to Russia? The answer consists of a mix of typical push factors on the Chinese side such as low wages, widespread poverty, high unemployment and a lack of jobs and pull factors on the Russian side such as employment opportunities in different industries and regions and higher wages. As in earlier times, more than a century ago, Chinese migration to Russia and particularly to the Russian Far East has an economic character.

In the late 1800s and early 1900s, Chinese labourers were mainly employed in agriculture, trade and services (Minakir 1996). As a result historically, a large share of Chinese migrant workers have been employed in the so-called 3-D jobs, namely dirty, dangerous and difficult (Kim 1994). According to Motritsch (2010), in the years preceding the revolution of 1917, Chinese labourers comprised the majority among workers employed in gold extraction (87.6 per cent), silicate mining and processing (92.5 per cent) and forestry (67.1 per cent); the main reason for use of a foreign labour force was the unavailability and high cost of Russian labourers. At the beginning of the twenty-first century (2012), the most frequent occupations of legal Chinese migrants – although adjusted to modern occupational structures – remained rather traditional: labourers in mining, construction, manufacturing and transport (27.4 per cent); agricultural, forestry and fishery labourers (15.3 per cent); administrative and commercial managers (7 per cent); metal processing and finishing plant operators and mechanical machinery assemblers (6.9 per cent). As an adaptation strategy to changing Russian migration legislation (especially related to trade occupations in 2007–2008), a gradual substitution of shuttle-traders for production-related migrants was observed over the period 2000 to 2009; the share of categories of migrants such as entrepreneurs, employees, students and manual workers increased. A gradual increase in the share of Chinese residing in rural areas (also reflected in the Censuses results) reflects both an increasing demand for workers in the agriculture, fishery and forestry sectors as well as an increasing practice of renting agricultural land to Chinese, especially in the Russian Far East (Kireev 2013). Ludmila Boni, chief scientific officer at the Institute of Far Eastern Studies, reported in April 2014 on more than 420,000 hectares of arable land rented by Chinese firms in Russia. In the future, China is likely to remain a supplier of migrants in primarily low-skilled occupations, since native Russians dominate in the medium- and high-skilled labour market segments while rejecting low-skilled jobs (Ioffe & Zayonchkovskaya 2010). This all reflects both a scarcity of "white-collar"/highly educated Chinese migrants (not more than 1 per cent as cited in Larin 2009) and a general tendency of Chinese migrants to fill the labour market niches left free by locals. There are also cases of symbioses, when Chinese entrepreneurs employ Russians to create fictitious joint enterprises or masquerade Chinese small enterprises as Russian ones in order to overcome restrictive regulations. According to Larin (2009), approximately 58 per cent of migrants worked for small and very small private enterprises belonging to both Russian and/or Chinese owners.

As most of the researchers note, workers come for short periods/temporary stays that include transit and suitcase trade (Kireev 2013). Gelbras (2002) speaks about Chinese migrants working in the Russian Far East as sojourners, not settlers. In the beginning of the 2000s, only a very low share of Chinese migrants stayed for more than four years in Russia. Larin (2009) notes that 29.8 per cent and 23 per cent of migrants stayed in Russia for more than five years during 2004 and 2007, respectively. It is only in Moscow that citizenship aspirations were the most pronounced (Gelbras 2004). In the Russian Far East, there were opportunities in commercial activity that attracted migrants. The apparently commuting type of migration served as an adaptation strategy in order to avoid high custom taxes and the official procedures restricting commodities flows. While Chinese businesspeople reported in surveys that they preferred doing business in Russia over China, they still indicated a preference for living in China (Larin 2009).

A growing category of Chinese migrants is composed of students. For example, there were 1,066 Chinese students alone at the Vladivostok State University of Economics and Service in the 2006–2007 academic year. In all of Russia, there were already approximately 12,000 students in the same period (undergraduate and graduate). The Minister of Education, Igor Remorenko, reported approximately 20,000 Chinese students throughout Russia in 2011. As Gelbras (2004) notes, such graduates, who could become important assets for the Russian economy, had immense difficulties finding jobs – especially in the city of Moscow – and were therefore forced to use illegal channels (possibly among Chinese networks) in the beginning of the 2000s. In the mid-2000s, most of the students returned to China after the completion of their education, a trend which has been considered one of the priorities of Chinese educational strategy since mid-1990s (Zweig & Wang 2013). Additionally, by 2012, cases in which Chinese citizens requested student visas in order to obtain legal status, in order to work but not study, practically disappeared. Moreover, as Shvedova (2013) notes, a survey conducted among Chinese students in 2011 revealed that Russia was not included in their top 10 desired schooling destinations.

It has been noted that those Chinese migrants who reside in Russia carefully preserve their cultural traditions and connections to their home country (Kireev 2013). Kireev cites a survey by P. Lyakh (2006–2007), which revealed that 33 per cent of respondents did not speak Russian at all or only knew words that they felt were most important.

However, when looking for economic opportunities, Chinese are found to "tend to build upon networks" established by previous migrants (Repnikova & Balzer 2009: 10). According to the survey of P. Lyakh, in 2006 to 2007, 47 per cent of respondents came to Russia with friends or relatives helping them, and 29 per cent respondents in turn advised their friends to come to Russia (cited in Kireev 2013).

In the literature, there is evidence of a rapid increase in the number of formal and semi-formal organizations covering a range of activities, from professional organisations/associations to organizations promoting Chinese language and culture. Kireev (2013) mentions 20 registered non-commercial organisations established in the Russian Far East from 1990 through 2000, which have represented the interests of migrants and provided juridical assistance. Since 2000, there have been signs of collaboration between these kinds of organisations and Russian governmental structures.

The adoption of an Agreement on the Mutual Recognition of Qualifications and Academic Degrees in 1995 marked the beginning of collaborations between educational institutions of different levels (higher, vocational; Kozlov & Nasakova 2008). In the framework of scientific and academic cooperation, the Chinese government involved a number of Russian specialists in joint scientific projects (Larin 2006). As part of the exchange, these specialists offered their know-how of barter trade, shops, restaurants and hotel management and creation, using the existing facilities of scientific institutes of the Far East Branch of the Russian Academy of Sciences as a base. However, the entrepreneurial knowledge offered by the Chinese was rarely implemented on the Russian side (Kozlov & Nasakova 2008). A 20-year-old Sino-Russian Treaty of Good-Neighborliness and Friendly Cooperation, signed in 2001, had an objective to develop further cross-border trade and cultural exchange, as well as high-level scientific projects (e.g. the development of a joint satellite navigation system "Glonass" and "Beidou"). Departments of Russian Language for Foreigners appeared in some universities of the Russian Far East, as did joint undergraduate and doctorate programs, for example, the Sino-Russian doctorate program of Xejluntsian University and the Far East State University in Kharbin and the Joint Transnational Program of Tomsk Polytechnic University and Jilin University. The number of initiatives and programs increased after 2006 to 2007 (the Year of China in Russia and vice versa).

In the beginning of the 2000s, several branches of the Sino-Russian Friendship Association (e.g. in Primorskiy and Khabarovskiy Kray and in the Amour region) already existed. In the mid-2000s, the Chinese government announced its goal to create a positive country image. In the framework of this initiative, at least 20 to 25 cultural centers were supposed to be created in Russia. The Confucius Institute in Vladivostok was opened on the grounds of the Far East State University in Vladivostok in 2006, having among its goals teaching Chinese to students interested in further education at Heilongjiang University. An expansion of Chinese language courses was enhanced after 2009 to 2010, when the Year of Russian Language in China and the Year of Chinese Language in Russia (Shvedova 2013) were announced. By 2013, there were already more than 20 Confucius Institutes in the territory of Russia far beyond the Far East. Moreover, in more than 40 universities and 20 primary schools, Chinese was adopted as the main foreign language.

7.2.   FDI to Russia

7.2.1.   *General facts on foreign investment in Russia*

The attractiveness of Russia for foreign direct investment (FDI) is based on the richness of its natural resources, as well as on the size of its consumer and producer markets (e.g. Zsuzsa 2003). Factors that have hampered potential FDI from unfolding include (perceived) high levels of corruption and crime, unfavourable tariff policies, general impediments to oil- and gas-sector penetration by foreign investors, deficiencies in the legislative environment and inter-regional disparities (Buccellato & Santangelo 2009; Ernst & Young 2013; Karhunen & Ledyaeva 2012).

It is only since the (mid-) 2000s that large-scale FDI began flowing into Russia. In 2005, the FDI stock per capita was approximately six times lower than the respective amount for the Czech Republic (Ledyaeva 2009). The amount of foreign direct investment grew nearly six times (in nominal terms, in current dollars) from 2000 to 2013 (from 4,427 to 26,208 million USD, respectively).

By 2009, 34 per cent of FDI accumulated stock was concentrated in manufacturing industries, 22.7 per cent in mining and quarrying, followed by real estate and trade (Bessonova & Gonchar 2013). Significant reallocations of FDI flows and stock followed after the onset of the 2008 global crisis. Net FDI flows to manufacturing, information and communication and professional scientific and technical activities started to decline, while those to construction, financial services and insurance and other service activities increased.

The recent growth of Russia's investment volume was partially catalysed by the establishment of the Russian Direct Investment Fund (RDIF) in 2011. The RDIF's goal is to stimulate "equity investments that generate strong returns, primarily in Russia". The International Advisory board includes CEOs of leading private equity firms and heads of some national sovereign wealth funds, including some from China.

As for the geographic distribution of FDI flows into Russia, there is no strong evidence of the flows concentrating in coastal and border regions – unlike in China or Central and Eastern Europe. The resource (oil and gas) -rich areas serve as the main investment magnet (Buccellato & Santangelo 2009). The top 10 FDI recipient regions are characterised by big consumer markets, developed infrastructure and a skilled labour force (Moscow, St. Petersburg, Samara, Omsk); low legislative risk (Novgorod); a highly developed metallurgy industry (Lipetsk);

the presence of big sea ports (Primorskiy, Sakhalin and Krasnodar regions); and resource abundance (the Sakhalin region, Magadan and Khabarovsk; Ledyaeva 2009). Over two decades, a process of redistribution of investments from eastern to western Russian regions can be observed. By 2009, nearly a half of the total FDI amount was allocated to the Central Federal District. The Far Eastern FD and Siberian FD followed with approximately 20 per cent and 9 per cent, respectively, of total FDI volume.

7.2.2.   *Extent of Chinese investments to Russia*

The BRIC countries (Brazil, Russia, India and China) still have a low interest in Russia as a host country for FDI. China is the most important current emerging market investor for Russia (Ernst & Young 2013); the volume of investments is steadily growing (Figure 7.1). In 2012 and 2013 alone, the volume of accumulated Chinese foreign investments increased by 740 and 5,027 million USD, respectively. By the end of 2013, the largest shares of accumulated foreign investments in Russia belonged to investors from Cyprus (18 per cent) and the Netherlands (17.8 per cent). Chinese investments held the fourth position (8.4 per cent) on this rating with a stock of 32,130 million USD.

Despite a secure place in the top 10 Chinese outward foreign direct investment (OFDI) destinations, in 2010, the stock of Chinese OFDI in Russia consisted of less than a third of Chinese OFDI in transition countries, or 0.9 per cent of the total OFDI stock. This low share corresponds to 660 million USD of investment volume and the fifth position in the rating of OFDI host countries, when offshore destinations and Hong Kong are excluded (Andreff 2013).

After the re-establishment of political and economic contacts in the beginning of the 1990s, regular Sino-Russian summits began to be organised to promote economic cooperation. Russian political leaders had warmly welcomed Chinese

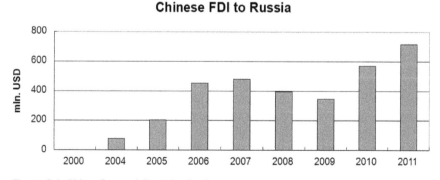

Figure 7.1 China, flows of direct foreign investments to Russia

Source: based on the data from the Ministry of Commerce of the People's Republic of China. FDI outflows from 2003 to 2006 did not include financial intermeditation, FDI outflows from 2007 to 2009 involved all sectors, million USD. www.gks.ru/publish/prezent/m-sotrudn/brics.pdf

investments, especially in the joint exploration of Russian natural resources and the construction of infrastructure facilities in the Russian Far East (Kuhrt 2007). This call for Chinese investment matched the guidelines of the "go global" strategy officially announced in China in the early 2000s. Governmental support was guaranteed to Chinese firms pursuing global expansion strategies and acquiring nationally lacking strategic assets and resources from abroad. Apart from natural resources, the acquisition and internalization of human resources (in particular with managerial experience relevant to market economy settings), advanced technologies and the establishment of competitive international brands were targeted (e.g. Lu et al. 2010). In 2007, a sovereign investment fund (the China Investment Corporation, CIC) was created, inducing a flow of trans-border mergers and acquisitions. The process was reinforced in 2010, when an "accelerated go-global strategy" went into effect (Andreff 2013).

At the same time, the Russian government made the attraction of large-scale Chinese investments into the country's economy one of its targets. The successful launch of the annual Russia-China Investment Forum in 2004 brought together more than 500 businesspeople and concluded with the signing of 32 investment programs consisting of a total investment of 4.36 million USD. The China-Russia Bilateral Investment Treaty was signed in 2006 (and entered into force on 1 May 2009). It secured the rights and duties that Russia owes Chinese investors. The accession of Russia to the WTO in 2012 improved the transparency of rules and standards and the predictability of the investment environment, thus welcoming increased investment activity. In 2013, the Russian Direct Investment Fund (RDIF) and the China Investment Corporation (CIC) created the Russian-Chinese Investment Fund (RCIF). The main goal of the RCIF is to "support Chinese investments in Russia, as well as promote job creation and technology transfer".

A number of significant trans-border mergers and acquisitions were achieved by Chinese companies in 2004 through 2013. The acquired firms were primarily in natural resources, power production and communication technologies. Among these were Udmurneft (oil producer, 3,500 million USD, acquired by Sinopec), Sintez (gas producer, 650 million USD, acquired by Hudian), Nobel Holdings (oil, 300 million USD, acquired by CIC), Digital Sky (communication technology, 300 million USD, acquired by Tencent), EuroSibEnergo (power producer, 170 million USD, acquired by Three Gorges) and Uralkali (potash fertilizer company, about 2,000 million USD, acquired by CIC). As novelties, several companies located sales-based facilities and production factories on the Russian territory. These included the white-goods and electronics manufacturer Hisense and the automotive production companies Chery Automobile and Geely (Andreff 2013).

Given the main goals of the go-global strategy, it is not surprising than presence of Chinese investors is found primarily to the east of the Urals (Andreff 2013). Already in the period from 1988 till 1994, Chinese capital was invested in 888 enterprises in the territorially close and rich-with-natural-resources Russian Far East, with an average investment of 50,000 USD and a total of 44.4 million USD in Chinese capital. Important agreements for cooperation in energy, timber, regional economic relations and joint ventures in electronics were signed at the beginning of the millennium. At the end of 2006, Chinese investment in Russia involved 657 projects worth approximately 1 billion USD (Mitchell 2007). Increasing governmental support was again promised to Chinese companies, enhancing investment in the fields of energy, timber processing, agricultural development, infrastructure construction and manufacturing in the Russian Far East and Siberia. The volume of the investments might have been even higher if the operations of foreign investors were not limited by the Russian authorities in sectors that were strategic for Chinese companies (Krkoska & Korniyenko 2008).

Local Russian governments in the border regions welcome the capital of both small and big Chinese investors. Ryazantsev (2014) describes the existing symbioses between Chinese entrepreneurs and local Russian officials in business sectors with quick payoff (trade, food services, tourism, hotel business). There are cases in which the officials ignore semi-legal and illegal methods of Chinese entrepreneurs' business operations in exchange for funds contributed to local budgets. As for the big-scale investments, in August 2013, the Minister for the Development of the Russian Far East and the president of the China Development Bank signed a cooperation agreement, which involves Chinese investment in large-scale projects in the Far East. The Chinese side plans to invest up to 5 billion USD into a number of infrastructure projects (ports, roads, heating and electricity systems, sport facilities etc.) in the framework of the Federal Program "Socioeconomic Development of the Far East and the Baikal Region until 2025" and the "Program of Cooperation between the Far East, Eastern Siberia, and the Northeast of China until 2018".

7.2.3. Cross-border cooperation and border trade

Unlike direct investments, trade flows between the two countries have been extensive since the beginning of the 1990s. At the end of the Soviet era, the USSR was supplying China with steel, mineral fertilizers, timber and aluminium, whereas China's export to the USSR was mainly consumer goods and foodstuffs (Kuhrt 2007). In 1992, China granted Russia the status of "most favorable nation". In 2005, China became Russia's fourth-largest trade partner, while Russia became China's eighth-largest trade partner (Mitchell 2007).

Already in the 1980s, local-scale trade between border regions accounted for approximately 20 per cent of trade turnover, although in that time barter was a primary form of goods exchange (Ryazantsev 2014). After the breakup of the Soviet Union, further development of cross-border trade on a large scale was hampered by insufficient transport and other infrastructure capacity problems on the Russian side (one of the issues highlighted during the first Sino-Russian summit in 1992). However, these were not obstacles for small-size entrepreneurs, the so-called shuttle traders, who owned trade spots at local Russian markets. Such trans-border "people's trade" has been stimulated extensively by Chinese local governments, for example through the establishment of free economic zones. Shuttle trade became both an instrument to satiate local Russian markets lacking consumer goods and a strategy for survival/gaining income at the beginning of transition.

The phenomenon involved hundreds of thousands of people (Tschernov 2006). A number of Chinese border cities were transformed into centers of economic activity focused on Russia. Billé (2014) gives an example of Heihe that, thanks to the flourishing of trans-border trade, underwent a fast transformation from a small settlement into a "thriving city" where even "street signage throughout the city is trilingual, in Chinese, Russian and English", the use of English being nation-wide policy (p. 157). The author also notes a common sense of resentment by inhabitants of the Russian city Blagoveshchensk right across the river, who widely believe that "Heihe has flourished on the backs of the Russians" (p. 158).

In general, "the Russian side has tended to view the border more as unavoidable evil" (Ryzhova & Ioffe (2009: 353). Apart from its cushioning effect against the shocks of the transition period, the authorities have always considered shuttle trade an economic activity creating criminogenic incentives such as the expansion of illicit entrepreneurial activities (Zabyelina 2012). In fact, multiple violations of legislation have taken place in this sphere. Chinese businesspeople were hiring both Chinese and Russian citizens, exploiting the availability of the free tourist entry visas introduced in 1993. "Tourists" could carry as much as 1,500 to 5,000 USD equivalent of commodities per trip without paying custom duties to Russian custom offices. Kim (1994) reports on 2,000 crossings by traders per day at the Sino-Russian border at Heihe and Suifenhe in 1993. Approximately 10,000 single male Chinese workers were legally employed in the trading business in the Russian Far East in that time. Expert estimates attribute 3 to 5 billion USD in 1993 and then 11.4 billion USD (22.3 per cent of total imports to Russia) in 1994 to shuttle trade (Tschernov 2006). Multiple Russian "clearance" companies appeared, which with the "help" of Russian customs officials facilitated the import of goods at a lower rate than the official tax. The practice existed for managing trade flows not only with China but also with other countries such as Spain, Italy and Germany. Surprisingly, Russian authorities tried to suppress this practice for Chinese traders as early as 1994, which led to a sharp fall in the import of Chinese goods during the following years (Kurt 2007). Additionally, regional elites of RFE and Siberia started to perceive the flows of Chinese migrants, trade and investments as undermining their economic and political bases; anti-Chinese propaganda flourished, influencing regional legislation towards migrants and trade (Sullivan & Renz 2010).

In 2006, border trade accounted for US$5.6 billion, or one third of overall trade (Mitchell 2007). Top Chinese regional officials, for example, from the northeastern Chinese Heilongjiang Province, emphasised the importance of further development of border trade in Russia's Far Eastern and Siberian regions. Among the main spheres/industries cited for further cooperation were agricultural development, energy, raw materials, technological exchange and labour transfers. In parallel with a mutual reassessment of the importance of border trade, Russian authorities continued to close some of the customs loopholes, as well as perform periodic searches and crackdowns on Chinese merchants (Bin 2009). Additionally, a new federal import law was introduced in 2006, establishing a 35 kilogram (versus the previous 50 kilogram) limit of imports per person per month.

By the end of the 2000s, high-level Chinese officials openly criticised the Russian government's constant efforts to hamper shuttle trade, which was seen as a channel of primarily illegal and counterfeit goods delivery. In June 2009, a sub-committee on customs operations was established to promote a healthier way of developing economic relationships. After a closure of Cherkizovsky market in Moscow at the end of June 2009, a measure that affected 100,000 merchants, 60,000 Chinese businessmen included, Qin Gang, the Chinese foreign ministry spokesman, urged Russians to "protect Chinese business people's interest in Russia". The market closure, which was performed "without warning", was perceived as "9/11" by many Chinese traders. Qin Gang stated that Russian authorities were "overdoing it", corrupting the dignity of Chinese business people involved in legal operations.

In 2010, under the new rules of the Customs Union (Russia, Belarus and Kazakhstan), the previous limit of 50 kilograms of imports per person was reinstated. However, the value of goods was not to exceed 1,500 euros. The previously allowed once-per-month frequency of a free customs-tax import of commodities was abolished; at present, customs authorities have the right to evaluate whether the goods are imported for private use and therefore should not be taxed by customs. The new rules were widely understood as a "death sentence" to the business of shuttle traders importing goods through Chinese borders with Russia and Kazakhstan.

Currently, a new business idea has been coming into force: Internet shuttle traders. An intermediate seller collects orders from clients of an Internet shop or a relevant group in a social network, makes the order and then distributes the goods among the clients. A number of business coaches offer trainings ("Importing Goods from China") for those interested in establishing such businesses.

7.3. Discussion

Although economic and political relationships between China and the Russian Federation were re-established only at the beginning of the 1990s – after a long period of hostility – the presence of Chinese capital and workers in Russia, especially in the Far East and Siberia, is not a new phenomenon.

What would Russia have to offer to Chinese migrants and investors? First of all, there are natural resources. In fact, Russia is one of the major suppliers of energy resources and hydrocarbons to China, as well as of timber and aluminium (Mitchel 2007). Flynt Leverett and Pierre Noël even called the development of this dimension of Sino-Russian collaboration a "new axis of oil" in the summer of 2006 issue of *The National Interest* magazine. Second, Russia – with its population of approximately 143 million – is a big consumption market, which, above all, gives a green light to the development of border trade. Additionally, the use of the Russian territory as a sales base is advantageous for some electronic and automotive manufacturing companies wanting to reach markets of Russia's neighbouring countries. Third, there is the relative geographical proximity and especially that of the Far Eastern and Siberian regions. This can result not only in lower transportation costs but also, above all, the availability of arable plots of rentable land that are adjacent (to China).[1] The latter was approved by the presidents of the two countries in 2009 within a program of cooperation between border regions for 2009 to 2018. According to Xinhua News Agency Reports, in 2010 alone, there were 426,000 hectares of Russian territory being rented by Chinese farmers. Most of the production is used by the farmers themselves, and some is sent to neighbouring Russian regions and to China. Furthermore, there are governmental incentives from both sides that could stimulate the exchange of workers with different levels of qualifications. Despite fast economic growth, poverty and unemployment are widespread in China. Russia, in turn, is experiencing a shrinking of its working-age population. Wages in the Russian labour market are competitive with Chinese ones, while workers with medium and low qualifications are in constant demand in Russia. Chinese workers usually fill the deficit of the local labour force in the so-called 3-D jobs (dirty, dangerous, difficult), namely in mining, construction, manufacturing, transport, agriculture, forestry and fishery (Kim 1994). Similar to a century ago, Chinese migration to Russia has an economic character.

From the beginning of the 1990s, the Chinese government has promoted the idea of a complementarity between the two economies (emphasizing geographical proximity). Top Russian officials, as early as the mid-1990s, implicitly called for the development of joint projects fostering the exploitation of Russian natural resources (Kuhrt 2007). The flow of direct investment was, however, weak during the 1990s, partially due to impediments to intensive participation by foreign investors in this strategic sector of the economy. Additionally, the underdevelopment of infrastructure on the Russian side (e.g. the transportation system) was reported in investor surveys as an impediment to the flawless extraction and export of raw resources (Ernst & Young 2013). A number of recent agreements do actively involve the participation of Chinese capital in the development of Russian Far Eastern and Siberian region infrastructure (e.g. the Federal Program "Socioeconomic Development of the Far East and the Baikal Region until 2025"). This is in line with the general concept of going global, pushing Chinese firms to invest abroad in order to provide multinational enterprises with resources lacking in China, as well as to expand to potentially larger consumer markets. In the framework of the go-global strategy, infrastructure development in the region of interest is not only pursued, but a number of mergers and acquisitions of Russian firms are already concluded over the last decade. The firms primarily belong to the economic sectors of natural resources, power production and communication technologies. As early as the 1990s, capital investments from China, especially small-scale investments, were inevitably followed by flows of migrant employees. The recently established Russian-Chinese Investment Fund (2013) aims to support Chinese investments in Russia and explicitly promotes related job creation for both locals and Chinese migrants. The inflow of Chinese workers does, in fact, seem to be one of the prerequisites of successful regional development. Before the collapse of the Soviet Union, the economy of the Russian Far East had a large share of production/industries related to the production of military hardware and the provision of fuel and other mineral products. The cut of subsidies to the region in the 1990s and the change in the structure of production towards raw material export caused an outflow of (skilled) workers from the region.

From the beginning of the 2000s, the Russian government has proclaimed an urgent need for the creation of industrial and scientific parks to the east of the Urals in order to diversify the structure of the Siberian economy (Mitchel 2007). In 2006, a State Commission for the Far East was established; in 2007, a federal targeted program with a budget of 22 billion USD was launched in order to increase the gross regional product 4.4-fold by 2025. Such plans are out of tune with Chinese investments, which are aggressively stimulated at the governmental level in the field of natural resource extraction and exploitation, reinforcing the vicious circle of resource dependence. Additionally, the creation of highly technological industrial areas is likely to be hampered by labour shortages of both low- and high-skill occupations and an undeveloped manufacturing base. High-skilled Chinese workers are unlikely to become a solution to the problem in the near future. Since the beginning of the 1990s, China has been inviting highly qualified Russian specialists and scientists in order to increase the quality of Chinese projects. At present, as discussed in section 7.2.3, the expansive growth of academic and scientific cooperation and the opening of joint higher-education programs contribute to a maturation in the pull of technical specialists in strategic areas (including physics and chemistry) with diplomas recognised by both countries. However, it is China that is more likely to reap the benefits. The Chinese government operates with dual objectives: offering scholarships and employment opportunities to Russian graduates with a knowledge of Chinese language – in particular, within the framework of joint PhD programs and initiatives undertaken by the Confucius Institutes (Kozlov & Nasakova 2008) – and stimulating the return of graduates in the framework of China's 2020 Education Reform Strategy (Larin 2009). Additionally, in late 2008, a "1000 Talents" program was launched by the Chinese Communist Party in order to stimulate scientists and academics, whose rate of return from overseas studies was previously low, in order to reestablish them in China (Zweig & Wang 2013). Documented difficulties in finding employment for Chinese graduates in attractive regions such as the city of Moscow and the necessity of using unofficial (Chinese) networks do not make the Russian labour market attractive in the eyes of this (desirable) category of migrants (Gelbras 2004).

As for low- and medium-skilled migrants, their flows and stocks are very sensitive to legal initiatives from both sides. "Chinatowns" are virtually non-existent in Russia. However, there are several centers of gravity for Chinese migrants (Moscow, the Far East, Siberia). Chinese are noted to settle compactly in a house/guest house and in the neighbourhood of Chinese-owned restaurants or polyvalent infrastructure centers (Kireev 2013). No balance between the sexes has been reached yet. However, the situation has been slowly changing, and the number of males residing in Russia with families (and children) has been increasing. However, most of the migrant communities still represent only one generation of migrants. Only a small share of migrants resides in Russia for a period longer than four years. Most of the Chinese working in the Russian Far East view their stay as temporary (a commuting type of migration). Local regional agreements in the Far East – such as the currently in-force cooperation agreement for 2009 through 2018 between China's northeastern region and the Russian Far East and Eastern Siberia – incorporate a long tradition of facilitation of cross-border tourism and trade, as well as temporary labour migrant exchanges (governmental policies from both sides purposely target the emigration of Chinese to Russia in frontier areas). Chinese migrants' reasons for coming to Russia are mainly economic and primarily include the availability of vacant working places, higher wages and the stimulation of border trade by Chinese officials (see section 7.2.3).

In the Russian Far East, however, a large portion of consumption goods still comes from China (due to simplified customs/tax procedures within the trade framework for frontier areas). A focus on the increasing volumes of bilateral trade (and especially border trade) uncovers a lack of infrastructure facilities and complex legislative formalities on the Russian side. Recent joint investment projects do target the development of infrastructure in the areas in question (e.g. the bridge over the Amur River). Small business entrepreneurs quickly adapt to changes in Russian legislation. As an example, one can point to temporary migration – to/ from China – as a tool of cross-border commodities delivery, the closure of a significant number of bazaars – after the introduction in 2007 of legislation prohibiting foreigners from selling in the markets – and the re-allocation of capital to restaurant businesses or construction (Kurt 2007).

However, the share of Chinese migrants who reported in the surveys that they would like to stay in the Russian Far East to reside for the long run doubled between the mid-1990s and mid-2000s (Kireev 2013). As the surveys reveal, nearly half of the Chinese migrants interviewed came to Russia following a friend's or relative's advice, and about one third of migrants themselves offered relocation advice or help to friends. Chinese seeking new economic opportunities tend to build networks established by preceding migrants. The top reasons for investors to invest in a region were the presence of previous investments and a possible partner company. This is in line with the findings of Quer, Claver and Rienda (2012), who found that in general, there is a positive association between Chinese outward direct investment and the presence of Chinese in the host country.

These findings are all pre-requisites for a transformation of the current migrant community into a future diaspora. Additionally, there is a growing number of formal and semi-formal national organizations with activities helping (e.g. with juridical consultations) their national migrants, although the structure of Chinese society in Russia is often described as unstable and decentralised. The creation of the Chinese diaspora in Russia (and in the Russian Far East in particular) is not yet completed (Kireev 2013). Given the general orientation of Russian migration policy towards the facilitation of inflows of migrants from CIS countries into low-skill occupations, especially in the western part of Russia, further concentration of Chinese migrants in border areas and a further solidification of the Chinese migrant community is likely.

In summary, it is noteworthy that Sino-Russian cooperation has been developing at an increasing pace. A memorandum of further cooperation between Chinese authorities and the Ministry of Development in the Russian Far East includes a cooperation agreement bringing Chinese investments into large-scale projects in the Far East that is likely to significantly improve the local infrastructure system. In combination with the measures undertaken in the framework of the Migration Policy Concept until 2025, this might make the Russian Far Eastern and Siberian regions more attractive for both internal and external migrants. A re-established partnership between Russian and Chinese universities is stimulating academic and scientific exchanges, as well as the development of joint highly technological projects. In addition, Russia's World Trade Organization membership since 2012 gives hope to investors for the further improvement of its investment climate. Given all these joint initiatives, it is likely that in due course, the role of Chinese investments and migration in the Russian economy – and in particular in Russia's Far Eastern and Siberian regions – will be increasing.

Note

1 www.kyivpost.com/opinion/op-ed/beijing-renting-russian-border-area-for-chinese-fa-68351.html

References

Andreff, W. (2013, November) *Comparing Outward Foreign Direct Investment Strategies of Russian and Chinese Multinational Companies: Similarities and Specificities.* Paper presented at EAEPE Conference – Beyond De-industrialisation: The Future of Industries, Paris. www.eaepeparis2013.com/papers/Full_Paper_Wladimir-Andreff.pdf

Bessonova, E., & Gonchar, K. (2013) Institutional Barriers to FDI Entry at the Regional Level in Russia. www.eaepeparis2013.com/papers/Full_Paper_Ksenia-Gonchar.pdf

Biao, X. (2003) Emigration from China: A Sending-Country Perspective, *International Migration*, 41 (3), 21–48.

Billé, F. (2014) Surface Modernities: Open-Air Markets, Containment, and Verticality in Two Border Towns in Russia and China, *Economic Sociology*, 15 (2), 154–72.

Bin, Y. (2009, October) China-Russia Relations: Market Malaise and Mirnaya Missiya. *Comparative Connections. A Quarterly E-Journal on East Asian Bilateral Relations.* http://csis.org/files/publication/0903qchina_russia.pdf

Buccellato, T., & Santangelo, F. (2009) *Foreign Direct Investments Distribution in the Russian Federation: Do Spatial Effects Matter?* SOAS. London: University of London, Discussion paper 94.

Chudinovskikh, O. (2012) *The Russian Federation. International Migration Report 2012.* SOPEMI. Moscow: Lomonosov Moscow State University/Higher School of Economics.

Concept. (2012) *Concept of the Russian Migration Policy until 2025. – Moscow, 2012.* An online version is on the website of the Office of the President of Russia. http://kremlin.ru/acts/15635

Di Bartolomeo, A., et al. (Eds.) (2014) *Regional Migration Report: Russia and Central Asia.* San Domenico di Fiesole (FI), Italy: European University Institute, Robert Schuman Centre for Advanced Studies, Migration Policy Centre.

Ernst & Young. (2013) *Russia Attractiveness Survey 2013.* – Report, Ernst & Young. www.ey.com/ru/en/issues/business-environment/russia-attractiveness-survey-2013

Gelbras, V. (2002) Chinese Migration and Chinese Ethnic Communities in Russia. In Iontsev, V. (Ed.) *The World in the Mirror of International Migration.* Scientific Series "International Migration of Population: Russia and the Contemporary World." Moscow: MAX Press, pp. 18–33.

Gelbras, V. (2004) Perspektivy kitajskoj migratsii na Dal'nem Vostoke. In *Otechestvennye zapiski*, 4. www.strana-oz.ru/?numid=19&article=905 [in Russian]

Ioffe, G., & Zayonchkovskaya, Zh. (2010) Immigration to Russia: Inevitability and Prospective Inflows, *Eurasian Geography and Economics*, 51 (1), 104–25.

Karhunen, P., & Ledyaeva, S. (2012) Corruption Distance, Anti-Corruption Laws and International Ownership Strategies in Russia, *Journal of International Management*, 16, 196–208.

Kim, W.B. (1994) Sino-Russian Relations and Chinese workers in the Russian Far East: A Porous Border, *Asian Survey*, 34 (12), 1064–76.

Kireev, A. (2013) Is There a Chinese Diaspora in the Russian Far East? *Oykumena*, 4 [in Russian].

Kozlov, L., & Nasakova, B. (2008) Possijskiy Daljnij Vostok kak objekt vneshnej kuljturnoj politiki Japonii i Kitaja. In Shinkovskyj, M., & Kotljar, N. (Eds.) *Rossijskij Daljnij Vostok v Aziatsko-Tihookeanskom regione na rubezhe vekov: politika, ekonomika, bezopasnostj*. Vladivostok: Daljnauka, pp. 183–197.

Krkoska, L., & Korniyenko, Y. (2008) China's Investment in Russia: Where Do They Go and How Important Are They? *China and Eurasia Forum Quarterly*, 6 (1), 39–49.

Kuhrt, N. (2007) *Russian Policy Towards China and Japan: The El'tsin and Putin Periods.* London: Routledge.

Larin, A. (2009) *Kitajskie migranty v Rossii. Istoriya i sovremennost'*. Moscow: Vostochnaya kniga [in Russian].

Larin, V. (2006) *V teni prosnuvshegosya drakona: Rossijsko-kitakskie otnosheniya na rubezhe XX–XXI vv.* Vladivostok: Dal'nauka [in Russian].

Ledyaeva, S. (2009) Spatial Econometric Analysis of Foreign Direct Investment Determinants in Russian Regions, *World Economy*, 32 (4), 643–66.

Lu, J., Liu, X., & Wang, H. (2010) Motives for Outward FDI of Chinese Private Firms: Firm Resources, Industry Dynamics, and Government Policies, *Management and Organization Review*, 7 (2), 223–48.

Minakir, P.A. (1996) *Chinese Immigration in the Russian Far East: Regional, National, and International Dimensions. Cooperation and Conflict in the Former Soviet Union: Implications for Migration.* Santa Monica, CA: RAND CF-130.

Mitchell, D. (2007) *Conference: The China Balance Sheet in 2007 and Beyond*, in Bergsten, C.F., Gill, B., Lardy, N.R., & Mitchell, D. (Eds.), Peterson Institute for International Economics, Washington, DC: Center for Strategic and International Studies/ Peterson Institute for International Economics, pp. 133–150.

Motritsch, E. (2010) Transforacija migracionnyh svjazej Dal'nego Vostoka Rossii so stranami blizhnego i daljnego zarubezhja, *Prostranstvennaja Ekonomika*, 2, 74–95 [in Russian].

Mukomel, V. (2012) *Labour Migration and the Host Country: The Russian Case.* Migration Policy Centre. CARIM-East Research Report; 2012/31. http://hdl.handle.net/1814/24874

Ponkratov, R. (2007) *Mezhdunarodnaja trudovaja migracija na Dal'nem Vostoke Rossii* (Doctoral thesis, Moscow State University, Moscow).

Quer, D., Claver, E., & Rienda, L. (2012) Political risk, cultural distance, and Outward Foreign Direct Investment: Empirical Evidence From Large Chinese Firms, *Asia Pacific Journal of Management*, 29 (4), 1089–104.

Repnikova, M., & Balzer, H. (2009) *Chinese Migration to Russia: Missed Opportunities*. Eurasian Migration Papers, No. 3. Washington, DC: Woodrow Wilson International Center for Scholars.

Ryazantsev, S. (2014) *Chinese Investment Strategies and Migration – Does Diaspora Matter? A Case Study on Russia*. MPC Research Reports 2014. San Domenico di Fiesole (FI): Robert Schuman Centre for Advanced Studies, European University Institute.

Ryzhova, N., & Ioffe, G. (2009) Trans-Border Exchange Between Russia and China: The Case of Blagoveshchensk and Heihe, *Eurasian Geography and Economics*, 50 (3), 348–64.

Shvedova, I. (2013) Internacionalizacija vysshego obrazovanija v Kitae. Vestnik Tomskogo gosudarstvennogo universiteta, *Istorija*, 1 (21), 132–38 [in Russian]. http://cyberleninka.ru/article/n/internatsionalizatsiya-vysshego-obrazovaniya-v-kitae

Sullivan, J., & Renz, B. (2010) Chinese Migration: Still the Major Focus of Russian Far East/Chinese North East relations? *Pacific Review*, 23 (2), 261–85.

Tschernov, V. (2006) Chelnoki i turisty (Shuttle-Traders and Tourists), *Rossiya v ATR*, 3 (3). http://chernov.ucoz.com/CHelnoki_i_turisty.pdf

Zabyelina, Y. (2012) Costs and Benefits of Informal Economy: Shuttle Trade and Crime at Cherkizovsky Market, *Global Crime*, 13 (2), 95–108.

Zsuzsa, L. (2003) Attraction vs Repulsion – Foreign Direct Investment in Russia, *Development and Finance*, 1, 51–62.

Zweig, D., & Wang, H. (2013) Can China Bring Back the Best? The Communist Party Organizes China's Search for Talent, *China Quarterly*, 215, 590–615.

Index

acquisitions 97, 109, 122, 142, 160, 188
Africa 20, 49, 102; Chinese emigration from 84; Chinese investments in 102
agencies, intermediary 15, 25
agency, travel 101–2
apparel 71
Association of Chinese Overseas Merchants in Hamburg 134
Association of Overseas Chinese 134
Association of Overseas Wenzhouese 70

Bank of Portugal 89
bazaar shops 91, 94, 95
bilateral trade 119, 194
brain drain 3, 26
"bridge" *see* Chinese diaspora, bridging role of
business networks 3–4, 38, 39, 117, 133; development of 35

Cantonese migration 19
CCP (Chinese Communist Party) 12, 21, 23, 193
China Development Bank 189
Chinese business, coping strategies of 8, 83, 89, 96, 107
Chinese business associations 85, 86, 103, 108, 130; in Portugal 102, 108
Chinese business community 38, 47, 49, 83, 85, 102, 105, 106, 109
Chinese businesses 63; diversification of 8; dualistic structure of 101; evolution of 86; and financial crisis 83, 91, 94; labour-intensive 75; monitoring of 76, 77
Chinese businessmen 39, 73, 189, 191; circular migration of 91; evolution of 60, 72; and the financial crisis 89, 103;

motives for emigration 152; in Poland 166, 167; in Portugal 8, 85, 91, 93, 101; propensity to start a business 95; in Russia 177, 184; transnational ties of 71, 96, 107; and visa policy 105
Chinese citizenship 118, 136
Chinese communities 5, 10, 21, 22, 28, 33, 44, 47, 48, 131, 141
Chinese companies 4; barriers to 189; and Chinese diaspora 47, 134, 138; clusters of 7; and financial crisis 97, 120; and illegal employment 67; investment activities of 136, 148, 165; investment decisions of 128; investment strategies of 142; and local market 8; management structure of 48; overseas 48; in Prato 59, 66; in Russia 184, 189; skilled workforce for 134; and SOEs 108; as subcontractors 58, 59, 60, 63, 64, 66, 67, 71, 164; technology-intensive 122
Chinese contract workers 15
Chinese diaspora 118; bridging role of 9, 10, 128, 130, 133, 134, 138, 142; and Chinese FDI 46; estimates of in Europe 18; in Germany 119, 123, 124, 129, 132; in Poland 148; in Russia 194; in South Asia 36
Chinese diaspora networks 5, 116, 131, 132, 133, 134, 136, 140, 141; in Germany 119, 129; in Southeast Asia 130; and transaction costs 118
Chinese economy 24, 26, 45, 93
Chinese emigration *see* emigration from China
Chinese enterprises *see* Chinese companies
Chinese entrepreneurs: in Italy 59; in Portugal 87, 93, 105; in Prato 59, 60, 72,

For Product Safety Concerns and Information please contact our EU
representative GPSR@taylorandfrancis.com
Taylor & Francis Verlag GmbH, Kaufingerstraße 24, 80331 München, Germany

www.ingramcontent.com/pod-product-compliance
Ingram Content Group UK Ltd.
Pitfield, Milton Keynes, MK11 3LW, UK
UKHW020957180425
457613UK00019B/724